Head First Software Architecture

Wouldn't it be dreamy if there was a book about software architecture that was more fun than getting a root canal and more revealing than reams of documentation? It's probably just a fantasy...

Raju Gandhi

Mark Richards

Neal Ford

Beijing · Boston · Farnham · Sebastopol · Tokyo

Head First Software Architecture

by Raju Gandhi, Mark Richards & Neal Ford

Published by O'Reilly Media, Inc., 1005 Gravenstein Highway North, Sebastopol, CA 95472.

O'Reilly Media books may be purchased for educational, business, or sales promotional use. Online editions are also available for most titles (*http://oreilly.com*). For more information, contact our corporate/institutional sales department: (800) 998-9938 or *corporate@oreilly.com*.

Series Creators:	Kathy Sierra, Bert Bates
Series Advisors:	Eric Freeman, Elisabeth Robson
Acquisitions Editor:	Melissa Duffield
Development Editor:	Sarah Grey
Cover Designer:	Susan Thompson, based on a series design by Ellie Volckhausen
Cover/Interior Illustrations:	José Marzan Jr.
Production Editor:	Christopher Faucher
Proofreader:	Rachel Head
Indexer:	nSight, Inc.
Page Viewers:	Buddy and Skye ("the dogs"), Princess Zara, baby Delphine, Sparks, Fauci, Linda Ruth, and Amadeus ("the cats")

Printing History:

March 2024: First Edition.

ISBN: 978-1-098-13435-8

[LSI]

[2024-03-04]

Other related books from O'Reilly

Fundamentals of Software Architecture

Software Architecture: The Hard Parts

Other books in O'Reilly's Head First series

Head First Android Development

Head First C#

Head First Design Patterns

Head First Git

Head First Go

Head First iPhone and iPad Development

Head First Java

Head First JavaScript Programming

Head First Learn to Code

Head First Object-Oriented Analysis and Design

Head First Programming

Head First Python

Head First Software Development

Head First Web Design

DEDICATION

From Mark and Neal

To all the conference attendees who patiently sat
through many drafts of this material

(2004-2024)

From Raju

To my Dad

જય શ્રી કૃષ્ણ

Authors of Head First Software Architecture

Mark Richards

Raju Gandhi

Neal Ford

Raju Gandhi

Raju is an architect, consultant, author, and teacher and a regularly invited speaker at conferences around the world. He believes in keeping things simple, and his approach is always to understand and explain the "why," as opposed to the "how." He lives in Columbus, Ohio, with his wonderful wife, Michelle; their sons, Mason and Micah; their daughter, Delphine; and three furry family members, Buddy, Skye, and Princess Zara. You can find his contact information at *RajuGandhi.com*.

Mark Richards

Mark is an experienced hands-on software architect and the founder of DeveloperToArchitect.com, a free website devoted to helping developers in their journeys to becoming software architects. He has been in the software industry since 1983 and has significant experience and expertise in application, integration, and enterprise architecture. Mark has authored numerous technical books and videos, including *Fundamentals of Software Architecture* and *Software Architecture: The Hard Parts* (O'Reilly), co-authored with Neal Ford. Mark also does training and has spoken at hundreds of conferences and user groups around the world.

Neal Ford

Neal Ford is director, software architect, and meme wrangler at ThoughtWorks, a global IT consultancy with a focus on end-to-end software development and delivery. He is also the designer and developer of many applications, articles, and video presentations and the author and/or editor of an increasingly large number of books, spanning a variety of subjects and technologies. His professional focus is designing and building large-scale enterprise applications. He is also an internationally acclaimed speaker who has spoken at more than 300 developer conferences worldwide and has delivered more than 2,000 presentations.

Table of Contents (the summary)

Table of Contents (the real thing)

Intro

Because software architecture is hard, your brain will trick you into thinking you can't learn it. Your brain's thinking, "Better to

focus on more important things, like what to eat for lunch and whether pigs have wings." The good news is that you CAN trick your brain into thinking software architecture is an important skill to learn, and in this chapter we're going to show you just how to do that.

software architecture demystified

1 Let's Get Started!

Software architecture is fundamental to the success of your system.
This chapter demystifies software architecture. You'll gain an understanding of architectural dimensions and the differences between architecture and design. Why is this important? Because understanding and applying architectural practices helps you build more effective and correct software systems—systems that not only function better, but also meet the needs and concerns of the business and continue to operate as your business and technical environments undergo constant change. So, without further delay, let's get started.

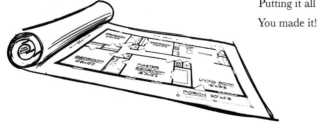

architectural characteristics
Know Your Capabilities

2

What does your architecture need to support? Architectural characteristics (the capabilities of an architecture) are the fundamental building blocks of any system. Without them, you cannot make architectural decisions, select an architectural style, or in many cases even create a logical architecture. In this chapter you'll learn how to define some of the more common characteristics (like scalability, reliability, and testability), how they influence a software architecture, how they help you make architectural decisions, and how to identify which ones are important for your particular situation. Ready to add some capabilities to your software architecture?

3

the two laws of software architecture
Everything's a Trade-Off

What happens when there are no "best practices"? The nice thing about best practices is that they're relatively risk-free ways to achieve certain goals. They're called "best" (not "better" or "good") for a reason—you know they work, so why not just use them? But one thing you'll quickly learn about software architecture is that it has no best practices. You'll have to analyze every situation carefully to make a decision, and you'll need to communicate not just the "what" of the decision, but the "why."

So, how *do* you navigate this new frontier? Fortunately, you have the laws of software architecture to guide you. This chapter shows you how to analyze trade-offs as you make decisions. We'll also show you how to create architectural decision records to capture the "hows" and "whys" of decisions. By the end of this chapter, you'll have the tools to navigate the uncertain territory that is software architecture.

logical components

The Building Blocks

4

Ready to start creating an architecture? It's not as easy as it sounds—and if you don't do it correctly, your software system could come crumbling to the ground, just like a poorly designed skyscraper or bridge.

In this chapter we'll show you several approaches for identifying and creating *logical components*, the functional building blocks of a system that describe how its pieces all fit together. Using the techniques described in this chapter will help you to create a solid architecture—a foundation upon which you can build a successful software system.

Put on your hard hat and gloves, get your tools ready, and let's get started.

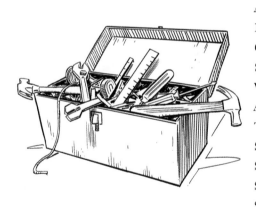

5

architectural styles

Categorization and Philosophies

There are lots of different architectural styles out there.

Each one exists for a reason and has its own philosophy about how and when it should be used. Understanding a style's philosophy will help you judge whether it's the right one for your domain. This chapter gives you a framework for the different kinds of architectural styles (which we'll be diving into for the remainder of this book), to help you make sense of these and all the other architectural styles you'll encounter as a software architect.

Let's fill in that final piece of the puzzle, shall we?

layered architecture

Separating Concerns

6

What if your problem is simple and time is of the essence?
Should you even bother with architecture? It depends on how long you want to keep what you build. If it's disposable, throw caution to the wind. If not, then choose the simplest architecture that still provides some measurable organization and benefit, without imposing many constraints on speed of delivery. The *layered architecture* has become that architecture because it's easy to understand and implement, leveraging design patterns developers already know. Let's peel back the layers of this architecture.

modular monoliths

Driven by the Domain

There's more than one way to build a monolith. So far, you've encountered the layered architecture, which aligns things *technically*. You can go a long way with a layered monolith, but when changes begin to involve lots of communication and coordination between different teams, you might need a little more horsepower under the hood—and perhaps even a different architectural style.

This chapter looks at the *modular monolith* architectural style, which divides applications up by *business concerns* as opposed to technical concerns. You'll learn what this means, what to look out for, and all the trade-offs associated with this style. Let's take the modular monolith for a spin, shall we?

microkernel architecture

Crafting Customizations

8

You can craft custom experiences, one capability at a time. Some architecture styles are particularly well suited for some capabilities, and the microkernel architecture is the world champion at customization. But it's also useful for a bewildering range of applications. Once you understand this architectural style, you'll start seeing it everywhere!

Let's dig into an architecture that lets your users have it *their* way.

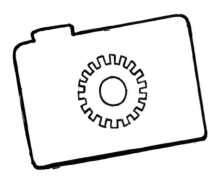

do it yourself

The TripEZ Travel App

9

Ready to extend your journey into software architecture? In this chapter, you're the software architect. You'll be determining architectural characteristics, building a logical architecture, making architectural decisions, and deciding whether to use a layered, modular, or microkernel architecture. The exercises in this chapter will give you an end-to-end view of what a software architect does and show you how much you've learned. Get ready to create an architecture for a startup company building a travel integration convenience site. *Bon voyage*—we hope you have a good trip building your architecture.

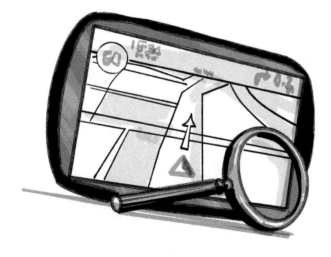

microservices architecture

Bit by Bit

10

How do you make an architecture easier to change?

Business is changing faster than ever, and software architectures need to keep up. In this chapter you'll learn how to create a flexible architecture that can change as your business changes, scale as your business grows, and remain operational even when system failures occur. Intrigued? We hope so, because in this chapter we're going to show you *microservices*—an architectural style that solves all of these problems and more. Let's get started on our journey through microservices, bit by bit.

event-driven architecture
Asynchronous Adventures

11

What if your architecture could do lots of things at the same time?
As businesses grow and become more successful, they need to be able to handle more and more users, without slowing down or crashing systems. In this chapter, you'll learn how to design high-performance systems that can scale as a business grows. Get ready for *event-driven architecture*, a highly popular distributed architecture style. It's very fast, highly scalable, and easy to extend—but it's also quite complex. You'll be learning about lots of new concepts in this chapter, including things like events, messages, and asynchronous communication, so you can create an architectural that can do many things at once. Fasten your seatbelt, and let's go on an asynchronous adventure through event-driven architecture.

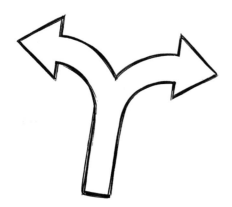

do it yourself

Testing Your Knowledge

12

Ready to test your skills in creating a distributed architecture? In this chapter, you're the software architect. You'll be determining architectural characteristics, building a logical architecture, making architectural decisions, and deciding whether to use microservices or event-driven architecture. The exercises in this chapter will give you an end-to-end view of what a software architect does and show you how much you've learned. Get ready to create an architecture for a student standardized test–taking system called Make the Grade. Good luck—we hope you get an A on your architecture!

appendix: leftovers

The Top Six Topics We Didn't Cover

There's a lot more to be said about software architecture. We promise you're done with this book. But reading this book is just the first step in your journey to thinking architecturally, and we couldn't in good conscience let you go without a little more preparation. So, we've gathered a few additional juicy bits into this appendix. Each of the topics that follow deserves as much attention as the other topics we've covered. However, our goal here is just to give you a high-level idea of what they're all about. And yes, this really *is* the end of the book. Except for the index, of course—it's a real page-turner!

how to use this book

Intro

In this section we answer the burning question:
"So why DID they put that in a software architecture book?"

Who is this book for?

If you can answer "yes" to both of these:

1 Do you want to learn what software architecture is all about?

2 Do you prefer **stimulating dinner-party conversation** to **dry, dull academic lectures**?

This book is for you.

Who should probably back away from this book?

If you can answer "yes" to any of these:

1 **Are you <u>completely</u> new to the tech industry?**

(While we firmly believe that software developers should understand the basics of software architecture, you might want to get a bit of experience developing software before diving into this book.)

2 Are you a seasoned software architect looking for a *reference* book?

3 Are you **afraid to try something new**? Would you rather sit in a corner licking 9-volt batteries than advance your career? Do you believe that a technical book can't be serious if it uses zoo animals to explain architectural characteristics like scalability and fault tolerance?

This book is **not** for you.

[Note from marketing: This book is for anyone with a credit card.]

We know what you're thinking

"How can *this* be a serious book on software architecture?"

"What's with all the graphics?"

"Can I actually *learn* it this way?"

Your brain thinks
THIS is important.

We know what your *brain* is thinking

Your brain craves novelty. It's always searching, scanning, *waiting* for something unusual. It was built that way, and it helps you stay alive.

So what does your brain do with all the routine, ordinary, normal things you encounter? Everything it *can* to stop them from interfering with the brain's *real* job—recording things that *matter*. It doesn't bother saving the boring things; they never make it past the "this is obviously not important" filter.

How does your brain *know* what's important? Suppose you're out for a day hike and a tiger jumps in front of you. What happens inside your head and body?

Neurons fire. Emotions crank up. *Chemicals surge.*

And that's how your brain knows...

This must be important! Don't forget it!

But imagine you're at home, or in a library. It's a safe, warm, tiger-free zone. You're studying. Getting ready for an exam. Or trying to learn some tough technical topic your boss thinks will take a week, 10 days at the most.

Just one problem. Your brain's trying to do you a big favor. It's trying to make sure that this *obviously* unimportant content doesn't clutter up scarce resources. Resources that are better spent storing the really *big* things. Like tigers. Like the danger of fire. Like how you should never have posted those "party" photos on your Facebook page. And there's no simple way to tell your brain, "Hey brain, thank you very much, but no matter how dull this book is and how little I'm registering on the emotional Richter scale right now, I really *do* want you to keep this stuff around."

Your brain thinks
THIS isn't worth
saving.

Great. Only 450 more dull, dry, boring pages.

We think of a "Head First" reader as a <u>learner</u>.

So what does it take to *learn* something? First you have to *get* it, then make sure you don't *forget* it. It's not about pushing facts into your head. Based on the latest research in cognitive science, neurobiology, and educational psychology, *learning* takes a lot more than text on a page. We know what turns your brain on.

Some of the Head First learning principles:

Make it visual. Images are far more memorable than words alone and make learning much more effective (up to 89% improvement in recall and transfer studies). They also make things more understandable. **Put the words within or near the graphics** they relate to, rather than on the bottom or on another page, and learners will be up to *twice* as likely to be able to solve problems related to the content.

Use a conversational and personalized style. In recent studies, students performed up to 40% better on post-learning tests if the content spoke directly to the reader, using a first-person, conversational style rather than taking a formal tone. Tell stories instead of lecturing. Use casual language. Don't take yourself too seriously. Which would *you* pay more attention to: a stimulating dinner party companion, or a lecture?

Get the learner to think more deeply. Unless you actively flex your neurons, nothing much happens in your head. A reader has to be motivated, engaged, curious, and inspired to solve problems, draw conclusions, and generate new knowledge. And for that, you need challenges, exercises, and thought-provoking questions, and activities that involve both sides of the brain and multiple senses.

Get—and keep—the reader's attention. We've all had the "I really want to learn this but I can't stay awake past page one" experience. Your brain pays attention to things that are out of the ordinary, interesting, strange, eye-catching, unexpected. Learning a new, tough, technical topic doesn't have to be boring. Your brain will learn much more quickly if it's not.

Touch their emotions. We now know that your ability to remember something is largely dependent on its emotional content. You remember what you care about. You remember when you *feel* something. No, we're not talking heart-wrenching stories about a boy and his dog. We're talking emotions like surprise, curiosity, fun, "what the...?" and the feeling of "I rule!" that comes when you solve a puzzle, learn something everybody else thinks is hard, or realize you know something that "I'm more technical than thou" Bob from engineering *doesn't*.

Metacognition: Thinking about thinking

If you really want to learn, and you want to learn more quickly and more deeply, pay attention to how you pay attention. Think about how you think. Learn how you learn.

Most of us did not take courses on metacognition or learning theory when we were growing up. We were *expected* to learn, but rarely *taught* to learn.

But we assume that if you're holding this book, you really want to learn what software architecture is all about. And you probably don't want to spend a lot of time on it. If you want to use what you read in this book, you need to *remember* what you read. And for that, you've got to *understand* it. To get the most from this book, or *any* book or learning experience, take responsibility for your brain. Your brain on *this* content.

The trick is to get your brain to see the new material you're learning as Really Important. Crucial to your well-being. As important as a tiger. Otherwise, you're in for a constant battle, with your brain doing its best to keep the new content from sticking.

So just how *DO* you get your brain to treat software architecture like it's a hungry tiger?

There's the slow, tedious way, or the faster, more effective way. The slow way is about sheer repetition. You obviously know that you *are* able to learn and remember even the dullest of topics if you keep pounding the same thing into your brain. With enough repetition, your brain says, "This doesn't *feel* important, but they keep looking at the same thing *over* and *over* and *over*, so I suppose it must be."

The faster way is to do ***anything that increases brain activity,*** especially different *types* of brain activity. The things on the previous page are a big part of the solution, and they're all things that have been proven to help your brain work in your favor. For example, studies show that putting words *within* the pictures they describe (as opposed to somewhere else on the page, like a caption or in the body text) causes your brain to try to make sense of how the words and picture relate, and this causes more neurons to fire. More neurons firing = more chances for your brain to *get* that this is something worth paying attention to, and possibly recording.

A conversational style helps because people tend to pay more attention when they perceive that they're in a conversation, since they're expected to follow along and hold up their end. The amazing thing is, your brain doesn't necessarily *care* that the "conversation" is between you and a book! On the other hand, if the writing style is formal and dry, your brain perceives it the same way you experience being lectured to while sitting in a roomful of passive attendees. No need to stay awake.

But pictures and conversational style are just the beginning…

Here's what WE did

We used ***visuals***, because your brain is tuned for visuals, not text. As far as your brain's concerned, a visual really *is* worth a thousand words. And when text and visuals work together, we embedded the text *in* the visuals because your brain works more effectively when the text is *within* the thing the text refers to, as opposed to in a caption or buried in a paragraph somewhere.

We used ***redundancy***, saying the same thing in *different* ways and with different media types, and *multiple senses*, to increase the chance that the content gets coded into more than one area of your brain.

We used concepts and visuals in ***unexpected*** ways because your brain is tuned for novelty, and we used visuals and ideas with at least *some **emotional** content*, because your brain is tuned to pay attention to the biochemistry of emotions. That which causes you to *feel* something is more likely to be remembered, even if that feeling is nothing more than a little ***humor***, ***surprise***, or ***interest***.

We used a personalized, ***conversational style***, because your brain is tuned to pay more attention when it believes you're in a conversation than if it thinks you're passively listening to a presentation. Your brain does this even when you're *reading*.

We included dozens of ***activities***, because your brain is tuned to learn and remember more when you ***do*** things than when you *read* about things. And we made the exercises challenging yet doable, because that's what most people prefer.

We used ***multiple learning styles***, because *you* might prefer step-by-step procedures, while someone else wants to understand the big picture first, and someone else just wants to see an example. But regardless of your own learning preference, *everyone* benefits from seeing the same content represented in multiple ways.

We included content for ***both sides of your brain***, because the more of your brain you engage, the more likely you are to learn and remember, and the longer you can stay focused. Since working one side of the brain often means giving the other side a chance to rest, you can be more productive at learning for a longer period of time.

And we included ***stories*** and exercises that present ***more than one point of view***, because your brain is tuned to learn more deeply when it's forced to make evaluations and judgments.

We included ***challenges***, with exercises, and we asked ***questions*** that don't always have a straight answer, because your brain is tuned to learn and remember when it has to *work* at something. Think about it—you can't get your *body* in shape just by *watching* people at the gym. But we did our best to make sure that when you're working hard, it's on the *right* things. That ***you're not spending one extra dendrite*** processing a hard-to-understand example or parsing difficult, jargon-laden, or overly terse text.

We used ***people***. In stories, examples, visuals, etc., because, well, because *you're* a person. And your brain pays more attention to *people* than it does to *things*.

Here's what YOU can do to bend your brain into submission

So, we did our part. The rest is up to you. These tips are a starting point; listen to your brain and figure out what works for you and what doesn't. Try new things.

Cut this out and stick it on your refrigerator.

1 Slow down. The more you understand, the less you have to memorize.

Don't just *read*. Stop and think. When the book asks you a question, don't just skip to the answer. Imagine that someone really *is* asking the question. The more deeply you force your brain to think, the better chance you have of learning and remembering.

2 Do the exercises. Write your own notes.

We put them in, but if we did them for you, that would be like having someone else do your workouts for you. And don't just *look* at the exercises. **Use a pencil.** There's plenty of evidence that physical activity *while* learning can increase the learning.

3 Read the "There Are No Dumb Questions."

That means all of them. They're not optional sidebars, ***they're part of the core content!*** Don't skip them.

4 Make this the last thing you read before bed. Or at least the last challenging thing.

Part of learning (especially the transfer to long-term memory) happens *after* you put the book down. Your brain needs time on its own, to do more processing. If you put in something new during that processing time, some of what you just learned will be lost.

5 Talk about it. Out loud.

Speaking activates a different part of the brain. If you're trying to understand something, or increase your chance of remembering it later, say it out loud. Better still, try to explain it out loud to someone else. You'll learn more quickly, and you might uncover ideas you hadn't known were there when you were reading about it.

6 Drink water. Lots of it.

Your brain works best in a nice bath of fluid. Dehydration (which can happen before you ever feel thirsty) decreases cognitive function.

7 Listen to your brain.

Pay attention to whether your brain is getting overloaded. If you find yourself starting to skim the surface or forget what you just read, it's time for a break. Once you go past a certain point, you won't learn faster by trying to shove more in, and you might even hurt the process.

8 Feel something.

Your brain needs to know that this *matters*. Get involved with the stories. Make up your own captions for the photos. Groaning over a bad joke is *still* better than feeling nothing at all.

9 Apply it every day!

There's only one way to learn how to *really* understand software architecture: **apply it every day**. You are going to be doing software architecture a lot in this book, and like with any other skill, the only way to get good at it is to practice. We're going to give you a lot of practice: every chapter has exercises that pose problems for you to solve. Don't just skip over them—a lot of the learning happens when you solve the exercises. We included a solution to each exercise—don't be afraid to **peek at the solution** if you get stuck! (It's easy to get snagged on something small.) But try to solve the problem before you look at the solution. And definitely get it working before you move on to the next part of the book.

Read me

This is a learning experience, not a reference book. We deliberately stripped out everything that might get in the way of learning whatever it is we're working on at that point in the book. And the first time through, you need to begin at the beginning, because the book makes assumptions about what you've already seen and learned.

We break things down, then build them back again.

We are fans of teasing things apart. This gives us the chance to focus on one aspect of software architecture at a time. We use a lot of visuals to explain various aspects of software architecture. We make sure you have a deep understanding of each aspect, and have the confidence to know when and how to use them. Only *then* do we start to bring things together, to explain the more complex ideas in software architecture.

We don't exhaustively cover everything.

We use the 80/20 approach. We assume that if you are going for a PhD in software architecture, this isn't going to be your only book. So, we don't talk about everything—just the stuff that you'll actually use, and that you need to hit the ground running. We want to hit the ground running.

The activities are NOT optional.

The exercises and activities are not add-ons; they're part of the core content of the book. Some of them are to help with memory, some are for understanding, and some will help you apply what you've learned. ***Don't skip the exercises.*** The crossword puzzles are the only thing you don't *have* to do, but they're good for giving your brain a chance to think about the words and terms you've been learning in a different context.

The redundancy is intentional and important.

One distinct difference in a Head First book is that we want you to *really* get it. And we want you to finish the book remembering what you've learned. Most reference books don't have retention and recall as a goal, but this book is about *learning*, so you'll see some of the same concepts come up more than once.

The examples are as generic as possible.

To teach you software architecture, we have to use business problems—otherwise, the concepts we introduce in this book would be too abstract and hard to follow. We've deliberately made the examples in this book generic, yet also interesting, fascinating, and downright fun. No matter your background, we are certain you will be able to relate to them when practicing software architecture, whatever kind of work you do.

The Brain Power exercises don't always have answers.

For some of them, there is no right answer, and for others, part of the learning experience is for you to decide if and when your answers are right. In some of the Brain Power exercises, you will find hints to point you in the right direction.

O'Reilly online learning

For more than 40 years, O'Reilly Media has provided technology and business training, knowledge, and insight to help companies succeed.

Our unique network of experts and innovators share their knowledge and expertise through books, articles, and our online learning platform. O'Reilly's online learning platform gives you on-demand access to live training courses, in-depth learning paths, interactive coding environments, and a vast collection of text and video from O'Reilly and 200+ other publishers. For more information, visit *http://oreilly.com*.

Do it yourself chapters

A unique aspect of this particular Head First book is what we call "do it yourself" chapters. These chapters (there are two of them) are entirely exercise-based and give you a chance to create an architecture from beginning to end, applying all the concepts you've learned up to that point.

In these chapters, *you're the software architect*. You'll determine architectural characteristics, build a logical architecture, and make architectural decisions, including what kind of architectural style to use. Doing the exercises in these chapters gives you an end-to-end view of what a software architect does and shows you how much you've learned.

In Chapter 9, the first "do it yourself" chapter, you'll create an architecture for a trip-management system called TripEZ (pronounced like "trapeze") that aims to make travel easier, especially for road warriors. This new online trip-management dashboard app will allow travelers to see and manage all of their travel reservations, organized by trip, through a browser or on their mobile devices.

In Chapter 12, the second "do it yourself" chapter, you'll create an architecture for a standardized-testing system called Make the Grade. All Dataville Public School students in specific grade levels take the same test to determine how well students, teachers, and the school are doing. This chapter will be a great way for you to *test* your knowledge (so to speak).

The technical review team

Meet our review team!

We were lucky enough to round up a powerhouse team of people to review this book, including **senior developers**, **software architects**, **renowned public speakers**, and **prolific book authors**.

These experts read every chapter, did the exercises, corrected our mistakes, and provided detailed commentary on every single page of this book. They also acted as our sounding board, letting us work through ideas, analogies, and narratives. They even helped us think through how this book should be organized.

Every single reviewer here made huge contributions to this book and vastly improved its quality. We deeply appreciate the countless hours they spent poring over the manuscript. We remain indebted to them.

Thank you!

Special thanks also to Moataz Sanad for finding lots of our typos!

Despite our (and our reviewers') best efforts, any and all errors and omissions are ours and ours alone.

Nate Schutta

Tanya Reilly

Christine Schutta

Clare Sudbery

Venkat Subramaniam

Patrick Viafore

Marc Loy

James Erler

Max Schubert

Joint acknowledgments

This book would not have been possible without the help, guidance, and support from a number of great individuals. We have a lot of people to thank, so let's get started!

Our editor:

Our first and foremost acknowledgment goes, along with our utmost thanks, to our brilliant editor **Sarah Grey**. Writing a book like *Head First Software Architecture* presented a number of unique challenges for us, and Sarah was there to guide us the entire time. She helped keep us on track when we deviated from the Head First style of writing (which was quite often) and made constant suggestions about every page's layout (really, we mean *every* page). Sarah took on the role of crossword expert and helped us out quite a bit with the *Make It Stick* poetry. We frequently referred to Sarah as our "fourth author," and in reality, she deserves much of the credit for the outcome of this book.

↖ The brilliant Sarah Grey

The O'Reilly team:

A big thanks to the entire O'Reilly Media team, including **Kristen Brown** and **Chris Faucher** for making sure that our book was production-worthy, and to **Rachel Head** for her keen and astute copyediting eye. And if, like us, you routinely use book indexes, you have **Tom Dinse** to thank for this one.

We'd also like to thank **Melissa Duffield** for her continued support and patience throughout this process, and for considering us for this long project.

Much appreciation to the **O'Reilly online training team**, especially **Yasmina Greco, Lindsay Ventimiglia**, and **all the producers**, for giving us a platform to teach software architecture to thousands of developers and architects around the world.

A shoutout to the **Early Release team**, who put out raw and unedited chapters as they were written for the audience on the O'Reilly platform to review. This gave many of our readers a chance to submit errata and feedback that made this book just that much better.

Finally, we would be remiss if we did not mention series editors **Elisabeth Robson** and **Eric Freeman**, who took the time to review our work and ensure that it aligned with the vision that is the Head First series—not to mention giving us some really useful InDesign tips. Thank you!

Individual acknowledgments

From Raju Gandhi:

It's hard for me to express how much of a privilege it has been to work on this project, and to be able to work with Mark and Neal—two of the smartest and most wonderful human beings, who not only were kind enough to consider me as a coauthor, but who since have spent countless hours teaching me the nuances of software architecture. Someday I hope I can repay that debt. For now, they have my deepest appreciation. A shoutout to so many friends, colleagues, unwitting mentors and teachers, and fellow speakers who've been a source of inspiration for me—**you all know you who are**. And finally, to my wife **Michelle**. We had baby **Delphine** while I was working on this project, and Michelle has certainly taken on more than her share as I spent many an hour working on this book. Thank you. I love you both.

From Mark Richards:

In addition to the joint acknowledgments, I would like to thank my friends and coauthors Raju and Neal. Raju brought prior Head First experience to the table from his great book *Head First Git*, and helped teach us the Head First style of writing and the ins and outs of InDesign. This is my third book with Neal, and as usual, working and collaborating with him was a very rewarding and enjoyable experience. I would also like to thank my lovely wife **Rebecca** for her patience and understanding while I was hidden away in my office for so many evenings writing this book instead of enjoying her company.

From Neal Ford:

I would like to thank first and foremost my coauthors, Mark and Raju, both of whom were a delight to work with and made this book possible. Mark is as always a fantastic collaborative juggernaut with a good sense of humor, both vital when writing is not our day job. I'd also like to thank our editor **Sarah**, who has an outsized role in this book series, for helping keep us in check. Thanks also to my extended families, both genetic and chosen, for their support and respite. That includes our weekly neighborhood cocktail club that moved to the parking lot during the pandemic and stayed there; it's great to catch up with what is happening nearby. And finally and primarily, I'd like to thank my wonderful wife **Candy**, who endures many long hours with me away from her and our cats, working on stuff like what you hold in your hand.

Good thing we only had three authors, or these acknowledgments would go on and on and on...

And finally, you, the readers. Your attention is a scarce resource, and we deeply appreciate the time you'll spend with this book. Happy learning.

1 software architecture demystified
Let's Get Started!

Software architecture is fundamental to the success of your system. This chapter demystifies software architecture. You'll gain an understanding of architectural dimensions and the differences between architecture and design. Why is this important? Because understanding and applying architectural practices helps you build more effective and correct software systems—systems that not only function better, but also meet the needs and concerns of the business and continue to operate as your business and technical environments undergo constant change. So, without further delay, let's get started.

Building your understanding of software architecture

To better understand software architecture, think about a typical home in your neighborhood. The structure of the home is its **architecture**—things like its shape, how many rooms and floors it has, its dimensions, and so on. A house is usually represented through a building plan, which contains all the lines and boxes necessary to know how to build the house. Structural things like those shown below are hard and expensive to change later and are the *important* stuff about the house.

The building metaphor is a very popular one for understanding software architecture.

This house has a nice architecture.

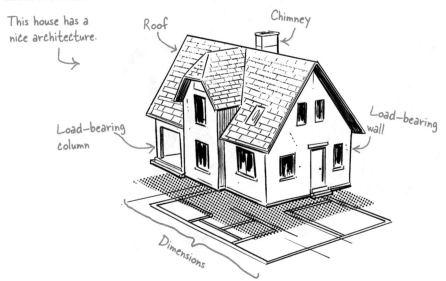

Roof

Chimney

Load-bearing column

Load-bearing wall

Dimensions

Not only is this house ugly, it's not very functional either.

Architecture is essential for building a house. Can you imagine building one without an architecture? It might turn out looking something like the house on the right.

Architecture is also essential for building software systems. Have you ever come across a system that doesn't scale, or is unreliable or difficult to maintain? It's likely not enough emphasis was placed on that system's architecture.

Exercise

Gardening is another useful metaphor for describing software architecture. Using the space below, can you describe how planning a garden might relate to software architecture? You can see what we came up with at the end of this chapter.

Solution on page 29

Building plans and software architecture

You might be wondering how the building plans of your home relate to software architecture. Each is a representation of the thing being built. So what does the "building plan" of a software system look like? Lines and boxes, of course.

A building plan specifies the structure of your home—the rooms, walls, stairs, and so on—in the same way a software architecture diagram specifies its structure (user interfaces, services, databases, and communication protocols). Both artifacts provide guidelines and constraints, as well as a vision of the final result.

Fun fact—a building plan used to be called a "blueprint," but that term is now obsolete (at least within building architecture).

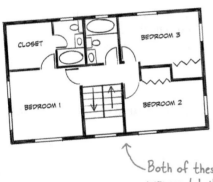

Both of these diagrams represent building plans.

Sharpen your pencil

What features of your home can you list that are *structural* and related to its *architecture*? You can find our thoughts at the end of this chapter.

Use this space to write down your ideas.

Did you notice that the floor plan for the house above doesn't specify the details of the rooms—things like the type of flooring (carpet or hardwood), the color of the walls, and where a bed might go in a bedroom? That's because those things aren't *structural*. In other words, they don't specify something about the **architecture** of the house, but rather about its **design**.

Don't worry—you'll learn a lot more about this distinction later in this chapter. Right now, just focus on the structure of something—in other words, its architecture.

Solution on page 29

The dimensions of software architecture

Most things around us are multidimensional. For example, you might describe a particular room in your home by saying it is 5 meters long and 4 meters wide, with a ceiling height of 2.5 meters. Notice that to properly describe the room you needed to specify all three dimensions—its height, length, and width.

You can describe software architecture by its dimensions, too. The difference is that software architecture has *four dimensions*.

❶ Architectural characteristics

This dimension describes what aspects of the system the architecture needs to support—things like scalability, testability, availability, and so on.

❷ Architectural decisions

This dimension includes important decisions that have long-term or significant implications for the system—for example, the kind of database it uses, the number of services it has, and how those services communicate with each other.

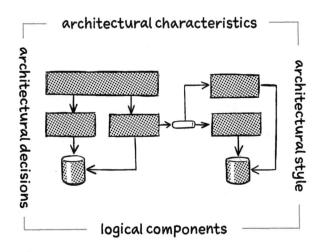

❸ Logical components

This dimension describes the building blocks of the system's functionality and how they interact with each other. For example, an ecommerce system might have components for inventory management, payment processing, and so on.

❹ Architectural style

This dimension defines the overall physical shape and structure of a software system in the same way a building plan defines the overall shape and structure of your home.

You'll learn about five of the most common architectural styles later in this book.

Puzzling out the dimensions

You can think of software architecture as a puzzle, with each dimension representing a separate puzzle piece. While each piece has its own unique shape and properties, they must all fit together and interact to build a complete picture.

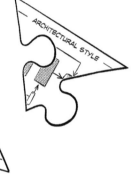

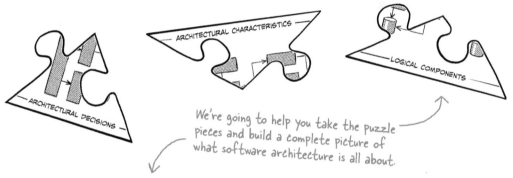

We're going to help you take the puzzle pieces and build a complete picture of what software architecture is all about.

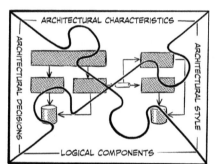

Everything is interconnected.

Did you notice how the pieces of this puzzle are joined in the middle? That's exactly how software architecture works: *each dimension must align.*

The architectural style must align with the architectural characteristics you choose as well as the architectural decisions you make. Similarly, the logical components you define must align with the characteristics and the architectural style as well as the decisions you make.

there are no
Dumb Questions

Q: Do you need all four dimensions when creating an architecture, or can you skip some if you don't have time?

A: Unfortunately, you can't skip any of these dimensions—they are all required to create and describe an architecture. One common mistake software architects make is using only one or two of these dimensions when describing their architecture. "Our architecture is microservices" describes a single dimension—the architectural style—but leaves too many unanswered questions. For example, what architectural characteristics are critical to the success of the system? What are its logical components (functional building blocks)? What major decisions have you made about how you'll implement the architecture?

The first dimension: Architectural characteristics

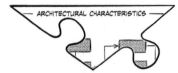

Architectural characteristics form the foundation of the architecture in a software system. Without them, you cannot make architectural decisions or analyze important trade-offs.

Imagine you're trying to choose between two homes. One home is roomy but is next to a busy, noisy motorway. The other home is in a nice, quiet neighborhood, but is much smaller. **Which characteristic is more important to you**—home size or the level of noise and traffic? Without knowing that, you can't make the right choice.

The same is true with software architecture. Let's say you need to decide what kind of database to use for your new system. Should it be a relational database, a simple key/value database, or a complex graph database? The answer will be based on what architectural characteristics are critical to you. For example, you might choose a graph database if you need high-speed search capability (we'll call that *performance*), whereas a traditional relational database might be better if you need to preserve data relationships (we'll call that *data integrity*).

performance
The amount of time it takes for the system to process a business request

availability
The amount of uptime of a system: usually measured in "nines" (so 99.9% would be three "nines")

scalability
The system's ability to maintain a consistent response time and error rate as the number of users or requests increases

Here are some of the more common architectural characteristics. You'll be learning all about these in Chapter 2.

Exercise

Check the things you think might be considered architectural characteristics—something that the *structure* of the software system supports.

- ☐ **Changing the font size in a window on the user interface screen**
- ☐ **Making changes quickly**
- ☐ **Handling thousands of concurrent users**
- ☐ **Encrypting user passwords stored in the database**
- ☐ **Interacting with many external systems to complete a business request**

⟶ Solution on page 30

The term **architectural characteristics** might not be familiar to you, but that doesn't mean you haven't heard of them before. Collectively, things like performance, scalability, reliability, and availability are also known as nonfunctional requirements, system quality attributes, and simply "the -ilities" because most end with the suffix *-ility*. We like the term *architectural characteristics* because these qualities help define the character of the architecture and what it needs to support.

Architectural characteristics are capabilities that are critical or important to the success of the system.

Make it Stick

To architect software you must first address:

Capabilities key to the new app's success

Who Does What?

Here's your chance to see how much you already know about many common architectural characteristics. Can you match up each architectural characteristic on the left with its definition on the right? You'll notice there are more definitions than characteristics, so be careful—not all of the definitions have matches.

Extensibility

We did this one for you.

Agility

Interoperability

Fault tolerance

Feasibility

Taking into account time frames, budgets, and developer skills when making architectural choices

The system's ability to keep its other parts functioning when fatal errors occur

The ease with which the system can be enhanced to support additional features and functionality

The amount of time it takes to get a response to the user

The system's ability to respond quickly to change (a function of maintainability, testability, and deployability)

The system's ability to interface and interact with other systems to complete a business request

Solution on page 30

The second dimension: Architectural decisions

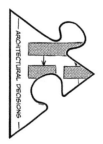

Architectural decisions are choices you make about structural aspects of the system that have long-term or significant implications. As constraints, they'll guide your development team in planning and building the system.

Should your new home have one floor or two? Should the roof be flat or peaked? Should you build a big, sprawling ranch house? These are good examples of architectural decisions because they involve the *structural* aspect of your home.

What should your home look like? This kind of decision is an architectural one.

You might decide that your system's user interface should not communicate directly with the database, but instead must go through the underlying services to retrieve and update data. This architectural decision places a particular constraint on the development of the user interface, and also guides the development team about how other components should access and update data in the database.

Here's an example of an architectural decision.

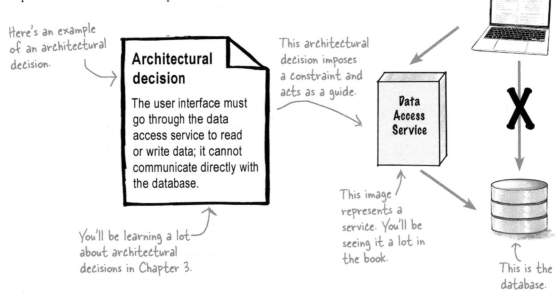

This architectural decision imposes a constraint and acts as a guide.

Architectural decision

The user interface must go through the data access service to read or write data; it cannot communicate directly with the database.

You'll be learning a lot about architectural decisions in Chapter 3.

Data Access Service

This image represents a service. You'll be seeing it a lot in the book.

This is the database.

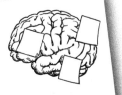

Make it Stick

Decisions are structural guides for dev teams.

They often focus on significant themes.

It's not uncommon to have several dozen or more documented architectural decisions within any system. Generally, the larger and more complicated the system, the more architectural decisions it will have.

BE the architect

Your job is to be the architect and identify as many architectural decisions as you can in the diagram below. Draw a circle around anything that you think might be an architectural decision and write what that decision might be.

Here's a hint—do you have questions about why certain things are done the way they are?

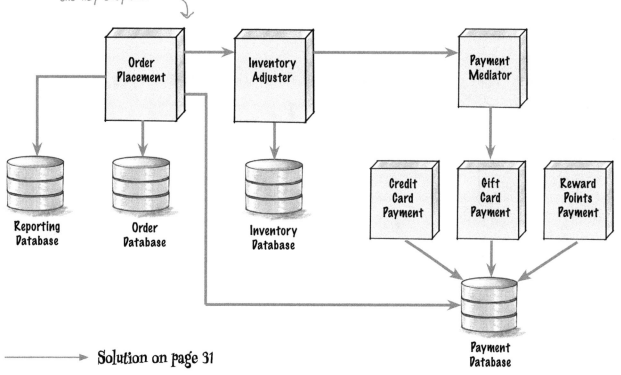

Solution on page 31

The third dimension: Logical components

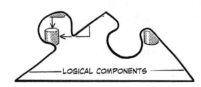

Logical components are the building blocks of a system, much in the same way rooms are the building blocks of your home. A logical component performs some sort of function, such as processing the payment for an order, managing item inventory, or tracking orders.

Logical components in a system are usually represented through a directory or namespace. For example, the directory `app/order/payment` with the corresponding namespace `app.order.payment` identifies a logical component named Payment Processing. The source code that allows users to pay for an order is stored in this directory and uses this namespace.

These rooms make up the building blocks of your home.

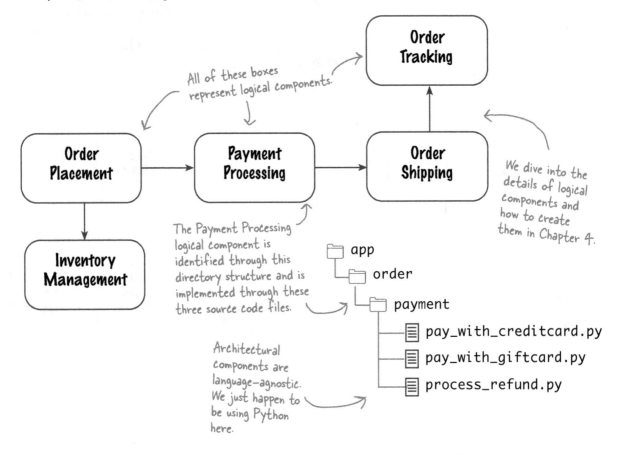

All of these boxes represent logical components.

The Payment Processing logical component is identified through this directory structure and is implemented through these three source code files.

We dive into the details of logical components and how to create them in Chapter 4.

Architectural components are language-agnostic. We just happen to be using Python here.

```
app
  order
    payment
      pay_with_creditcard.py
      pay_with_giftcard.py
      process_refund.py
```

Sharpen your pencil

You've just created the following two components for a new system, and your development team wants to start writing class files to implement them. Can you create a directory structure for them so they can start coding? Flip to the end of the chapter for our solution.

> **Customer Profile**

> **Customer Preferences**

Use this space to write down your answer. ↙

→ Solution on page 32

A logical component should always have a well-defined role and responsibility in the system—in other words, a clear definition of what it does.

This component is responsible for "pick and pack." It locates items in a warehouse (that's the "pick" part), then determines the correct box size for the items so they can be shipped (that's the "pack" part).

> **Order Fulfillment**

This is the role and responsibility statement for the Order Fulfillment component.

Make it Stick

Logical components are blocks in conjunction.

They hold the source code for each business function.

there are no Dumb Questions

Q: What is the difference between the system functionality and the domain?

A: The **domain** is the problem you are trying to solve, and the **system functionality** is *how* you are solving that problem. In other words, the domain is the "what," and the system's functionality is the "how."

The fourth dimension: Architectural styles

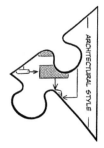

Homes come in all shapes, sizes, and styles. While there are some wild-looking houses out there, most conform to a particular style, such as Victorian, ranch, or Tudor. The style of a home says a lot about its overall structure. For example, ranch homes typically have only one floor; colonial and Tudor homes typically have chimneys; contemporary homes typically have flat roofs.

Each region of the world has its own set of home styles—check 'em out at https://en.wikipedia.org/wiki/List_of_house_styles.

What style home do you live in?

Architectural styles define the overall shape and structure of a software system, each with its own unique set of characteristics. For example, the **microservices** architectural style scales very well and provides a high level of *agility*—the ability to respond quickly to change—whereas the **layered** architectural style is less complex and less costly. The **event-driven** architectural style provides high levels of scalability and is very fast and responsive.

Don't worry—you'll be learning all about these architectural styles later in the book. We've devoted chapters to each of them.

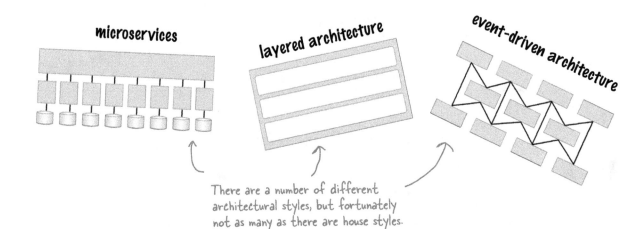

microservices

layered architecture

event-driven architecture

There are a number of different architectural styles, but fortunately not as many as there are house styles.

Because the architectural style defines the overall shape and characteristics of the system, it's important to get it right the first time. Why? Can you imagine starting construction on a one-story ranch home, and in the middle of construction changing your mind and deciding you're going to build a three-story Victorian house instead? That would be a major undertaking, and likely exceed your budget and affect when you can move into the house.

Software architecture is no different. It's not easy changing from a monolithic layered architecture to microservices. Like the house example, this would be quite an undertaking.

Make it Stick

Styles shape the system and help serve its purposes.

You might choose a monolith or microservices.

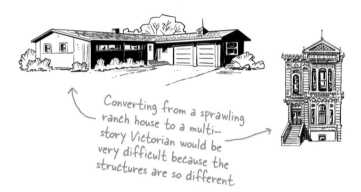

Converting from a sprawling ranch house to a multi-story Victorian would be very difficult because the structures are so different.

Later in the book, we'll show you how to properly select an architectural style based on characteristics that are important to you.

Which brings us back to an earlier point—all of the dimensions of software architecture are interconnected. You can't select an architectural style without knowing what's important to you.

Brain Power

The tightly wound tendons and muscles in a lion's legs enable it to reach speeds as fast as reach speeds as fast as 50 miles (80 kilometers) per hour and leap up to 36 feet (11 meters) in a single bound. This characteristic allows lions to survive by catching fast prey.

Look around you—what else has a structure or shape that defines its characteristics and capabilities?

Fun fact: A lion doesn't have much stamina and can only run fast in short bursts. If you can last longer than the lion chasing you, then you just might survive.

Who Does What?

We were trying to describe our architecture, but all the puzzle pieces got mixed up. Can you help us figure out which dimension does what by matching the statements on the left with the software architecture dimensions on the right? Be careful—some of the statements don't have a match because they are not related to architecture.

— This is about availability.

This system must be available for our overseas customers.

We did this one for you.

ARCHITECTURAL CHARACTERISTICS

Customers are complaining about the background color of the new user interface.

The product owner insists that we get new features and bug fixes out to our customers as fast as possible.

Our system uses an event-driven architecture.

LOGICAL COMPONENTS

We need to support up to 300,000 concurrent users in this system.

The single payment service will be broken apart into separate services, one for each payment type we accept.

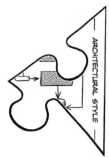

ARCHITECTURAL STYLE

We are going to start offering reward points as a new payment option when paying for an order.

We are breaking up the orderPlacement class into three smaller class files.

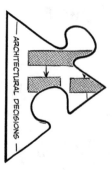

ARCHITECTURAL DECISIONS

The user interface shall not communicate directly with the database.

Solution on page 33

If I'm responsible for the design of a software system, does that mean I'm responsible for its architecture as well? Aren't those the same thing?

No, architecture and design are different.

You see, architecture is less about appearance and more about structure, while design is less about structure and more about appearance.

The color of a room's walls, the placement of furniture, and the type of flooring (carpet or wood) are all aspects of design, whereas the physical size of the room and the placement of doors and windows are part of architecture—in other words, the *structure* of the room.

Think about a typical business application. The architecture, or structure, is all about how the web pages communicate with backend services and databases to retrieve and save data, whereas the design is all about what each page looks like: the colors, the placement of the fields, which design patterns you use, and so on. Again, it becomes a matter of structure versus appearance.

Your question is a good one, because sometimes it gets confusing trying to tell what is considered architecture and what is considered design. Let's investigate these differences.

A design perspective

Suppose your company wants to replace its outdated order processing system with a new custom-built one that better suits its specific needs. Customers can place orders and can view or cancel orders once they have been placed. They can pay for an order using a credit card, a gift card, or both payment methods.

Lucky you. You've been put in charge of building the new order processing system. This is the big break you've been looking for, and you're anxious to get started.

From a *design* perspective, you might build a Unified Modeling Language (UML) class diagram like the one below to show how the classes interact with each other to implement the payment functionality. While you could write source code to implement these class files, this design says nothing about the *physical structure* of the source code—in other words, how these class files would be organized and deployed.

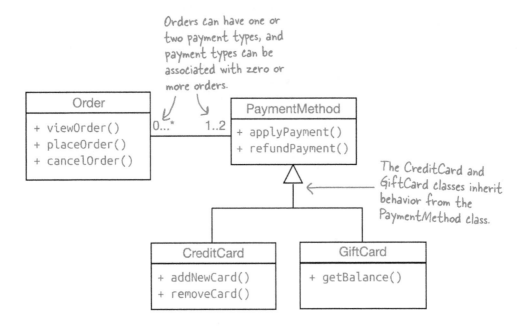

Orders can have one or two payment types, and payment types can be associated with zero or more orders.

The CreditCard and GiftCard classes inherit behavior from the PaymentMethod class.

An architectural perspective

Unlike design, architecture is about the *structure* of the system—things like services, databases, and how services communicate with each other and the user interface.

Let's think about that new order processing system again. What would the *system* look like? From an *architectural* perspective, you might decide to create separate services for each payment type within the order payment process and have an orchestrator service to manage the payment processing part of the system, like in the diagram below.

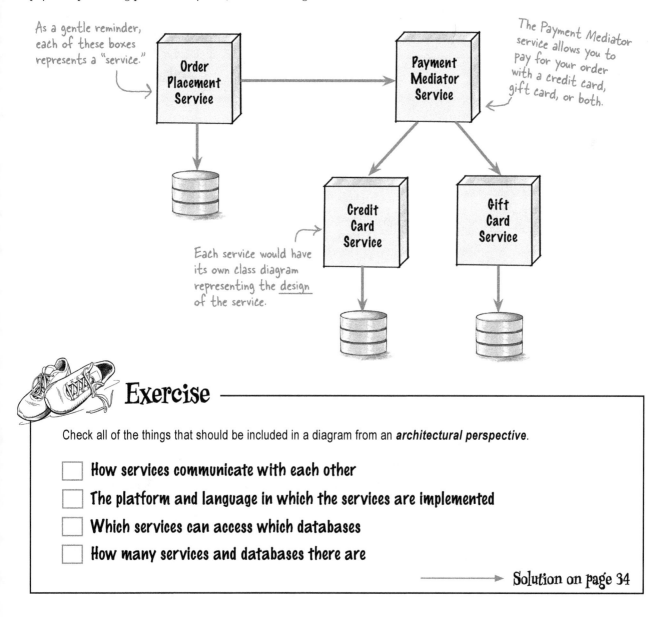

As a gentle reminder, each of these boxes represents a "service."

The Payment Mediator service allows you to pay for your order with a credit card, gift card, or both.

Each service would have its own class diagram representing the design of the service.

Exercise

Check all of the things that should be included in a diagram from an *architectural perspective*.

- [ ] **How services communicate with each other**
- [ ] **The platform and language in which the services are implemented**
- [ ] **Which services can access which databases**
- [ ] **How many services and databases there are**

Solution on page 34

The spectrum between architecture and design

Some decisions are certainly architectural (such as deciding which architectural style to use), and others are clearly design-related (such as changing the position of a field on a screen or changing the type of a field within a class). In reality, most decisions you encounter will fall between these two examples, within a *spectrum* of architecture and design.

Things on this side are more about architecture.

Things on this side are more about design.

Architecture

Design

You'll find most of your decisions fall within the spectrum right about here.

Don't worry if you don't know all the answers to this exercise—you'll learn more about this topic on the next page.

Sharpen your pencil

Circle all of the things that you think fall somewhere in the middle of the spectrum *between* architecture and design.

Breaking up a class file

Deciding to use a graph database

Selecting a user interface framework

Migrating to microservices

Redesigning a web page

Choosing a persistence framework

Breaking apart a service

Choosing an XML parsing library

Solution on page 34

Why should I care where in the spectrum between architecture and design my decision lies? Does it really matter that much?

Yes, it matters a lot. You see, knowing where along the spectrum between architecture and design your decision lies helps determine *who* should be responsible for ultimately making that decision. There are some decisions that the development team should make (such as designing the classes to implement a certain feature), some decisions that an architect should make (such as choosing the most appropriate architectural style for a system), and others that should be made together (such as breaking apart services or putting them back together).

Where along the spectrum does your decision fall?

Is it strategic or tactical?

Strategic decisions are long term and influence future actions or decisions. *Tactical* decisions are short term and generally stand independent of other actions or decisions (but may be made in the context of a particular strategy). For example, deciding how big your new home will be influences the number of rooms and the sizes of those rooms, whereas deciding on a particular lighting fixture won't affect decisions about the size of your dining room table. The more strategic the decision, the more it sits toward the architecture side of the spectrum.

Sometimes waking up in the morning requires a lot of effort—we'll call those "architecture" mornings.

How much effort will it take to construct or change?

Architectural decisions require more effort to construct or change, while design decisions require relatively less. For example, building an addition to your home generally requires a high level of effort and would therefore be more on the architecture side of the spectrum, whereas adding an area rug to a room requires much less effort and would therefore be more on the design side.

Does it have significant trade-offs?

Trade-offs are the pros and cons you evaluate as you are making a decision. Decisions that involve significant trade-offs require much more time and analysis to make and tend to be more architectural in nature. Decisions that have less-significant trade-offs can be made quicker, with less analysis, and therefore tend to be more on the design side.

We're going to walk you through the details of all three of these factors in the next several pages.

Brain Power

Can you think of a decision that doesn't involve a trade-off, no matter how small or insignificant? Here's a hint: if you think you've found a decision that doesn't involve a trade-off, keep looking.

Strategic versus tactical

The more strategic a decision is, the more architectural it becomes. This is an important distinction, because decisions that are strategic require more thought and planning and are generally long term.

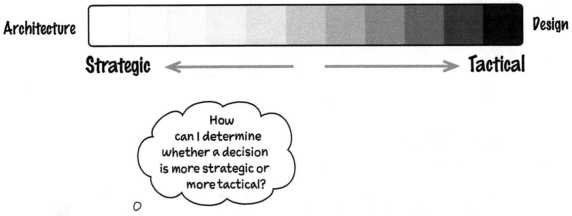

Architecture — **Design**

Strategic ← ——— → **Tactical**

How can I determine whether a decision is more strategic or more tactical?

Good question. You can use these three questions to help determine if something is more strategic or tactical. Remember, the more strategic something is, the more it's about architecture.

1. **How much thought and planning do you need to put into the decision?**

   If making the decision takes a couple of minutes to an hour, it's more tactical in nature. If thought and planning require several days or weeks, it's likely more strategic (hence more architectural).

2. **How many people are involved in the decision?**

   The more people involved, the more strategic the decision. A decision you can make by yourself or with a colleague is likely to be tactical. A decision that requires many meetings with lots of stakeholders is probably more strategic.

3. **Does your decision involve a long-term vision or a short-term action?**

   If you are making a quick decision about something that is temporary or likely to change soon, it's more tactical and hence more about design. Conversely, if this is a decision you'll be living with for a very long time, it's more strategic and more about architecture.

Sharpen your pencil

Oh dear. We've lost all of our marbles and we need your help collecting them and putting them back in the right spot. Using the three questions on the previous page as a guide, can you figure out which jar each marble should go in?

Picking a programming language for your new project

Deciding to get your first dog

Deploying in the cloud or on premises

Redesigning your user interface

Migrating your system to microservices

Choosing a parsing library

Using a design pattern

Strategic

Somewhere in between

Tactical

Solution on page 35

High versus low levels of effort

Renowned software architect and author Martin Fowler once wrote that "software architecture is the stuff that's hard to change." You can use Martin's definition to help determine where along the spectrum your decision lies. The harder something is to change later, the further it falls toward the architecture side of the spectrum. Conversely, the easier it is to change later, the more it's probably related to design.

Martin Fowler's website (https://martinfowler. com/architecture) has lots of useful stuff about architecture.

Suppose you are planning on moving from one architectural style to another; say, from a traditional *n*-tiered layered architecture to microservices. This migration effort is rather difficult and will take a lot of time. Because the level of effort is high, this would be on the far end of the *architecture side* of the spectrum.

Oh dear, this is going to take a lot of effort. Changing things that are architectural is difficult.

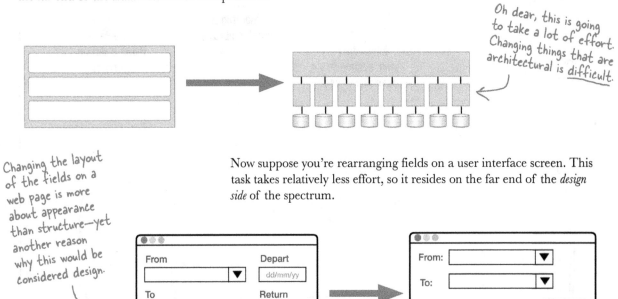

Changing the layout of the fields on a web page is more about appearance than structure—yet another reason why this would be considered design.

Now suppose you're rearranging fields on a user interface screen. This task takes relatively less effort, so it resides on the far end of the *design side* of the spectrum.

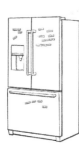

Code Magnets

We had all of these magnets from our to-do list arranged from high effort to low effort, and somehow they all fell on the floor and got mixed up. Can you help us put them back in the right order based on the amount of effort it would take to make each change?

Draw arrows to put the high-effort tasks at the top of the page, and the lower-effort ones toward the bottom of the page.

High effort

Resolving a merge conflict in Git

Replacing your user interface framework

Migrating your system to a cloud environment

Deciding which mustard to buy

Renaming a method or function

Breaking apart a single service into separate ones

Moving from a relational to a graph database

Breaking apart a class file

Low effort

Solution on page 36

Significant versus less-significant trade-offs

Some decisions you make might involve significant trade-offs, such as choosing which city to live in. Others might involve less significant trade-offs, like deciding on the color of your living room rug. You can use the level of significance of the trade-offs in a particular decision to help determine whether that decision is more about architecture or design. The more significant the trade-offs, the more it's about architecture; the less significant the trade-offs, the more it's about design.

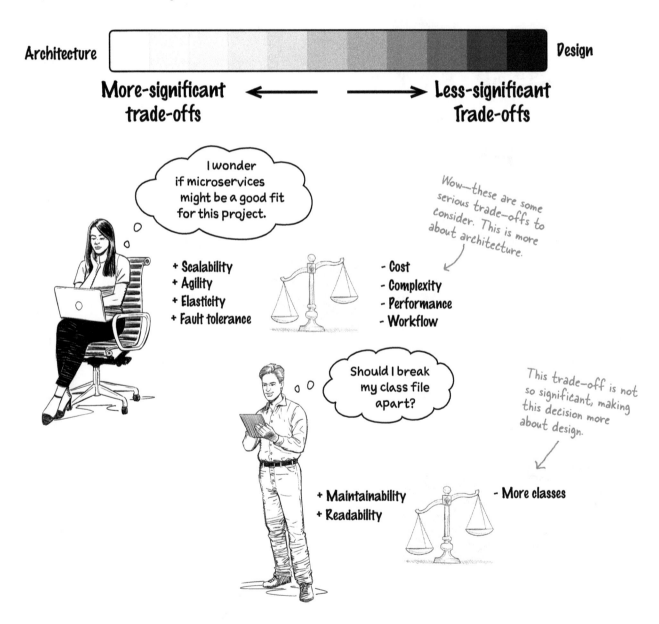

Exercise

Decisions, decisions, decisions. How can we ever tackle all of these decisions? One thing we think might help is to identify the decisions that involve significant trade-offs, since those will require more thinking and will take longer. Can you help us by identifying which decisions have significant trade-offs and which don't?

Is this a significant trade-off?

☐ Yes   ☐ No   **Picking out what clothes to wear to work today**

☐ Yes   ☐ No   **Choosing to deploy in the cloud or on premises**

☐ Yes   ☐ No   **Selecting a user interface framework**

☐ Yes   ☐ No   **Naming a variable in a class file**

☐ Yes   ☐ No   **Choosing between vanilla and chocolate ice cream**

☐ Yes   ☐ No   **Deciding which architectural style to use**

☐ Yes   ☐ No   **Choosing between REST and messaging**

☐ Yes   ☐ No   **Using full data or only keys for the message payload**

☐ Yes   ☐ No   **Selecting an XML parsing library**

☐ Yes   ☐ No   **Deciding whether or not to break apart a service**

☐ Yes   ☐ No   **Choosing between atomic or distributed transactions**

☐ Yes   ☐ No   **Deciding whether or not to go out to dinner tonight**

⟶ Solution on page 37

Putting it all together

Now it's time to put all three of these factors to use to figure out whether a decision is more about architecture or more about design. This tells development teams when to collaborate with an architect and when to make a decision on their own.

Let's say you decide to use asynchronous messaging between the Order Placement service and the Inventory Management service to increase the system's responsiveness when customers place orders. After all, why should the customer have to wait for the business to adjust and process inventory? Let's see if we can determine where in the spectrum this decision lies.

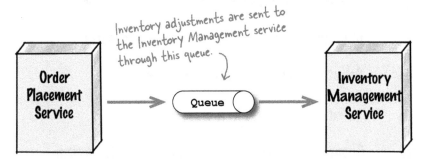

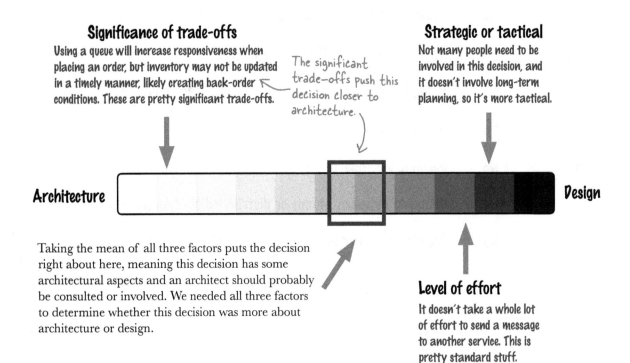

Significance of trade-offs

Using a queue will increase responsiveness when placing an order, but inventory may not be updated in a timely manner, likely creating back-order conditions. These are pretty significant trade-offs.

The significant trade-offs push this decision closer to architecture.

Strategic or tactical

Not many people need to be involved in this decision, and it doesn't involve long-term planning, so it's more tactical.

Taking the mean of all three factors puts the decision right about here, meaning this decision has some architectural aspects and an architect should probably be consulted or involved. We needed all three factors to determine whether this decision was more about architecture or design.

Level of effort

It doesn't take a whole lot of effort to send a message to another service. This is pretty standard stuff.

You made it!

Congratulations—you made it through the first part of your journey to understanding software architecture. But before you roll up your sleeves to dig into further chapters, here's a little quiz for you to test your knowledge so far. For each of the statements below, circle whether it is true or false.

True or False

True	False	Design is like the structure of a house (walls, roof, layout, and so on), and software architecture is like the furniture and decoration.
True	False	Most decisions are purely about architecture or design. Very few exist along a spectrum between architecture and design.
True	False	The more strategic your decision, the more it's about architecture; the more tactical, the more it's about design.
True	False	The more effort it takes to implement or change your decision, the more it's about design; the less effort, the more it's about architecture.
True	False	*Trade-offs* are the pros and cons of a given decision or task. The more significant the trade-offs become, the more it's about architecture.

⟶ Solution on page 38

Bullet Points

- Software architecture is less about appearance and more about structure, whereas design is more about appearance and less about structure.

- You need to use four dimensions to understand and describe software architecture: architectural characteristics, architectural decisions, logical components, and architectural style.

- Architectural characteristics form the foundational aspects of software architecture. You must know which architectural characteristics are most important to your specific system, so you can analyze trade-offs and make the right architectural decisions.

- Architectural decisions serve as guideposts to help development teams understand the constraints and conditions of the architecture.

- The logical components of a software architecture solution make up the building blocks of the system. They represent things the system does and are implemented through class files or source code.

- Like with houses, with software there are many different architectural styles you can use. Each style supports a specific set of architectural characteristics, so it's important to make sure you select the right one (or combination of them) for your system.

- It's important to know if a decision is about architecture or design, because that helps determine who should be responsible for the decision and how important it is.

Software Architecture Crossword

Congratulations! You made it through the first chapter and learned about what software architecture is (and isn't). Now, why don't you try architecting the solution to this crossword?

Across

2. An architectural style determings the system's overall _____
4. _____-driven is an architectural style
5. Architectural characteristics are sometimes called this
10. Architectural decisions are usually _____ term
12. If something takes a lot of _____ to implement, it's probably architectural
13. You're learning about software _____
15. You'll make lots of architectural _____
16. A system's _____ components are its building blocks
18. The number of rooms in your home is part of its _____
19. Architecture and design exist on a _____

Down

1. Strategic decisions typically involve a lot of these
3. Building this can be a great metaphor
6. Decisions can be strategic of _____
7. How many dimensions it takes to describe a software architecture
8. A website's user _____ involves lots of design decisions
9. The overall shape of a house or a system, like Victorian or microservices
11. It's important to know whether a decision is about architecture or this
13. You might want to become one after reading this book
14. You analyze these when making an architectural decision
17. Trade-offs are about the _____ and cons

⟶ Solution on page 39

Exercise
Solution

From page 2

Gardening is another useful metaphor for describing software architecture. Using the space below, can you describe how a garden might relate to software architecture?

The overall layout of a garden can be compared to the architectural style, whereas each grouping of like plants (either by type or color) can represent the architectural components. Individual plants within a group represent the class files implementing those components.

Gardens are influenced by weather in the same way a software architecture is influenced by changes in technology, platforms, the deploymnent environment, and so on. Also, if you don't pay attention to the garden, weeds grow—just like structural decay within your architecture.

Sharpen your pencil
Solution

From page 3

What features of your home can you list that are *structural* and related to its *architecture*?

The size and shape of your kitchen (who doesn't complain about how small their kitchen is?)

How many floors it has (as you get older, stairs might be a problem)

Where the front door is and if the entranceway is wheelchair accessible

The size of your bedroom closet (if you have lots of clothes)

The height of your ceilings (especially if you happen to be very tall)

How many bathrooms it has (adding a new bathroom is really hard to do)

An attic for storing all of the stuff you never use

Outside deck or patio (unless you live in the Arctic, of course)

Exercise Solution

From page 6

Check the things you think might be considered architectural characteristics—something that the *structure* of the software system supports.

☐ **Changing the font size in a window on the user interface screen**

☒ **Making changes quickly** ← — This is known as <u>agility</u> in architecture.

☒ **Handling thousands of concurrent users** ← — This is known as <u>elasticity</u>.

☐ **Encrypting user passwords stored in the database**

☒ **Interacting with many external systems to complete a business request** ← This is known as <u>interoperability</u>.

Who Does What? Solution

From page 7

Here's your chance to see how much you already know about many common architectural characteristics. Can you match up each architectural characteristic on the left with its definition on the right? You'll notice there are more definitions than characteristics, so be careful—not all of the definitions have matches.

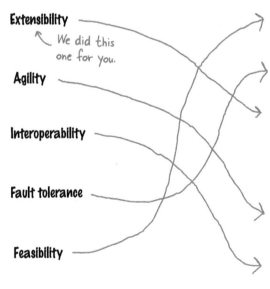

Extensibility — We did this one for you.

Taking into account time frames, budgets, and developer skills when making architectural choices

Agility

The system's ability to keep its other parts functioning when fatal errors occur

Interoperability

The ease with which the system can be enhanced to support additional features and functionality

Fault tolerance

The amount of time it takes to get a response to the user

Feasibility

The system's ability to respond quickly to change (a function of maintainability, testability, and deployability)

The system's ability to interface and interact with other systems to complete a business request

From page 9

BE the architect Solution

Your job is to be the architect and identify as many architectural decisions as you can in the diagram below. Draw a circle around anything that you think might be an architectural decision and write what that decision might be.

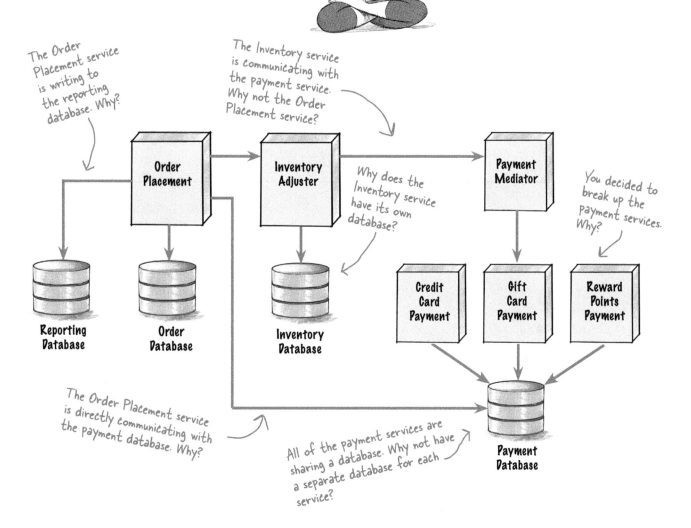

The Order Placement service is writing to the reporting database. Why?

The Inventory service is communicating with the payment service. Why not the Order Placement service?

Order Placement

Inventory Adjuster

Why does the Inventory service have its own database?

Payment Mediator

You decided to break up the payment services. Why?

Reporting Database

Order Database

Inventory Database

Credit Card Payment

Gift Card Payment

Reward Points Payment

The Order Placement service is directly communicating with the payment database. Why?

All of the payment services are sharing a database. Why not have a separate database for each service?

Payment Database

From page 11

Sharpen your pencil
Solution

You've just created the following two components for a new system, and your development team wants to start writing class files to implement them. Can you create a directory structure for them so they can start coding?

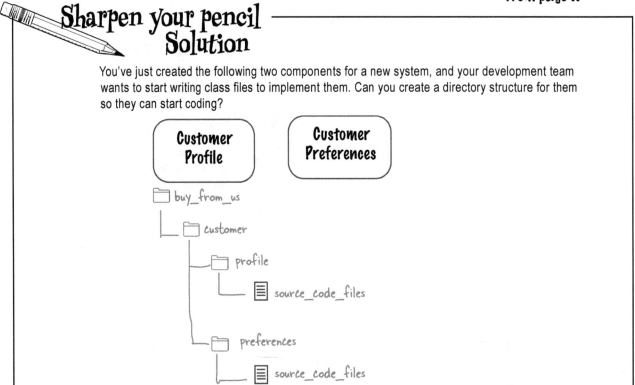

Who Does What? Solution

From page 14

We were trying to describe our architecture, but all the puzzle pieces got mixed up. Can you help us figure out which dimension does what by matching the statements on the left with the software architecture dimensions on the right? Be careful—some of the statements don't have a match because they are not related to architecture.

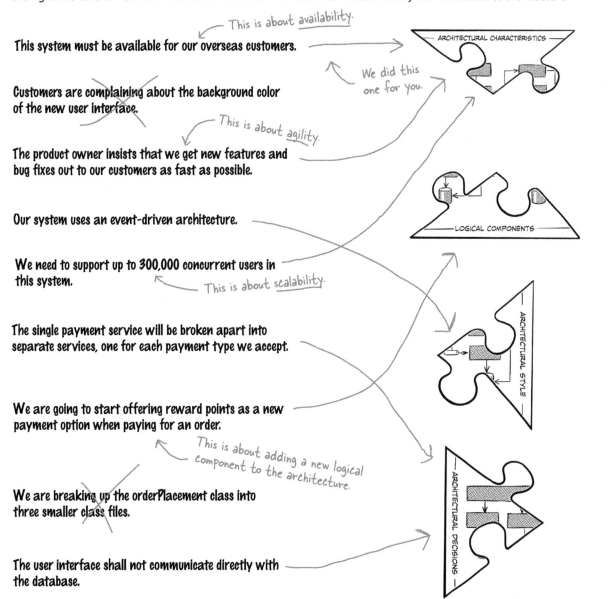

This is about availability.

This system must be available for our overseas customers.

ARCHITECTURAL CHARACTERISTICS

We did this one for you.

Customers are complaining about the background color of the new user interface.

This is about agility.

The product owner insists that we get new features and bug fixes out to our customers as fast as possible.

Our system uses an event-driven architecture.

LOGICAL COMPONENTS

We need to support up to 300,000 concurrent users in this system.

This is about scalability.

The single payment service will be broken apart into separate services, one for each payment type we accept.

ARCHITECTURAL STYLE

We are going to start offering reward points as a new payment option when paying for an order.

This is about adding a new logical component to the architecture.

We are breaking up the orderPlacement class into three smaller class files.

ARCHITECTURAL DECISIONS

The user interface shall not communicate directly with the database.

Exercise Solution

From page 17

Check all of the things that should be included in a diagram from an *architectural perspective*.

☒ **How services communicate with each other**

☐ **The platform and language in which the services are implemented** ← *How something should be implemented is a design perspective.*

☒ **Which services can access which databases**

☒ **How many services and databases there are**

Sharpen your pencil Solution

From page 18

Circle all of the things that you think fall somewhere in the middle of the spectrum *between* architecture and design.

This is design.

Breaking up a class file

Choosing a persistence framework

Deciding to use a graph database

Breaking apart a service

Redesigning a web page

Selecting a user interface framework

This is architecture.

Migrating to microservices

Choosing an XML parsing library

These are design.

Sharpen your pencil
Solution

Oh dear. We've lost all of our marbles and we need your help collecting them and putting them back in the right spot. Using the three questions on page 20 as a guide, can you figure out which jar each marble should go in?

These require some planning and usually involve a few other people.

This decision involves the entire family.

This requires a lot of planning, is more visionary, and involves a lot of people.

Picking a programming language for your new project

Deciding to get your first dog

Deploying in the cloud or on premises

You can usually make these decisions alone.

Redesigning your user interface

Migrating your system to microservices

Choosing a parsing library

Using a design pattern

Good luck.

Strategic

Somewhere in between

Tactical

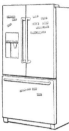

Code Magnets
Solution

From page 23

We had all of these magnets from our to-do list arranged from high effort to low effort, and somehow they all fell on the floor and got mixed up. Can you help us put them back in the right order based on the amount of effort it would take to make each change?

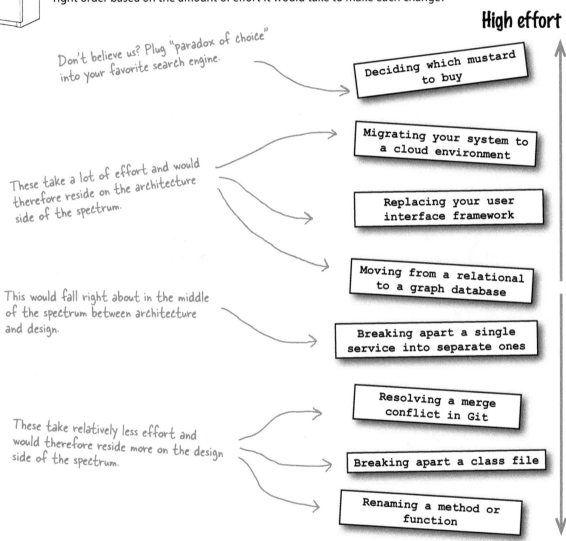

High effort

Don't believe us? Plug "paradox of choice" into your favorite search engine.

Deciding which mustard to buy

These take a lot of effort and would therefore reside on the architecture side of the spectrum.

Migrating your system to a cloud environment

Replacing your user interface framework

Moving from a relational to a graph database

This would fall right about in the middle of the spectrum between architecture and design.

Breaking apart a single service into separate ones

Resolving a merge conflict in Git

These take relatively less effort and would therefore reside more on the design side of the spectrum.

Breaking apart a class file

Renaming a method or function

Low effort

Exercise Solution

Decisions, decisions, decisions. How can we ever tackle all of these decisions? One thing we think might help is to identify the decisions that involve significant trade-offs, since those will require more thinking and will take longer. Can you help us by identifying which decisions have significant trade-offs and which ones don't?

Significant Tradeoffs?

Okay, so maybe this is a difficult decision sometimes.

☐ Yes	☒ No	**Picking out what clothes to wear to work today**
☒ Yes	☐ No	**Choosing to deploy in the cloud or on premisis**
☐ Yes	☒ No	**Selecting a user interface framework**
☐ Yes	☒ No	**Deciding on the name of a variable in a class file**
☐ Yes	☒ No	**Choosing between vanilla and chocolate ice cream**
☒ Yes	☐ No	**Deciding which architectural style to use**
☒ Yes	☐ No	**Choosing between REST and messaging**
☒ Yes	☐ No	**Using full data or only keys for the message payload**
☐ Yes	☒ No	**Selecting an XML parsing library**
☒ Yes	☐ No	**Deciding whether or not to break apart a service**
☒ Yes	☐ No	**Choosing between atomic or distributed transactions**
☐ Yes	☒ No	**Deciding whether or not to go out to dinner tonight**

There are certainly trade-offs here, so this one could go either way.

These can impact scalability, performance, and overall maintainability.

Are you getting hungry yet?

This can impact data integrity and data consistency, but also scalability and performance.

True or False Solution

From page 27

True (False) Design is like the structure of a house (walls, roof, layout, and so on), and software architecture is like the furniture and decoration.

This is backwards.

True (False) Most decisions are purely about architecture or design. Very few exist along a spectrum between architecture and design.

Most decisions lie within the spectrum between architecture and design.

(True) False The more strategic your decision, the more it's about architecture; the more tactical, the more it's about design.

True (False) The more effort it takes to implement or change your decision, the more it's about design; the less effort, the more it's about architecture.

This is backwards.

(True) False *Trade-offs* are the pros and cons of a given decision or task. The more significant the trade-offs become, the more it's about architecture.

 Software Architecture Crossword Solution

From page 23

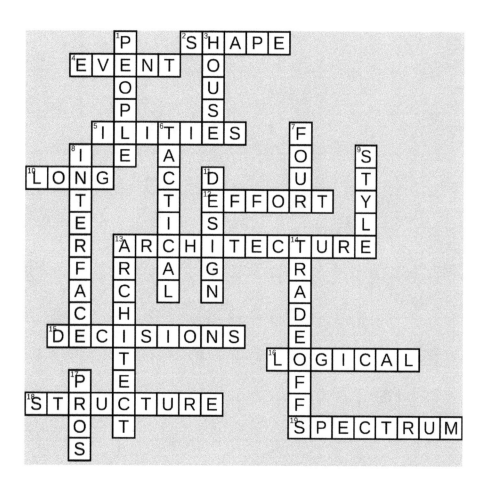

2 architectural characteristics
Know Your Capabilities

What does your architecture need to support? Architectural characteristics (the capabilities of an architecture) are the fundamental building blocks of any system. Without them, you cannot make architectural decisions, select an architectural style, or in many cases even create a logical architecture. In this chapter you'll learn how to define some of the more common characteristics (like scalability, reliability, and testability), how they influence a software architecture, how they help you make architectural decisions, and how to identify which ones are important for your particular situation. Ready to add some capabilities to your software architecture?

Causing Lafter

Sillycon Symposia is a startup with a Bay Area feel whose business plan combines technology-themed conferences with comedy. By gathering like minds, Sillycon provides unique offerings for each group and keeps them engaged by keeping them laughing.

How hard could it be to start a social networking site?!

Part of the business plan includes building Lafter, a social media network related to (but not limited to) the conferences Sillycon hosts. The business stakeholders put together a **requirements document** for it:

The good news is that they've got the logo figured out. The rest is up to you.

Sillycon Symposia is hosting a social media network of like-minded technologists named Lafter.

A pretty standard level of detail for a requirements document

Users: Hundreds of speakers, thousands of users

Requirements:

Users can register for usernames and approve the privacy policy

Users can add new content on Lafter as a "Joke" (long-form post) or "Pun" (short-form post)

Followers can "HaHa" (indicating strong approval) or "Giggle" (a milder approval message) content they like

Speakers at Sillycon Symposia events have a special icon

Speakers can host forums on the platform related to their content

Users can post messages of up to 281 characters

Users can also post links to external content

Additional Context:

International support

Very small support staff

"Bursty" traffic: extremely busy during live conferences

Cubicle conversation

Mara   Sam   Alex

Alex: Look what just landed in my inbox—the Powers That Be want me to be the architect for the Sillycon Symposia social media app, Lafter.

Sam: You have the requirements? You should jump right into the design of the system—it seems really straightforward.

Mara: Well, you can really only do that for the simplest of applications, and I don't think this one qualifies. Remember the diagram I drew on the whiteboard the other day?

These are the nonfunctional requirements.

architectural characteristics

These represent the problem domain.

architectural decsions

architectural style

These are the decisions we make after doing a trade-off analysis.

logical components

Architectural characteristics and logical components together help us decide on the architectural style.

You need to analyze both architectural characteristics and logical components before you can choose an architectural style as a starting point.

You can implement just about any application in any architectural style, but some are more suitable than others. Choosing the style before performing this type of analysis is a classic case of putting the cart before the horse.

Sam: Can't we just be super-agile, start with something tiny, and then keep iterating on it until we have the entire system?

Mara: The iterative approach you talk about doesn't quite work like that for architectural characteristics analysis. For example, it's difficult to make a system highly scalable if it wasn't designed for that.

Alex: That makes sense. I guess I need to roll up my sleeves and analyze some architectural characteristics—thanks!

What are architectural characteristics?

You have a problem. You decide, "I'm going to write some software to solve this problem!" The *thing* you're writing software about is called the **domain**, and designing for it will occupy much of your effort—that is, after all, why you're writing software. However, it's not the only thing an architect must consider—they must also analyze **architectural characteristics**. Here are a few examples of architectural characteristics that show how different domains have different, but often overlapping, architectural characteristics.

These make up one of the dimensions that help describe your architecture.

Notice how many of them end with "–ility".

Auditability
Banks must provide a way to verify transactions.

Data integrity
Financial transactions must be consistent and accurate.

Security
Banks require stringent security to protect financial concerns.

Bank

Both domains have scalability as an architectural characteristic they must support.

Scalability

Banks must support large numbers of concurrent users.

Online auctions must support a large number of bidders.

Usability
Auction sites must be easy to use for quick and efficient entry of bids.

Online auction

Consistency
Bids must be captured consistently and in order for auctions to work.

Reliability
Auction sites must be reliable—users don't like it if their connection drops in the middle of an auction.

Defining architectural characteristics

Part of your job as an architect is structural design for software systems, for which there are two parts: *logical components* and *architectural characteristics*. Logical components represent the domain of the application—the motivation for writing the software system (we cover these in Chapter 4). If you combine architectural characteristics with logical components, you have the structural considerations for an architecture.

Architectural characteristics are the important parts of the construction process of a software system or application, irrespective of the problem domain. They represent its operational capabilities, internal structure decisions, and other necessary characteristics.

We'll show you lots of examples of architectural characteristics in the upcoming pages, but first we want to cover the concept itself.

We define architectural characteristics in **three parts**, as shown here.

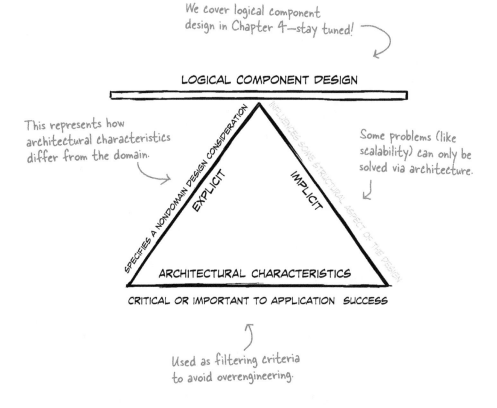

We cover logical component design in Chapter 4—stay tuned!

LOGICAL COMPONENT DESIGN

This represents how architectural characteristics differ from the domain.

SPECIFIES A NONDOMAIN DESIGN CONSIDERATION

EXPLICIT

INFLUENCES SOME STRUCTURAL ASPECT OF THE DESIGN

IMPLICIT

Some problems (like scalability) can only be solved via architecture.

ARCHITECTURAL CHARACTERISTICS

CRITICAL OR IMPORTANT TO APPLICATION SUCCESS

Used as filtering criteria to avoid overengineering.

Let's look at each of these edges one at a time.

Characteristics are nondomain design considerations

To define architectural characteristics, we first need to look at what they are **not**. The *requirements* specify what the application should do; *architectural characteristics* specify operational and design criteria for success, how to implement the requirements, and why certain choices were made. For example, an application's level of performance is an important architectural characteristic that often doesn't appear in requirements documents.

Structural design in architecture can be divided into **domain and non-domain considerations**. Architectural characteristics represent your design effort to create the capabilities necessary for the project to succeed.

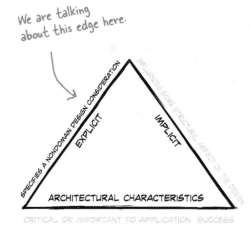

We are talking about this edge here.

Mara: OK, the business analysts and subject matter experts have toiled away to create both a requirements document and the beginning of a domain design. But we need to work with them to figure out what architectural characteristics we need to support.

Sam: Isn't that part of the domain design? Why does an architect need to get involved at this point?

Alex: Well, our business analysts have never worked on a software porject, so they probably won't understand the impact of one decision versus another.

Mara: That's correct—often what seems like a minor difference to a business person makes a big difference for an architect! What they want may turn out to be difficult to support in architecture. That's why it's important for architects to be involved early and often in the design process.

Sam: What kinds of things are we looking for?

Alex: Part of the definition of *architectural characteristics* is "nondomain design considerations." Let's look at what they've designed and see if they've considered things like performance and scalability.

Characteristics influence architectural structure

The primary reason architects try to describe architectural characteristics has to do with architectural considerations: does this characteristic require special structural support to succeed? For example, security is a concern in virtually every project, and all systems must take baseline precautions during design and coding. However, security becomes an *architectural* characteristic when the architect needs to make a special effort to accommodate it.

Consider the following potential architecture diagrams for Lafter, which include functionality for marketing upcoming promotions and rules for when each promotion applies. An architect could design this as a **monolithic architecture**—one with a single deployable unit and matching database—or as a series of independent services.

For the monolithic architecture, the entire application would have to be redeployed when the promotion rules change, because monoliths are built and deployed as a single unit. However, in a **distributed architecture**, only the Promotions service would be affected, and it could be redeployed independently.

We've moved on to the second edge here.

SPECIFIES A NONDOMAIN DESIGN CONSIDERATION

INFLUENCES SOME STRUCTURAL ASPECT OF THE DESIGN

EXPLICIT

IMPLICIT

ARCHITECTURAL CHARACTERISTICS

CRITICAL OR IMPORTANT TO APPLICATION SUCCESS

This is a monolithic architecture.

If Promotions needs to fix a bug in production, the whole application needs to be redeployed.

Promote event

Add event user

Promotions

Post message

In a distributed architecture, each service is deployed independently.

Promote event

Add event user

Post message

Promotions

In this case, Promotions can go to production anytime they like!

You must consider many trade-offs when making architectural decisions, such as whether to use a monolithic versus distributed physical architecture.

Limit characteristics to prevent overengineering

Applications *could* support a huge number of architectural characteristics…but they shouldn't. Every architectural characteristic the system must support adds complexity.

The sheer number and variety of architectural characteristics means there are many tempting choices. But as architects, we should try to pick as *few* architectural characteristics as possible, rather than as many as possible. This is because architectural characteristics are:

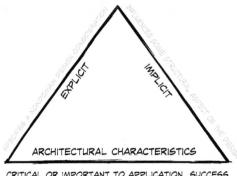

ARCHITECTURAL CHARACTERISTICS

CRITICAL OR IMPORTANT TO APPLICATION SUCCESS

We are talking about the third edge. Almost there!

Impossible to standardize

Different organizations use different terms for the same architectural characteristics. For example, *performance* and *responsiveness* might indicate the same behavior.

It's a good idea to create a "ubiquitous language" (shared vocabulary) for architectural characteristics within your organization—this gives you a fighting chance at creating a usable standard list.

Your takeaway? You often cannot choose one architectural characteristic without considering how it may affect others.

Synergistic

Architectural characteristics affect other architectural characteristics and domain concerns. For example, if you want to make an application more secure, the required changes will almost certainly affect performance negatively (more on-the-fly encryption and other similar changes will lead to performance overhead).

Even the number of categories of architectural characteristics has increased over the last few years, with additions such as cloud constraints and capabilities.

Overabundant

Possible architectural characteristics are extraordinarily abundant, and new ones appear all the time. For example, a few years ago there was no such thing as on-demand elasticity via a cloud provider.

We'll be discussing some categories of architectural characteristics soon.

A common hazard for architects is *overengineering*: supporting too many architectural characteristics and complicating the overall design to little or no benefit. Knowing which architectural characteristics are **critical or important to application success** acts as a filtering tool. It help us *eliminate* features that would be nice to have but just end up adding needless complexity to the system.

Beware of resume-driven development (RDD)! It's fun to play with new stuff, and we should keep learning, but trying to support too many architectural characteristics in our systems will not align with larger priorities or help the application succeed.

Synergy can be dangerous!

Architects would love to design for architectural characteristics irrespective of the domain design. Unfortunately, the real world refuses to cooperate. When we say that architectural characteristics are *synergistic*, we mean that changes to one might require changes to other architectural characteristics and/or the domain. No matter how clever you are, no architect can make every single architecture scalable. Some architectures can't scale as successfully as others because of physical constraints such as memory and bandwidth.

Be careful when you change one architectural characteristic; consider how that change may affect other parts of your architecture. The same applies to making changes to domain design, such as component boundaries and distribution—changes to the domain may synergistically affect your architectural characteristics. For example, if you change your application to begin storing users' payment information, the security and data integrity architectural characteristics will also change.

Brain Power

Many things in the the real world are **synergistic**—that is, combining them yields something different than the sum of the parts. See if you can think of some real-world examples of synergy. *Hint: These might include things that are still identifiable (like peanut butter and chocolate) or things that merge (such as emulsions like oil and vinegar).*

Use this space to jot down your ideas.

Consider explicit and implicit capabilities

Some things are *explicit*—stated clearly—whereas others are *implicit*—assumed based on context or other knowledge. Imagine if you saw a bunch of mail and packages piling up outside the door of a home—what conclusions would you draw?

Explicit

Packages are stacked outside a door.

The door is locked.

Implicit

No one is home.

This family orders a bunch of stuff online.

Is this family on vacation?

Explicit architectural characteristics are specified in the requirements for the application.

Implicit architectural characteristics are factors that influence an architect's decisions but aren't explicitly called out in the requirements. Security is often an implicit architectural characteristic: even if it isn't mentioned in the requirements, architects know that we shouldn't design an insecure system.

You must use your knowledge of the problem domain to uncover these architectural characteristics during the analysis phase. For example, a high-frequency trading firm may not specify how critical it is for transactions to complete within milliseconds, but the architects in that problem domain know how important this is.

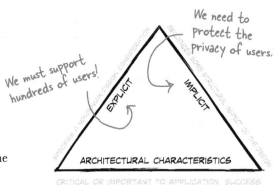

---

there are no
Dumb Questions

Q: What about important things like good internal structure that no one thinks to ask for?

A: Some implicit architectural characteristics are more subtle, but just as important. For example, architects should pay attention to the application's internal structure as developers create it, to ensure that sloppy coding and other deficiencies don't degrade the longevity of the application. However, virtually no requirements list will specify "Don't mess up the internal modularity of the system as you build it!" or "Make sure the software is maintainable!"

The International Zoo of "-ilities"

Like the animals in a zoo, architectural characteristics exist along a broad spectrum. Just as animals range from primates to reptiles, architectural characteristics range from low-level code characteristics, such as modularity, to sophisticated operational concerns, such as scalability and elasticity. Unfortunately, there is no "universal list" of architectural characteristics, nor are there any real standards for what many of these terms mean (although people have tried). Instead, each organization interprets these terms for itself.

Additionally, the software ecosystem is constantly adding new concepts, terms, measures, and verifications, providing new opportunities to define *even more* architectural characteristics.

Think this is a big list? Check out https://iso25000.com/index.php/en/iso-25000-standards/iso-25010.

scalability	accessibility	observability
availability	maintainability	testability
interoperability	reusability	portability
security	simplicity	feasibility
stability	reliability	usability
agility	integrity	performance
traceability	localizability	auditability

This is **not** the complete list. There is **no** complete list!

Sam: We're supposed to define architectural characteristics for Lafter, but I can't seem to find a standard list anywhere.

Alex: Gosh, there are so many possibilities...

Mara: That's why I like to categorize them. Remember the old zoo maps that broke the zoo into "houses" and "enclosures" for each type of animal? That same kind of categorization can work here. It's sort of like the genus and species of architectural characteristics.

"Ladies and gentlemen, boys and girls, children of all ages—welcome to the International Zoo of '-ilities'!"

Structural pen

Operational house

Process enclosure

Cross-cutting savannah

Process architectural characteristics

Process architectural characteristics are where the software development process intersects with software architecture. They reflect the decisions about the mechanics of building software.

 modularity
The degree to which the software is composed of discrete components. Modularity affects how architects partition behavior and organize logical building blocks.

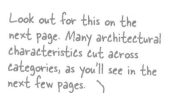 **testability**
How complete the system's testing is and how easy these tests are to run, including unit, functional, user acceptance, and exploratory tests.

"Testability" refers to testing at development time (such as unit testing), rather than formal quality assurance.

 agility
A composite architectural characteristic that encompasses testability, deployability, modularity, and a host of other architectural characteristics that facilitate and enable agile software development practices.

Agility is a composite architectural characteristic we'll discuss later in this chapter—stay tuned!

Look out for this on the next page. Many architectural characteristics cut across categories, as you'll see in the next few pages.

 deployability
How easy and efficient it is to deploy the software system.

This is one of the many architectural characteristics that make up "agility."

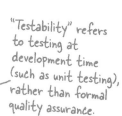 **extensibility**
How easy it is for developers to extend the system. This may encompass architectural structure, engineering practices, internal design, and governance.

 decouple-ability
Coupling describes how parts of the system are joined together. Some architectures define how to *decouple* parts in specific ways to achieve certain benefits; this architectural characteristic measures the extent to which this is possible in a software system.

Yes, we know this is a made-up word. That happens a lot in software architecture!

Structural architectural characteristics

Structural architectural characteristics affect the internal structure of the software system, including factors like the degree of coupling between components and the relationships between different integration points.

security

How secure the system is, holistically. Does the data need to be encrypted in the database? How about for network communication between internal systems? What type of authentication needs to be in place for remote user access?

Security appears in every application, as an implicit or explicit architectural characteristic.

maintainability

How easy it is for architects and developers to apply changes to enhance the system and/or fix bugs.

Portability can apply to any part of the system, including the user interface and implementation platform.

portability

How easy it is to run the system on more than one platform (for example, Windows and macOS).

This is one of those characteristics that belong to more than one category.

extensibility

How easy it is for developers to extend the system. This may encompass architectural structure, engineering practices, internal design, and governance.

Some architectural characteristics cover development concerns rather than purely domain concerns.

localization

How well the system supports multiple languages, units of measurement, currencies, and other factors that allow it to be used globally.

Another flavor of localization is internationalization (i18n).

Operational architectural characteristics

Operational architectural characteristics represent how architectural decisions influence what operational team members can do.

availability

What percentage of the time the system needs to be available and, if 24/7, how easy it is to get the system up and running quickly after a failure.

Usually represented as a number of "nines" (99.999% uptime = 5 nines, a bit under 6 minutes/year).

recoverability

How quickly the system can get online again and maintain business continuity in case of a disaster. This will affect the backup strategy and requirements for duplicated hardware.

A good example of the axiom that you can take any adjective and add "–ility" to make a new architectural characteristic!

robustness

The system's ability to handle errors and boundary conditions while running, such as if the power, internet connection, or hardware fails.

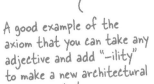

performance

How well the system achieves its timing requirements using the available resources.

As you will see shortly, "performance" has many different aspects.

When these are important, they are very important.

reliability/safety

Whether the system needs to be fail-safe, or if it is mission critical in a way that affects lives. If it fails, will it endanger people's lives or cost the company large sums of money? Common for medical systems, hospital software, and airplane applications.

Some "–ilities" are easier to achieve than others. This one is often difficult.

scalability

How well the system performs and operates as the number of users or requests increases.

Our Lafter application will definitely need this!

Cross-cutting architectural characteristics

As much as we'd like a nice, orderly zoo of architectural characteristics, platypuses still show up! Lots of important characteristics defy categorization.

security

How secure the system is, holistically. Does the data need to be encrypted in the database? How about for network communication between internal systems? What type of authentication needs to be in place for remote user access?

This is one of those architectural characteristics that are always present. It also happens to be a cross-cutting concern.

Authentication and authorization are aspects of security.

legal

How well the system complies with local laws about data protection and about how the application should be built or deployed.

authentication/authorization

How well the system ensures users are who they say they are and makes sure they can access only certain functions within the application (by use case, subsystem, web page, business rule, field level, etc.).

privacy

How well the system hides and encrypts transactions so that internal employees like data operators, architects, and developers cannot see them.

Many countries and regions have strict laws governing privacy, making consistency for international applications tricky.

Many government agencies around the world require a baseline level of accessibility.

accessibility

How easy is it for all your users to access the system, including those with disabilities, like colorblindness or hearing loss.

usability

How easy is it for users to achieve their goals. Is training required? Usability requirements need to be treated as seriously as any other architectural issue.

This is a great example of how ambiguous architectural characteristics can be: "usability" can also refer to user experience design.

Who Does What?

So many architectural characteristics! We had a nice database that listed the ones that are most important for Lafter, along with their definitions, but somehow the index became corrupted and we lost the linkage. Can you help restore them by drawing a line from each architectural characteristic to its definition?

scalability

Describes how well the components in the system create well-defined groupings and boundaries between components.

deployability

The system's ability to recover from problems such as a power, internet connection, or hardware failure.

modularity

How easy is it for all users to access the system, including those with disabilities like colorblindness or hearing loss.

robustness

How easy it is for architects and developers to apply changes to enhance the system and/or fix bugs.

accessibility

Describes how well the system handles a large number of concurrent users while maintaining reasonable performance.

maintainability

Describes the cadence, efficiency, and reproducibility of deployments.

Solution on page 74

Q: Where can I find a standard list of architectural characteristics?

A: No standard list really exists (despite several futile efforts) because the software development ecosystem constantly shifts and changes. Anyone trying to create a standard list is trying to hit a moving target.

Q: Isn't security required for every application?

A: It depends! While it's a common concern, if you design a free intra-office lunch-ordering system, the only security concern lies with others finding out that you order an egg salad sandwich every day.

Q: Doesn't every application require availabilty?

A: You guessed it—it depends! Again, availability is a common concern for most applications, but if the mythical sandwich-ordering system mentioned above fails, the only real downside is that everyone has to get their own lunch.

Q: Can I choose any combination of architectural characteristics for my application?

A: Some architectural characteristics oppose one another. For example, architects find it challenging to design for both high performance and scalability. Determining the most important architectural characteristics for a system is only part of the design process. Combining them with logical component design will point you to an appropriate architectural style.

Q: What does it mean if you don't choose an architectural characteristic like availability in your requirements?

A: The architectural characteristics you choose provide a guideline for the appropriate architectural style. If an architect doesn't choose availability, it doesn't mean they will purposefully design the system to have poor availability. Rather, it's an indication of priority: trading off one architectural characteristic for another.

Exercise

Welcome to "Take It or Leave It!" The rules of this game are simple—we'll give you a business requirement that might come up for the Lafter application, and two architectural characteristics. As you know, everything in architecture is a trade-off, so if you attempt to optimize one, you probably won't do as well with the other. Your job is to tell us which characteristic you rate as a higher priority for that requirement. You'll find our thoughts at the end of the chapter.

"We need to get this to market ASAP!"	fault tolerance	agility
"Money's tight, folks!"	scalability	simplicity
"Oh, wow, this conference is going to be our biggest yet."	high availability	maintainability
"We want to start storing users' credit card information."	security	recoverability
"This site is going to be very popular upon launch."	agility	elasticity

Solution on page 75

Geek Note

The software architecture world lacks a standard term for what we call *architectural characteristics*. Here are some of the terms people often use, and why we don't care for them.

Most teams still call them *nonfunctional requirements*, which is misleading because architectural characteristics are indeed functional—they just don't concern the domain. Calling them nonfunctional downplays their importance. Other teams call them *system quality attributes*, which implies an activity that happens at the end of the project rather than the beginning. Another common name is *cross-cutting requirements*, which is the one we dislike the least—but it contains the word *requirement*, which entangles it with domain behaviors, which come from requirements, as opposed to *capabilities*, which are defined by architectural characteristics.

I see that there are lots of architectural characteristics... but how do I know which ones are critical or important to my project?

Recall that some architectural characteristics are "implicit." Many implicit characteristics emerge from these two sources.

Architectural characteristics don't just appear out of thin air. In fact, there are three different sources from which you should look to derive them.

❶ The problem domain

Part of your job is analyzing a problem to determine what architectural characteristics the system requires. Many structural design decisions come directly from the problem domain.

❷ Environmental awareness

Many requirements come from having a good understanding of the environment in which you're operating. For example, are you working for a fast-moving startup, or a large enterprise with a lot at stake?

❸ Holistic domain knowledge

Sure, you're working with a particular problem domain—but we can assure you that the domain is a lot bigger than your particular focus. Let's say you're building out a payment system. While understanding what's required of you is important, you'll reveal architectural characteristics if you understand the financial world, finance industry regulations, and customers' habits.

Let's look at each of these sources in turn.

Sourcing architectural characteristics from the problem domain

Architects derive many of the necessary architectural characteristics from the problem domain—it is, after all, the motivation for writing the software in the first place. That means you must *translate* the items stated in requirements documents into their corresponding architectural characteristics. For example, the Lafter requirements specify "thousands of users." As an architect, you must dig deeper to more accurately determine how many users are expected (scalability), how many of them will be there at the same time (concurrency), and how rapidly they'll show up (elasticity).

Exercise

Domain requirements are often a rich source of architectural characteristics. For example, our Lafter application needs to support large numbers of users, so scalability will be one necessary characteristic. Can you uncover more? Here are the requirements again:

Users: hundreds of speakers, thousands of users

Requirements:	**Architectural characteristics**
Users can register for usernames and approve the privacy policy	Scalability
Users can add new content on Lafter as a "Joke" (long-form post) or "Pun" (short-form post)	
Followers can "HaHa" (indicating strong approval) or "Giggle" (a milder approval message) content they like	
Speakers at Sillycon Symposia events have a special icon	
Speakers can host forums on the platform related to their content	
Users can post messages of up to 281 characters	
Users can also post links to external content	
Additional Context:	
International support	
Very small support staff	
"Bursty" traffic: extremely busy during live conferences	

Solution on page 76

Sourcing architectural characteristics from environmental awareness

You know a lot about where you work (maybe too much, in some cases!), and that will naturally drive your architectural characteristics analysis. For example, an architect working for a fast-moving startup will prioritize agility whether it is specified or not.

Sorry, but this means you're going to have to start paying attention in those business prioritization meetings!

It is important to understand **organizational priorities** so we can make more durable decisions. For example, let's say we must decide how to integrate two subsystems. The choices are a customized but highly suited protocol or an industry-standard protocol that will require a little more effort. In a vacuum, we might choose the first. However, if we know that the organization's goal is to engage heavily in mergers with other companies, that fact could tip our decision toward the more open solution.

Architects can't make decisions in a vacuum— context is always important.

Some architects stay within particular domains exactly because they have the advantage of domain knowledge.

Sourcing architectural characteristics from holistic domain knowledge

You have also no doubt absorbed a lot of **domain knowledge**: information that isn't explicitly spelled out in the requirements but that you implicitly understand about important aspects of the domain.

Suppose Lafter has decided to run a promotion at a local university to entice students to sign up (they go to a lot of conferences, and some of them have a sense of humor). We need to design an application that handles sign-ups for the promotion day. To make the math easy, assume that the school has 1,000 students and they have 10 hours to sign up. Should we design the system using a consistent scale, implicitly assuming that the students will distribute themselves evenly during the sign-up process? (Have we *met* any university students?)

Never underestimate some university students' ability to procrastinate.

One of the most dangerous discoveries in life is how much you can procrastinate and still (mostly) get the job done.

Based on real-world experience, we can guess that this won't work. Think about what you know about the target demographic. Some students are hyperdiligent; some tend to procrastinate. Thus, the actual design must handle an elastic burst of students in the first hour (as the Type A individuals rush to get in line), stay mostly idle for the bulk of the day, and then handle another elastic burst just before the sign-up window closes, to accommodate all the stragglers.

Architects must make use of all available information sources to understand the full range of trade-offs inherent in our architectural decisions.

Solutions versus requirements

Customers often come to architects with *solutions* rather than requirements. For example, back in the 1970s, the US Air Force commissioned a fighter jet and included a requirement that it be capable of achieving speeds up to Mach 2.5. The designers tried, but the technology of the time just wasn't sufficient to meet the requirement. They went back to the Air Force and asked: "Why does it need to go Mach 2.5?" The answer was, "Well, these things are expensive, so we want it to be able to flee a fight if necessary." With that knowledge in mind, they went back and designed the F-16 fighter jet. It had a maximum speed of Mach 2.1, but it was the most maneuverable and fastest-accelerating jet ever created.

When users bring us solutions rather than requirements, it's architects' job to imitate an annoying toddler and keep asking "But why?!?" enough times to uncover the *actual* requirements hidden within the solutions.

Exercise

It's sometimes difficult to distinguish requirements from solutions. Here are some responses you might get when you ask "why?" that could indicate something might be one or the other. Can you identify which indicate requirements and which solutions?

"We need a system to track user preferences and customizations, then save them between sessions."

☐ **requirement**　　　　　　　　☐ **solution**

"Do we really need to build our own survey service? Surely we can find one that does what we need."

☐ **requirement**　　　　　　　　☐ **solution**

"An enterprise service bus would solve some of our current problems (albeit with some changes and work-arounds) and it offers extreme extensibility."

☐ **requirement**　　　　　　　　☐ **solution**

"According to the friendly sales rep, this software package does all the things accounting needs, now and in the near future."

☐ **requirement**　　　　　　　　☐ **solution**

⟶ Solution on page 77

Composite architectural characteristics

Alex: The business analyst asked if we can make sure the system is "reliable." What do they mean?

Sam: Wow, I can think of a lot of ways to define "reliable" for a piece of software.

Mara: This happens a lot. A **composite** is a combination of two or more things, and often architectural characteristics combine with each other to create (seemingly) new ones. We call these **composite architectural characteristics**.

What does *reliable* mean? We can measure many different aspects of reliability, like how available the system is, how consistent the user interface workflows are, and how well it handles data integrity.

Alex: How do I identify these?

Mara: To identify composites, ask: "Can I objectively measure this architectural characteristic?" While we often discuss performance as a single value, it's actually a composite—because we have to be more specific to get to something measurable. An example of a measurable architectural characteristic is *first contentful paint*, which measures the time it takes for a web page to load on a mobile device.

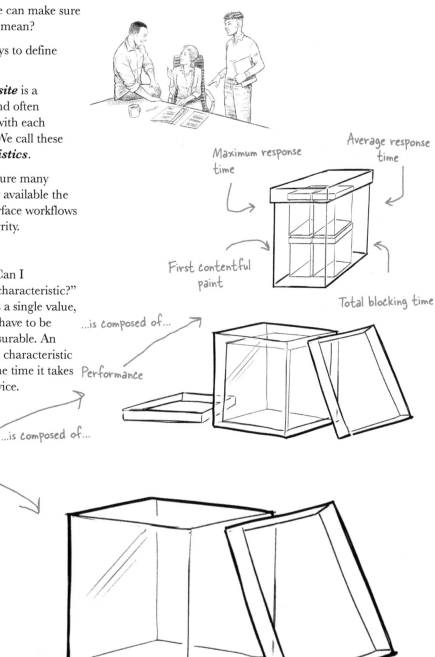

Maximum response time

Average response time

First contentful paint

Total blocking time

...is composed of...

Performance

...is composed of...

Usability

Priorities are contextual

It's impossible to choose the same set of architectural characteristics for
every project. The set of architectural characteristics you choose for a
particular application, and how you prioritize each one, will differ based
on context.

Sharpen your pencil

Context matters. At the top, we've listed several architectural characteristics. Below that
are three application scenarios. For each scenario, rank each characteristic based on how
important it is for that type of application. *Hint: Some applications won't need all of them.*

Scalability		Performance

Extensibility

Security   Data integrity

Scenario #1

An ecommerce site in a
competitive market

1 _____

2 _____

3 _____

4 _____

5 _____

Scenario #2

A system for an enterprise
whose goal is to grow via
mergers

1 _____

2 _____

3 _____

4 _____

5 _____

Scenario #3

An application to
automate standardized
testing and grading for
university admissions

1 _____

2 _____

3 _____

4 _____

5 _____

Solution on page 78

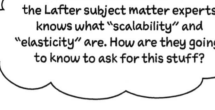

Wait a minute. None of the Lafter subject matter experts knows what "scalability" and "elasticity" are. How are they going to know to ask for this stuff?

Congratulations, you have yet *another* job.

You're right to be skeptical about how sophisticated an understanding your coworkers have of architectural concepts. That means you have one more job as an architect: translation!

As much as it would be nice for our colleagues to learn our language, architects are generally the ones who have to translate the business's goals into *identifiable and measurable* architectural characteristics.

Lost in translation

It's not unusual for business experts and analysts to state (or subtly suggest) a requirement without realizing it, hidden in plain English. It's your job, as a software architect, to read between the lines, find the requirements, and translate them into architectural characteristics. Here are a few examples.

When business analysts and subject matter experts say:	Software architects translate:	
"Lafter is constantly changing to meet new marketplace demands."	• Agility • Modularity • Extensibility	Good modularity allows for faster change without rippling side effects.
"Due to new regulatory requirements, we must complete end-of-day processing on time."	• Performance • Recoverability • Scalability	We must perform well but also recover quickly in case of error.
"Our plan is to engage heavily in mergers and acquisitions in the next three years."	• Résumé-ability • Integratability • Interoperability	"The ability to update your résumé." Many people would rather not work in a place undergoing constant mergers.
"We have a very tight time frame and a fixed scope and budget for this project."	• Feasibility • Simplicity • Affordability	More of an architect-the-person characteristic.

Of course, no one would <u>ever</u> ask for this impossible combination… ahem.

Feasibility—evaluating whether something is possible—is an underutilized architecture "-ility."

Architects often have a unique perspective of what's possible within a given time frame.

Not only do my business analysts not understand the technical terms for architectural characteristics, they ask for way too many things!

More requirements are NOT better.

What happens when an architect takes a list of possible architectural characteristics for Lafter to a group of business users and asks them, "Which of these do you want for the system?"

They invariably answer: "All of them!"

As nice as it would be to be able to accommodate that request, it's not a good idea to try.

Remember, architectural characteristics are *synergistic* with each other and with the problem domain. That means **the more architectural characteristics the system must support, the more complex its design must be.**

When undertaking structural design for a system, architects must find a balance between domain priorities and the architectural characteristics necessary for success.

Architectural characteristics and logical components

Before we tell you how to go about trying to balance architectural characteristics with each other and the domain, we want to show you how architectural characteristics and logical components are two sides of the same coin. You see, both of them aim to support the problem domain (also known as the reason you are writing software to begin with).

Architectural characteristics = capabilities

Architectural characteristics describe the *kinds of capabilities* your solution will support, rather than the *behavior* of the application, which is based on requirements.

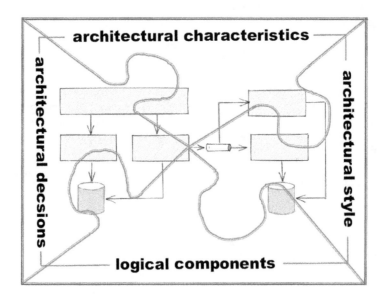

Logical components = behavior

Logical components, covered in depth in Chapter 4, represent the design of the system you are attempting to implement in software in order to solve the fundamental problem at hand.

Balancing domain considerations and architectural characteristics

Architects use architectural characteristics and logical component analysis to determine the appropriate architectural style, and the Lafter application is no exception. You need to strike a balance between the two.

Imagine the left side to be domain considerations and the right side to be architectural characteristics.

No architectural characteristics

Sometimes we don't take the time to analyze architectural characteristics before designing the system, leading to expensive and time-consuming rework as we discover that our system fails to exhibit the necessary architectural characteristics.

Projects that ignore needed architectural characteristics can deliver failure faster.

Remember, architectural characteristics are synergistic with domain <u>and</u> other architectural characteristics.

Good balance between...

In this scenario, we have achieved a balance in our design decisions between architectural characteristics and domain considerations.

...architectural characteristics and domain considerations

This allows us to achieve operational and structural goals without overengineering.

Too many architectural characteristics

Unfortunately, architects sometimes retreat to an ivory tower and spend too much time analyzing architectural characteristics, or identifying too many of them to be useful. This leads to overengineering, wasting time and effort that could be spent on implementation and ongoing maintenance.

Many systems that try to support too many architectural characteristics end up with too little space left to support the domain.

Limiting architectural characteristics

When the business stakeholders want *all* of the possible architectural characteristics, how can you limit their enthusiasm?

The magical number 7

One useful guideline for the conversation between architects and business analysts is to **limit the number of architectural characteristics they can choose to seven**. Why seven? Psychological research indicates that people remember items in chunks of seven (one of the reasons that early phone numbers were seven digits). It's also large enough to provide some variety without creating a paradox of choice by offering too many.

"The Magical Number Seven, Plus or Minus Two: Some Limits on Our Capacity for Processing Information" is a famous paper from 1956 by psychologist George Miller.

We created a worksheet to help architects work with other stakeholders to arrive at a reasonable number. This is a demo; you'll get to use it on the next page.

Once you've settled on the most important driving characteristics, you get to pick three. Just put 1, 2, and 3 next to the ones that matter the most to you.

Driving characteristics are architectural characteristics that drive important design decisions.

Implicit characteristics become driving characteristics if they influence structural decisions.

Top 3	Driving Characteristics	Implicit Characteristics
☐	_____	*feasibility (cost/time)*
☐	_____	*security*
☐	_____	*maintainability*
☐	_____	*observability*
☐	_____	
☐	_____	
☐	_____	

We've found these four to be pretty common implicit characteristics. Feel free to replace these with whatever makes sense for you.

Sharpen your pencil

On page 60, you identified architectural characteristics for Sillycon Symposia's social media application, Lafter. To make sure you've achieved a good balance, limit your list to seven characteristics. Then, check the boxes next to the top three most important.

Top 3	Driving Characteristics	Implicit Characteristics
☐	_____	*feasibility (cost/time)*
☐	_____	*security*
☐	_____	*maintainability*
☐	_____	*observability*
☐	_____	
☐	_____	
☐	_____	

These are implied characteristics. Move them to the Driving Characteristics column if you think they are <u>critical</u> to the success of the system.

Pick the top three most important ones (in any order).

Possible Candidate Architectural Characteristics

performance	data integrity	deployability
responsiveness	data consistency	testability
availability	adaptability	configurability
fault tolerance	extensibility	customizability
scalability	interoperability	recoverability
elasticity	concurrency	auditability

Solution on page 79

Bullet Points

- *Architectural characteristics* represent one part of the structural analysis that architects use to design software systems. (We'll talk abou the other part, logical components, in Chapter 4.)

- Architectural characteristics describe a system's capabilities.

- Some architectural characteristics overlap with operational concerns (such as availability, scalability, and so on).

- There are many catagories of architectural characteristics. No one can make a comprehensive list, because the software development ecosystem is constantly changing.

- When identifying architectural characteristics, architects look for factors that influence structural design.

- Architects should be careful not to specify too many architectural characteristics, because they are *synergistic*—changing one requires other parts of the system to change.

- Some architectural characteristics are *implicit*: not explicitly stated in requirements, yet part of an architect's design considerations.

- Some architectural characteristics may appear in multiple categories.

- Many architectural characteristics are *cross-cutting*: they interact with other parts of (and decisions in) the organization.

- Architects must derive many architectural characteristics from requirements and other domain design considerations.

- Some architectural characteristics come from *domain and/or environmental knowledge*, outside of the requirements of a specific application.

- Some architectural characteristics are *composites*: they consist of a combination of other architectural characteristics.

- Architects must learn to translate "business speak" into architectural characteristics.

- Architects should limit the number of architectural characteristics they consider to some small number, such as seven.

Characteristics Crossword

Ready to have some fun and test your knowledge about what you've learned? Try this crossword puzzle about architectural characteristics.

Across

3. An architectural characteristic that might be implicit
4. _____ engineering is an architectural problem
8. Choosing architectural characteristics means assigning each one a _____
9. Magic number of characteristics to ask for
11. A nonfunctional requirement is also called an architectural _____
15. Some architectural characteristics are _____-cutting
17. What architects should ask when users suggest solutions instead of requirements
18. A system might need to _____ up and down to meet demand
19. _____ tolerance is an architectural demand

Down

1. Uneven traffic often comes in _____
2. A Lafter post can be a "joke" or a "_____"
3. Architectural characteristics influence the system's _____
5. Architectural characteristics can be explicit or _____
6. _____ integrity is an architectural characteristic
7. A site with large numbers of _____ users might need to be scalable
10. Many governments regulate data _____
12. An architectural characteristic is critical or important to the system's _____
13. Combining architectural characteristics and logical components gives you an architectural _____
14. The thing you're writing software about
16. Web page loading time is often called "first contentful _____"

Solution on page 80

From page 56

Who Does What? Solution

So many architectural characteristics! We had a nice database that listed the ones that are most important for Lafter, along with their definitions, but somehow the index became corrupted and we lost the linkage. Can you help restore them by drawing a line from each architectural characteristic to its definition?

scalability

Describes how well the components in the system create well-defined groupings and boundaries between components.

deployability

The system's ability to recover from problems such as a power, internet connection, or hardware failure.

modularity

How easy is it for all users to access the system, including those with disabilities like colorblindness or hearing loss.

robustness

How easy it is for architects and developers to apply changes to enhance the system and/or fix bugs.

accessibility

Describes how well the system handles a large number of concurrent users while maintaining reasonable performance.

maintainability

Describes the cadence, efficiency, and reproducibility of deployments.

From page 58

Exercise Solution

Welcome to "Take It or Leave It!" The rules of this game are simple—we'll give you a business requirement that might come up for the Lafter application, and two architectural characteristics. As you know, everything in architecture is a trade-off, so if you attempt to optimize one, you probably won't do as well with the other. Your job is to tell us which characteristic you rate as a higher priority for that requirement.

"We need to get this to market ASAP!"   fault tolerance   *(agility)*

"Money's tight, folks!"   scalability   *(simplicity)*

"Oh, wow, this conference is going to be our biggest yet."   *(high availability)*   maintainability

"We want to start storing users' credit card information."   *(security)*   recoverability

"This site is going to be very popular upon launch."   agility   *(elasticity)*

From page 60

Exercise Solution

Domain requirements are often a rich source of architectural characteristics. For example, our Lafter application needs to support large numbers of users, so scalability will be one necessary characteristic. Can you uncover more? Here's what we came up with.

Users: hundreds of speakers, thousands of users

Requirements:

Users can register for usernames and approve the privacy policy

Users can add new content on Lafter as a "Joke" (long-form post) or "Pun" (short-form post)

Followers can "HaHa" (indicating strong approval) or "Giggle" (a milder approval message) content they like

Speakers at Sillycon Symposia events have a special icon

Speakers can host forums on the platform related to their content

Users can post messages of up to 281 characters

Users can also post links to external content

Additional Context:

International support

Very small support staff

"Bursty" traffic: extremely busy during live conferences

Architectural characteristics

Scalability

Elasticity

Authorization

Authentication

Internationalization

Customizability

From page 62

Exercise Solution

It's sometimes difficult to distinguish requirements from solutions. Here are some responses you might get when you ask "why?" that indicate something might be one or the other. Can you identify which indicate requirements and which solutions?

"We need a system to track user preferences and customizations, then save them between sessions."

☒ **requirement** ☐ **solution**

"Do we really need to build our own survey service? Surely we can find one that does what we need."

☒ **requirement** ☐ **solution**

"An enterprise service bus would solve some of our current problems (albeit with some changes and workarounds) and it offers extreme extensibility."

☐ **requirement** ☒ **solution**

"According to the friendly sales rep, this software package does all the things accounting needs, now and in the near future."

☐ **requirement** ☒ **solution**

Exercise Solution

From page 64

Context matters. At the top, we've listed several architectural characteristics. Below that are three application scenarios. For each scenario, rank each characteristic based on how important it is for that type of application. *Hint: Some applications won't need all of them.* Here are our rankings.

Scalability		Performance
	Extensibility	
Security		Data integrity

Scenario #1

An ecommerce site in a competitive market

1 ___Security___

2 ___Performance___

3 ___Scalability___

4 _____

5 _____

Scenario #2

A system for an enterprise whose goal is to grow via mergers

1 ___Extensibility___

2 ___Scalability___

3 _____

4 _____

5 _____

Scenario #3

An application to automate standardized testing and grading for university admissions

1 ___Data integrity___

2 ___Security___

3 ___Performance___

4 _____

5 _____

Exercise Solution

From page 71

On page 60, you identified architectural characteristics for the Sillycon Symposia Lafter social media application. To make sure you have achieved a good balance, limit the number to seven. Then, check the boxes next to the top three most important.

Top 3	Driving Characteristics	Implicit Characteristics
☒	Scalability	*feasibility (cost/time)*
☒	Security ⟵	*security*
☐	Elasticity	*maintainability*
☒	Responsiveness	*observability*
☐	Performance	
☐	Portability	
☐	Accessibility	

⟵ Remember, no single correct answer exists. The question is: can you justify your choices?

Possible Candidate Architectural Characteristics

performance	data integrity	deployability
responsiveness	data consistency	testability
availability	adaptability	configurability
fault tolerance	extensibility	customizability
scalability	interoperability	recoverability
elasticity	concurrency	auditability

Characteristics Crossword Solution

From page 73

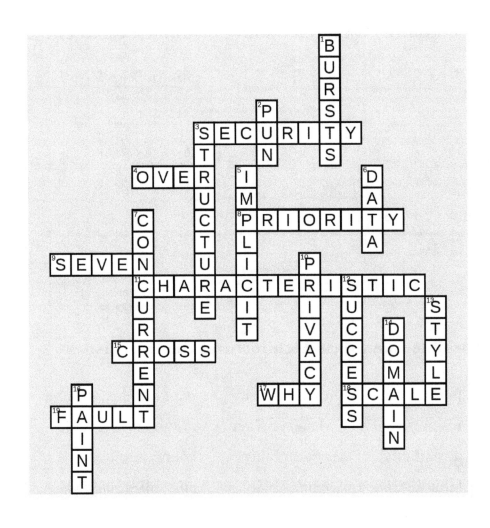

3

the two laws of software architecture
Everything's a Trade-Off

What happens when there are no "best practices"? The nice thing about best practices is that they're relatively risk-free ways to achieve certain goals. They're called "best" (not "better" or "good") for a reason—you know they work, so why not just use them? But one thing you'll quickly learn about software architecture is that it has no best practices. You'll have to analyze every situation carefully to make a decision, and you'll need to communicate not just the "what" of the decision, but the "why."

So, how *do* you navigate this new frontier? Fortunately, you have the laws of software architecture to guide you. This chapter shows you how to analyze trade-offs as you make decisions. We'll also show you how to create architectural decision records to capture the "hows" and "whys" of decisions. By the end of this chapter, you'll have the tools to navigate the uncertain territory that is software architecture.

It starts with a sneaker app

Archana works for Two Many Sneakers, a company with a very successful mobile app where shoe collectors ("sneakerheads") can buy, sell, and trade collectible sneakers. With millions of shoes listed, customers can find the shoes they really want or upload photos to help sell the ones they don't.

The app's initial architecture was a single service as shown below:

Two Many Sneakers' slogan: You only have two feet, but you can never have too many sneakers!

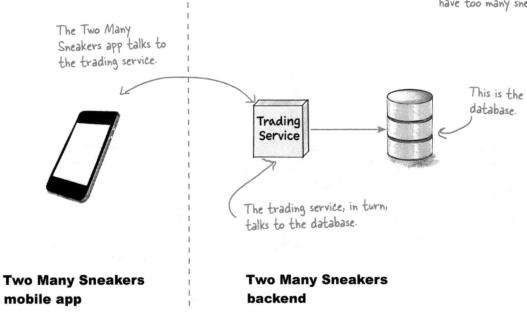

The Two Many Sneakers app talks to the trading service.

This is the database.

The trading service, in turn, talks to the database.

Two Many Sneakers mobile app

Two Many Sneakers backend

The Two Many Sneakers app knows to talk to the trading service to fetch and update data (like a photo of a mint-condition pair of Nikes). The trading service, in turn, fetches data and updates the database.

Business is booming. Sneakerheads are always willing to change up their collections, and Two Many Sneakers' customer base has grown quickly. Now customers are demanding real-time notifications, so they'll know whenever someone lists a pristine pair of those Air Jordans they've been pining for.

Security is always a concern in online sales. Nobody wants knockoffs, and credit card numbers need to be protected. To stay a few steps ahead of any scammers, Two Many Sneakers' management team wants to prioritize improving the app's *fraud detection* capabilities. They plan to use data analytics to help detect fraud by spotting anomalies in user behavior and filtering out bots.

Work has already begun—all the team needs to do now is set up the trading service to notify the new notification and analytics services anytime something of interest happens in the app.

The database is still part of the architecture. We just left it out in this diagram.

New Air Jordans just got listed? Inform everyone interested with an update.

Trading Service

Notification Service

Analytics Service

Any and all trades need to be sent to the analytics service. Nobody likes being scammed.

Piece of cake! I'll just use messaging to inform the notification and analytics services every time a new pair of shoes is listed on the app. Genius!

Archana

What do we know so far?

We need to figure out how these services will communicate with one another. Let's recap what we know (and don't know) so far:

- The current architecture is rather simple—the trading service talks to its own database, and that's that. We need the trading service to send information to the notification service and the analytics service.

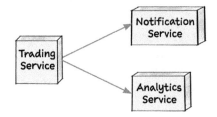

- Word in the office is that there's a chance that the finance department (which is responsible for compliance) will want updates from the trading service. In other words, whatever architecture we come up with will need to be *extensible*.

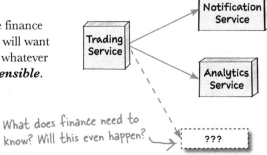

What does finance need to know? Will this even happen?

- We don't know what data to send the notification and analytics services—do the two services get the same kind of data, or wildly different data? And we don't know where things stand with finance, so that's another unknown.

```
{
    "sellerId": 12345,
    "buyerId": 6789,
    "itemId": 1492092517,
    "price": "$125.00"
}
```

What should this look like?

To be clear, there are some things we know and plenty we don't. Welcome to the world of software architecture.

Speaking of architecture, we'll be done, say, next Thursday—right?

As the system's architects, we need to identify its architectural characteristics. (You learned about those in Chapter 2.)

Exercise

Which of the following architectural characteristics stand out as important for this particular problem? *Hint: There are no right answers here, because there is a lot we don't know or aren't sure of yet.* Take your best guess—we've provided our solution at the end of this chapter. We'll get you started:

Lots of downstream services need to know about sneaker trades. This sounds important!

extensibility

modularity

upgradability

low coupling

security

performance

Solution on page 116

Brain Power

All the characteristics in the previous exercise sound pretty good, right? Seriously, who'd say no to upgradability?

But for each one, ask yourself— *is this characteristic critical to the project's success?* Or is it a nice-to-have?

What's more, some characteristics *conflict*. A highly secure application with loads of encryption and secure connections probably won't be highly performant. Go back and see if any of your choices are at odds. If so, you can only pick one.

Flashback to Chapter 2? You bet it is!

there are no Dumb Questions

Q: **Even this simple exercise seems to have a lot of moving parts. We know some things, we think we know some other things, and there's a lot that we certainly don't know. How do we go about thinking about architecture?**

A: You're right. In almost all real-life scenarios, your list of architectural characteristics will probably contain a healthy mix of "this is what we want" and "this is something we *might* want." Even your customers can't answer the question of what they will *eventually* want. (Wouldn't that be nice?) This is the "stuff you don't know you don't know," also known as the "unknown unknowns."

It's not unusual for an "unknown unknown" to rear its head midway through a project and derail even the best-laid plans. The solution? *Embrace agility* and its iterative nature. Realize that nothing, particularly software architecture, remains static. What worked today might prove to be the biggest hurdle to success tomorrow. That's the nature of software architecture: it constantly evolves and changes as you discover more about the problem and as your customers demand more of you.

Communicating with downstream services

Our goal is to get the trading system to notify the reporting and analytics systems automatically. For now, let's assume we decide to use messaging. But that presents a dilemma—should our messaging use queues or topics?

It's OK if you don't know much about messaging, queues, or topics. We'll tell you what you need to know.

Before we go further, let's make sure we're on the same page about the differences between queues and topics. Most messaging platforms offer two models for a ***publisher*** of a message (in this case, that's the trading service) to communicate with one or more ***consumers*** (the downstream services).

The first option is a ***queue***, or a point-to-point communication protocol. Here, the publisher knows who is receiving the message. To reach multiple consumers, the publisher needs to send a message to one queue for each consumer. If the trading service wants to use queues to tell the analytics service and the reporting service about trades, this is what the setup will look like:

If it helps, think of queues as being like a group text—you pick everyone you want to inform, type your message, and hit "send."

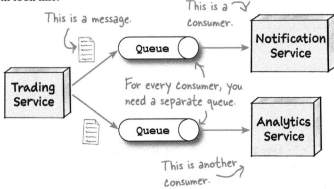

When using the second option, ***topics***, you are signing on for a *broadcasting* model. The publisher simply produces and sends a message. If another service downstream wants to hear from the publisher, it can ***subscribe*** to the topic to receive messages. The publisher doesn't know (or care) how many services are listening.

Topics are similar to posting a picture on your go-to social networking site. Anyone following you will see that picture, since they've "subscribed" to your timeline.

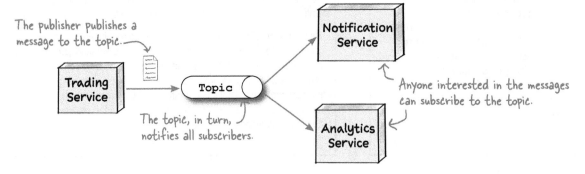

Both options sound good—so how do we pick? Let's find out.

Analyzing trade-offs

You can't have your cake and eat it too. The world is full of compromises—we often optimize for one thing at the cost of another. Want to take and store lots of pictures on your phone? Either get more storage, which costs more, or compress them, which lowers the image quality.

Software architecture is no different. Every choice you make involves significant compromises or, as we like to call them, **_trade-offs_**. So what exactly does this mean for you?

If this sounds familiar, it should be! It was part of our discussion of significant versus less-significant trade-offs in Chapter 1.

If you know which architectural characteristics are most important to your project, you can start thinking of solutions that will maximize some of those attributes. But if a solution lets you maximize one characteristic (or more), it will come at the cost of other characteristics. For example, a solution that allows for great scalability might also make deployability or reliability harder.

No matter what solution you come up with, it *will* come with trade-offs—upsides *and* downsides.

Your job is twofold: know the trade-offs associated with every solution you come up with, and then pick the solution that best serves the most important architectural characteristics.

Rich Hickey, creator of the Clojure programming language, once said, "Programmers know the benefits of everything and the trade-offs of nothing." We'd like to add: "Architects need to understand both."

You can't have it all. You'll have to decide which architectural characteristics are most important, and choose the solution that best allows for those characteristics.

Trade-off analysis: Queue edition

Trade-off analysis isn't just about finding the *benefits* of a particular approach. It's also about seeking out the *negatives* to get the full picture. Let's look at each option in turn, starting with queues.

With queues, for every service that the trading service needs to notify, we need a separate queue. If the notification service and the analytics service need different information, we can send different messages to each queue. The trading service is keenly aware of every system to which it communicates, which makes it harder for another (potentially rogue) service to "listen in." (That's useful if security is high on our priority list, right?) Oh, and since each queue is independent, we can monitor them separately and even scale them independently if needed.

The trading service is *tightly coupled* to its consumers—it knows exactly how many there are. But we're not sure if we'll need to send messages to the compliance service, too. If that happens, we'll have to rework the trading service to start sending messages to a *third* queue. In short, if we choose queues, we're giving up on extensibility.

Just a friendly reminder of what using queues would look like, so you don't have to flip back and forth.

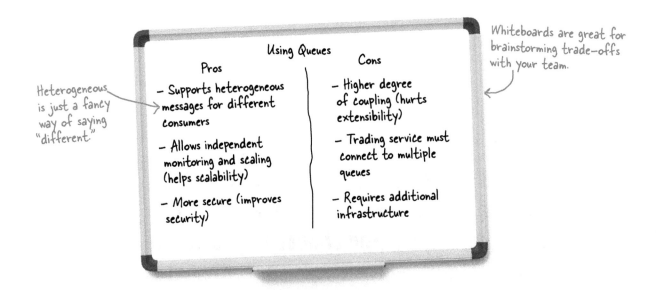

Heterogeneous is just a fancy way of saying "different."

Using Queues

Pros
- Supports heterogeneous messages for different consumers
- Allows independent monitoring and scaling (helps scalability)
- More secure (improves security)

Cons
- Higher degree of coupling (hurts extensibility)
- Trading service must connect to multiple queues
- Requires additional infrastructure

Whiteboards are great for brainstorming trade-offs with your team.

See what we mean when we say "trade-off analysis"?

Trade-off analysis: Topic edition

What about using topics? Well, the upside is clear—the trading service only delivers messages to a topic, and anyone interested in listening for a message from the trading service simply *subscribes* to that topic. Compliance wants in? They can simply subscribe: no need to make any changes to the trading service. Low coupling for the win.

But topics have a few downsides, too. For one thing, *you can't customize the message* for any particular service—it's a one-size-fits-all, take-it-or-leave-it proposition. Scaling, too, is one-size-fits-all, since you have only one thing to scale. And anyone can subscribe to the topic without the trading service knowing—which, in some circumstances, is a potential security risk.

Back to the whiteboard!

This is what using a topic looks like.

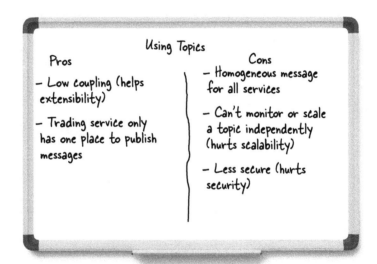

Using Topics

Pros
- Low coupling (helps extensibility)
- Trading service only has one place to publish messages

Cons
- Homogeneous message for all services
- Can't monitor or scale a topic independently (hurts scalability)
- Less secure (hurts security)

Sharpen your pencil

Spend a few minutes comparing the results of our trade-off analysis. Notice how both options support some characteristics but trade off on others? Now we're going to present you with some requirements—see if you can decide if you'd pick queues or topics to support each one.

Requirements

"Security is important to us."   Queues / Topics

"Different downstream services need different kinds of information."   Queues / Topics

"We'll be adding other downstream services in the future."   Queues / Topics

⟶ Solution on page 116

The first law of software architecture

Queues or topics? Enough with the suspense already. The answer is—*it depends!*

What's important to the business? If **security** is paramount, we should probably go with queues. Two Many Sneakers is growing by leaps and bounds and has loads of other services interested in its sneaker trades, so **extensibility** is its biggest priority. That means we should pick the topic option.

Time is also a factor: if we need to get to market quickly, we might pick a simpler architecture (simplicity) over one that offers high availability. (Having an application that guarantees three "nines" of uptime only matters if you have customers, right?)

The key takeaway is that in software architecture, you'll always be balancing trade-offs. That leads us to the **First Law of Software Architecture**.

One of your authors often sports this T-shirt in public. (If you get any printed, please send us one medium and two extra-large!)

> THE FIRST LAW
> OF
> SOFTWARE
> ARCHITECTURE:
>
> EVERYTHING IN
> SOFTWARE
> ARCHITECTURE
> IS A
> TRADE-OFF

If you find a decision in software architecture that doesn't have a trade-off, you haven't looked at it hard enough.

In software architecture, nice, clean lines are rare and there are no "best practices." Every choice you make will involve many factors—often conflicting ones. The First Law is an important lesson, so take it to heart. Write it down on a sticky note and put it on your monitor. Get a backwards tattoo of it on your forehead so you'll see it in the mirror! Whatever it takes.

Sharpen your pencil

This time, we'd like you to do some trade-off analysis on your own. We chose messaging as the communication protocol between our trading service and its consumers. Messaging is asynchronous. Choosing between asynchronous and synchronous forms of communication comes with its own set of trade-offs! We've given you two whiteboards, one for each form of communication, and we've listed a bunch of "-ilities." We'd like you to consider how each architectural characteristic would work in both contexts. Is this characteristic a pro or a con (or neither) in synchronous communications? What about in asynchronous communications? Place each "-ility" in the appropriate column. *Hint: Not all of them apply to this decision.* We put the first pro on the whiteboard for you. When you're done, you can see our answers at the end of the chapter.

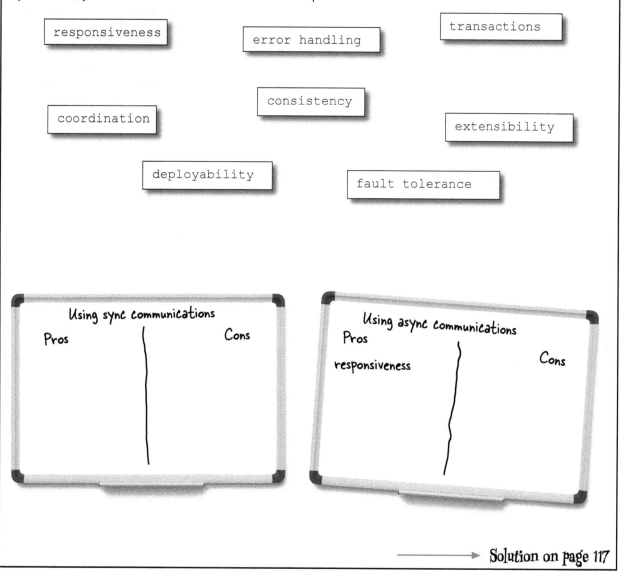

```
responsiveness          error handling              transactions


                        consistency
    coordination                                 extensibility


       deployability              fault tolerance
```

Using sync communications
Pros | Cons

Using async communications
Pros
responsiveness | Cons

Solution on page 117

Q: I've heard of the Architecture Tradeoff Analysis Method (ATAM). Is that what you're talking about?

A: ATAM is a popular method of trade-off analysis. With ATAM, you start by considering the business drivers, the "-ilities," and the proposed architecture, which you present to the stakeholders. Then, as a group, you run through a bunch of scenarios to produce a "validated architecture." While ATAM offers a good approach, we believe it comes with certain limitations—one being that it assumes the architecture is static and doesn't change.

Rather than focusing on the process of ATAM, we prefer to focus on results. The objective of any trade-off analysis should be to arrive at an architecture that best serves your needs. You'll probably go through the process several times as you discover more and more about the problem and come up with different scenarios.

Another popular approach is the Cost Benefit Analysis Method (CBAM). In contrast to ATAM, CBAM focuses on the cost of achieving a particular "-ility."

We recommend you look at both methods and perhaps consider combining them—ATAM can help with trade-off analysis, while CBAM can help you get the best return on investment (ROI).

Just remember—the process is not as important as the goal, which is to arrive at an architecture that satisfies the business's needs.

It always comes back to trade-offs

Some people always pick a particular technique, approach, or tool regardless of the problem at hand. Often they choose something they've had a lot of success with in the past. Sometimes they have what we affectionately call "shiny object syndrome," where they think that some new technology or method will solve all their problems.

Regardless of past achievements or future promises, just remember—*for every upside, there's a downside*. The only questions you need to answer are "Will the upsides help you implement a successful application?" and "Can you live with the downsides?"

Whenever someone sings the praises of a certain approach, your response should be: *"What are the trade-offs?"*

To be clear, we aren't saying you shouldn't use new tools and techniques. That's progress, right? Just don't forget to consider the trade-offs as you decide.

Making an architectural decision

Debating the pros and cons with your team in front of a whiteboard is fun and all, but at some point, you *must* make an **architectural decision**.

We mentioned architectural decisions in Chapter 1, but let's dive a little deeper. As you architect and design systems, you will be making lots of decisions, about everything from the system's overall structure to what tools and technologies to use. So what makes a decision an *architectural* decision?

In most cases, any choice you make that affects the *structure* of your system is an architectural decision. Here are a couple of example decisions:

> You got it: we're talking about the second dimension of software architecture.

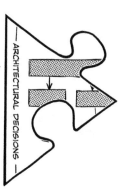

ARCHITECTURAL DECISIONS

> To jog your memory, picking whether you'd like a one— or two-story house would be an architectural decision.

```
We will use a cache to reduce the load on
the database and improve performance.
```

> Notice how this decision introduces an additional piece of infrastructure. It's also something the implementing team must keep in the back of their minds when accessing or writing data.

```
We will build the reporting service as a
modular monolith.
```

> This one is pretty obvious— it literally describes the structure of a service.

> As we put it in Chapter 1: "Architectural decisions serve as guideposts to help development teams understand the constraints and conditions of the architecture."

> I believe we have a decision—we're going to split the order shipping service apart from the order tracking service.

Notice how these decisions act as *guides* rather than rules. They aid teams in making choices, without being too specific. Most (but not all) of the architectural decisions you'll make will revolve around the structure of your systems.

What else makes a decision architectural?

Usually, architectural decisions affect the *structure* of an architecture—are we going with a monolith, or will we leverage microservices? But every so often, you might decide to maintain a particular architectural characteristic. If security is paramount, for example, Two Many Sneakers might make a decision like this:

> **We will use queues for asynchronous communication between services.**

Recall that topics are a broadcasting mechanism, allowing any service to subscribe and listen in on a topic.

This decision isn't about structure—it's driven by the need for security. Since there's a queue for every subscriber, we know who the consumers are.

At other times, you might decide on a *specific* tool, technology, or process if it affects the architecture or indirectly helps you achieve a particular architectural characteristic. For example:

> **We will use Node.js as the development framework for the MVP.**

Perhaps you need to get to market quickly, or maybe you have a large pool of engineers with expertise in this particular technology stack.

MVP stands for "minimum viable product."

Everything in this chapter so far has led to this important moment—making an architectural decision. You start with a trade-off analysis. Then you consider the pros and cons of each option in light of other constraints, like business and end user needs, architectural characteristics, technical feasibility, time and budgetary constraints, and even development concerns. Then, *finally*, you can make a decision.

Geek Note

Michael Nygard, author of the book *Release It!* (Pragmatic Programmer), defines an architecturally significant decision as "something that has an effect on how the rest of the project will run" or that can "affect the structure, non-functional characteristics, dependencies, interfaces, or construction techniques" of the architecture. To learn more, we recommend reading his blog post, "Documenting Architecture Decisions" (*https://www.cognitect.com/blog/2011/11/15/documenting-architecture-decisions*).

Hold up. Whiteboards are great, but there has to be a more permanant way of recording the trade-off analysis, the decision, and most importantly, <u>why</u> that choice was made. Whiteboards seem awfully temporary, no?

You bring up several good points. It's important to record our decisions in a more permanent way. In addition, trade-off analysis is an involved process. It'd be a real waste if we lost all that work just because someone got a little hasty with the eraser.

But you make another key observation: while the decision itself is important, *why* we made that decision might be even more important. Which leads us to...

The second law of software architecture

Making decisions is one of the most important things software architects do.

Let's say you and your team do a trade-off analysis and conclude that you're going to use a cache to improve your application's performance. The result of your analysis is that your system starts using a cache somewhere. The **what** is easy to spot.

That decision is important, but so are the circumstances in which you made the decision, its impact on the team implementing it, and **why**, of all the options available to you, you chose what you did.

This leads us to the ***Second Law of Software Architecture***.

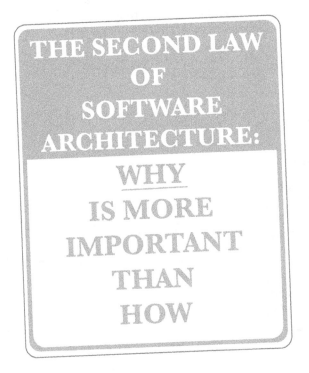

You see, future architects (or even "future you") might be able to discern what you did and even how you did it—but it'll be very hard for them to tell *why* you did it that way. Without knowing that, they might waste time exploring solutions you've already rejected for good reasons, or miss a key factor that swayed your decision.

This is why we have the Second Law. You need to understand *and* record the "why" of each decision so it doesn't get lost in the sands of time.

So how do we go about *capturing* architectural decisions? We'll dive into that next.

Architectural decision records (ADRs)

Do you remember everything you did last week? No? Neither do we. This is why it's important to document stuff—especially the important stuff.

Thanks to the Second Law of Software Architecture, we know we need a way to capture not just the decision, but the reason we made it. Architects use ***architectural decision records*** (ADRs) to record such decisions because it gives us a specific template to work with.

We cannot emphasize enough how important keeping these records is.

An ADR is a document that describes a specific architectural decision. You write one for every architectural decision you make. Over time, they'll build up into an ***architectural decision log***. Remember that architectural decisions form the second dimension to describe your architecture. ADRs are the documentation that supports this dimension.

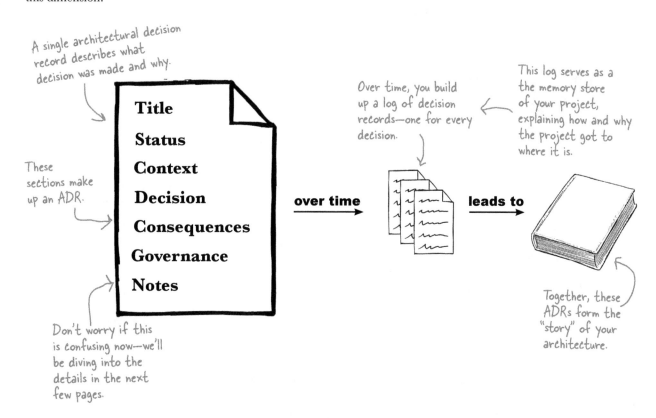

A single architectural decision record describes what decision was made and why.

These sections make up an ADR.

Title

Status

Context

Decision

Consequences

Governance

Notes

Don't worry if this is confusing now—we'll be diving into the details in the next few pages.

over time →

Over time, you build up a log of decision records—one for every decision.

leads to →

This log serves as a the memory store of your project, explaining how and why the project got to where it is.

Together, these ADRs form the "story" of your architecture.

An ADR has seven sections: Title, Status, Context, Decision, Consequences, Governance, and finally Notes. Every aspect of an architectural decision, including the decision itself, is captured in one of these sections. Let's take a look, shall we?

Cubicle conversation

Alex

Mara

Sam

Guess what? You're going to be helping the team write their ADR. Keep an eye out for those exercises.

Alex: Doing the trade-off analysis between queues and topics took it out of me.

Mara: Me too. Trade-off analysis can be arduous, but I'm glad we got it done. This is a big architectural decision. It's crucial that we understand the pros and cons of every choice.

Sam: Yeah, yeah. So we decided to use queues, right? Now can we get back to programming?

Mara: Slow down a second. You're right—we've made a decision. Now we should record our decision in an ADR.

Sam: But why? We already know what we're going to do. That seems like a lot of work.

Alex: Look, we know why we chose to go with queues. It's the option that best supports the architectural characteristics we want to maximize in the system, right?

Mara: Correct. But while *we* know why we made that decision, what about anyone else who might come along and wonder why we chose queues over topics, like future employees? *That's* why we should record our thinking.

Sam: I can see that being useful.

Alex: Great! So can we start drafting our ADR?

Writing ADRs: Getting the title right

Every ADR starts with a *title* that describes the decision. Craft this title carefully. It should be meaningful, yet concise. A good title makes it easy to figure out what the ADR is about, which is especially handy when you're frantically searching for an answer!

Let's dive deeper into what a good ADR title looks like. Imagine a team is writing a service that provides surveys to customers. They've done a trade-off analysis and have decided to use a relational database to store survey results. Here's what their ADR title might look like:

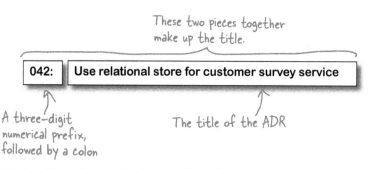

These two pieces together make up the title.

| 042: | Use relational store for customer survey service |

A three-digit numerical prefix, followed by a colon

The title of the ADR

The title should consist mostly of nouns. Keep it terse: you'll have plenty of opportunities to go into detail later. It should *describe* what the ADR is about, much like the headline of a news article or blog post. Get that right, and the rest will follow.

The title should start with a number—we suggest using three digits, with leading zeros where needed. This allows you to number your ADRs *sequentially*, starting with 001 for your first ADR, all the way to 999. Every time you add a new ADR, you increment the number. This makes it easy for anyone reading your records to know which decisions came before others.

there are no Dumb Questions

Q: What happens if we end up writing more than 999 ADRs?

A: That's a lot of ADRs! If that were to happen, you'd need to revise a bunch of titles (and potentially filenames). In our experience, a three-digit prefix is plenty.

Q: Can I reuse an ADR number?

A: Every ADR should get a unique identifier. This makes it easier to reference them without confusion.

More about this when we discuss the Status section.

Exercise

In the following exercises, you're going to help the team at Two Many Sneakers write an ADR. They've decided to use asynchronous messaging, with queues between the trading service and downstream services. Assume this is the *12th* ADR the team is writing. What title would you give this ADR? Don't forget to number it! Use this space to jot down your thoughts. You can see what we came up with at the end of this chapter.

Solution on page 118

Writing ADRs: What's your status?

Great! You've settled on a descriptive title. Next, you'll need to decide on the **status** of your ADR. The status communicates where the team stands on the decision itself.

But wait—isn't the point of the ADR to record a *decision*? Well, kinda. But making decisions is a process.

ADRs do record architectural decisions, but they also act as **documentation**, making it easier to share and collaborate. Others might need to look at or even sign off on an ADR. Let's start by considering the different statuses an ADR can have.

Title
Status
Context
Decision
Consequences
Governance
Notes

Request for Comment (RFC)

Use this status for ADRs that need additional input—perhaps from other teams or some sort of advisory board. Usually, these ADRs affect multiple teams or address a cross-cutting concern like security. An ADR in RFC status is typically a draft, open for commentary and critique from anyone invited to do so. An ADR in RFC status should **always** have a "respond by" deadline.

This is like planning an evening out. You know you'd like to go out and which friends you want to invite, but you hope they'll suggest a restaurant.

You ask everyone to respond by Tuesday so you can make reservations. (The deadline is important, since Ted can never make up his mind about anything.)

Proposed

After everyone has a chance to comment, the ADR's status moves to Proposed. This means the ADR is waiting for approvals. You might edit it or even overhaul the decision if you discover a limitation that makes it a no-go. In other words, you still haven't made a decision, but you're getting there.

You have a plan for the evening, but you haven't hit "send" on the invite yet—just in case the weather turns.

Accepted

Does exactly what it says on the tin. A decision has been made, and everyone is on board who needs to be. An Accepted status also tells the team tasked with implementing this decision that they can get started.

Oh yeah. Everyone has RSVP'd. Time to find a cool outfit!

If there's no need for feedback from others, you can set the ADR's status to Accepted as soon as the decision is made. Most ADRs stay at Accepted, but there is one more status to be aware of: Superseded.

Writing ADRs: What's your status? (continued)

You've arrived at a decision, which you diligently record in an ADR. Signed, sealed, delivered—you're done.

But then things change.

Maybe the business is growing and the board decides to focus more on scalability than on time to market. Maybe the company is entering international markets and needs to comply with EU data privacy and retention regulations. Whatever the reason, the decision you made is no longer appropriate. What now?

Well, you write another ADR. The old ADR is ***superseded*** by the new one, and you record it as such. Suppose the customer survey team realizes that a relational database is no longer fulfilling their needs, so they do another trade-off analysis and decide to switch to a document store. Here are the titles and statuses of the old and new ADRs:

The previous ADR

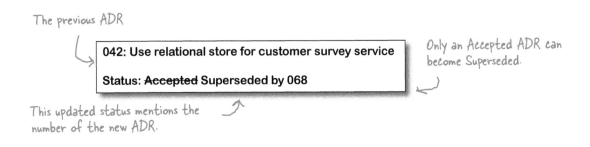

Only an Accepted ADR can become Superseded.

This updated status mentions the number of the new ADR.

This ADR overrides the previous ADR.

Note: We'll be showing you ADR 068 for the rest of the chapter, while you help the Two Many Sneakers team with their ADR.

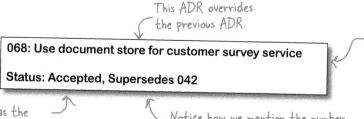

Now the new ADR has the status Accepted.

Notice how we mention the number of the superseded ADR here.

Linking ADRs is an important part of a project's "memory." It helps everyone remember what has already been tried.

An accepted ADR can move into Superseded status if a future ADR changes the decision it documents. It's important for both ADRs to highlight which ADR did the *superseding* and which ADR has been *superseded*. This bidirectional linking allows anyone looking at a superseded ADR to quickly realize that it's no longer relevant, and tells them exactly where to look for details on the new decision. Anyone looking at the superseding ADR can follow the link back to the superseded ADR to understand everything involved in solving that particular problem.

there are no Dumb Questions

Q: All this superseding and numbering seems overly complicated. Why not just edit the original ADR?

A: We use a three-digit prefix in the ADR title because it helps sequence things. Let's say ADR 007 no longer applies to your situation, but you've made a bunch of architectural decisions in the meantime. The last ADR in your architectural decision log is ADR 013.

Now you need to reevaluate ADR 007. Say you choose to edit it, as opposed to superseding it with ADR 014. What would happen?

Chronologically speaking, you amend ADR 007 *after* accepting ADR 013. But if someone tried to follow the decision process by reading the ADRs, they'd be seeing them in the wrong order!

Readers might think that the new decision came first. It wouldn't convey that you made one decision and then had to change it for some reason. Giving it a new number makes it clear that the old ADR 007 was no longer relevant after ADR 013. Confused yet?

Q: So you're telling me that an Accepted ADR is *immutable*: once accepted, it is not permitted to change. Is that right?

A: Look at you! That's exactly it. Except for when the status of an ADR goes from Accepted to Superseded, a decision recorded in an ADR is immutable. Sure, you might edit the ADR to include additional information, but for the most part, other than the status, things shouldn't change much.

Exercise

In the previous exercise, you hashed out the title of Two Many Sneakers' ADR about using queues for messaging. Let's say you get the green light. Write down the title you chose in the space below and give your ADR a status:

Title: _____

Status: _____

Three months later:

Whoops! The requirements have changed. Your latest trade-off analysis reveals that topics would be a better fit. Everyone has signed off on this, so you need to supersede your ADR with a new ADR. This is the 21st ADR your team has worked on. Write down the title and the new status of the old ADR:

Title: _____

Status: _____

Now write down the title and status of the newly introduced ADR:

Title: _____

Status: _____

⟶ Solution on page 118

Writing ADRs: What's your status? (recap)

There's a lot going on with ADR statuses, so we've created a handy visualization to help you out.

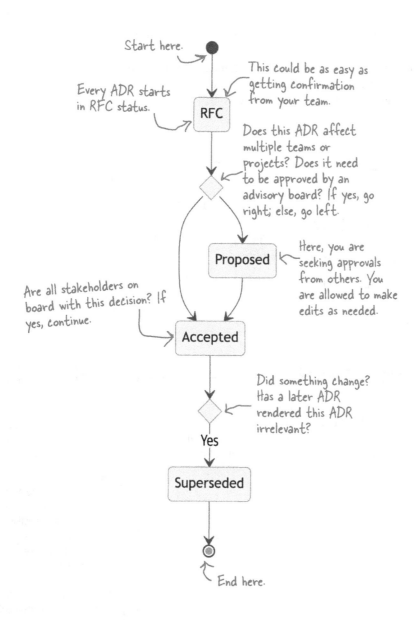

Start here.

Every ADR starts in RFC status.

This could be as easy as getting confirmation from your team.

RFC

Does this ADR affect multiple teams or projects? Does it need to be approved by an advisory board? If yes, go right; else, go left.

Proposed

Here, you are seeking approvals from others. You are allowed to make edits as needed.

Are all stakeholders on board with this decision? If yes, continue.

Accepted

Did something change? Has a later ADR rendered this ADR irrelevant?

Yes

Superseded

End here.

Writing ADRs: Establishing the context

Context matters. Every decision you've ever made, you made within a certain context and with certain constraints. When you chose what to have for breakfast this morning, the context might have included how hungry you were, how your body felt, your lunch plans, and whether you're trying to increase your fiber intake. It's no different for software architecture.

The Context section in the ADR template is your place to explain the circumstances that drove you to make the decision the ADR is capturing. It should also capture any and all factors that influenced your decision. While technological reasons will usually find their way onto this list, it's not unusual to include cultural or political factors to help the reader understand where you're coming from.

Title
Status
Context
Decision
Consequences
Governance
Notes

Let's continue working on the ADR we started with in the Status section.

> ## Context
>
> We need to simplify how we store customer survey responses. The data currently resides in a relational store, and its rigid schema requirements have become challenging as we evolve the surveys (for example, introducing different or extended surveys for our premium customers).
>
> There are various options available to us, like the `JSONB` data type in PostgreSQL or document stores such as MongoDB.

The Context section answers the question, "Why did we have to make this choice to begin with?"

Note—we aren't describing our decision just yet! We have a whole section for that.

Sharpen your pencil

Continue building out the ADR for Two Many Sneakers. Use the space below to write a Context section for the team's decision to use queues for communication between the trading service and other services. (Then compare it with our take at the end of this chapter.)

→ Solution on page 119

there are no Dumb Questions

Q: **What about all that time and effort I spent on the whiteboard? Is that part of the context?**

A: If you need to document your trade-off analysis, we suggest you introduce a new section called "Alternatives." In it, list all the alternatives you considered, followed by your lists of pros and cons.

Using a separate section to detail the trade-off analysis delineates it cleanly and avoids cluttering the Context section.

Writing ADRs: Communicating the decision

We've finally arrived at the actual decision. Let's start by looking at the customer survey team's completed Decision section:

Title
Status
Context
Decision
Consequences
Governance
Notes

Decision

— Notice the authoritative voice!

We will use a document database for the customer survey.

The marketing department requires a faster, more flexible way to make changes to the customer surveys.

Moving to a document database will provide better flexibility and speed, and will better facilitate changes by simplifying the customer survey user interface.

The Decision section covers the "why" of the decision itself: remember the Second Law?

If this ADR's status is RFC or Proposed, the decision hasn't been made (yet). Even so, the Decision section starts by *clearly expressing the decision being made*. The tone of the writing should reflect that. It's best to use an authoritative voice when stating the decision, with active phrases like "we will use" (as opposed to "we believe" or "we think").

The Decision section is also the place to explain why you're making this decision, paying tribute to the Second Law of Software Architecture: "Why is more important than how." Future you, or anyone else who reads the ADR, will then understand not just the decision but the *justification* for it.

In the Context section, you explained why this decision was on the table. The Decision section, which immediately follows it, explains the decision itself. Together, they allow the reader to frame the decision correctly.

This is also a great place to list others who signed off on this decision. For example, "The marketing department requires..." is an example of CYA. ◄— "Cover Your Assets"! :)

The ADR is not an opinion piece

Remember that the ADR is not a place for anyone's opinions on the state of things. It's easy to slip into that mode, especially when justifying a decision. Even when explaining context, it can sometimes be hard to stay objective.

Treat an ADR like a journalist treats a news article—stick to the facts and keep your tone neutral.

Exercise

It's time for you to write the Decision section of the ADR for Two Many Sneakers. Here are the main factors the team considered when making their decision:

- Queues allow for heterogeneous messages.
- Security is an important architectural characteristic for the stakeholders.

We've given you some space to write out a Decision section, including the corresponding justification. This section should answer the question, "Why queues?" *Hint: Be sure to focus on the decision and the "why."* See the solution at the end of the chapter for our own take.

Feel free to glance back at the trade-off analysis we did earlier in the chapter to refresh your memory.

Solution on page 119

there are no
Dumb Questions

Q: I'm not entirely clear on the difference between the context and the "justification" we provide in the Decision section. Aren't those the same thing?

A: Maybe an example will help. Say it's your best friend's birthday, and you and a few others decide to go out to a fancy dinner to celebrate. That's the **context**—the circumstances surrounding the decision you have to make.

Before you decide on the details, you might make a list of possible restaurants (the **alternatives** available to you), thinking about how well the cuisines they offer match everyone's preferences. This would be akin to a trade-off analysis.

You pick a pan-Asian bistro: that's the **decision**. You choose that particular restaurant because its menu has vegetarian and gluten-free options, and it allows anyone with dietary restrictions to make substitutions. That's the **justification** for your decision.

Writing ADRs: Considering the consequences

Every decision has ***consequences***. Did you work out extra hard yesterday? If so, you might be sore this morning. (But maybe a little bit proud of yourself, too!)

It's important to realize the consequences—good and bad—of architectural decisions and document them. This increases ***transparency*** by ensuring that everyone understands what the decision entails, including the team(s) affected by it. Most importantly, it allows everyone to assess whether the decision's positive consequences will outweigh its negative consequences.

The consequences of an ADR can be limited in scope or have huge ramifications. Architectural decisions can affect all kinds of things—teams, infrastructure, budgets, even the implementation of the ADR itself. Here's an incomplete list of questions to ask:

Title
Status
Context
Decision
Consequences
Governance
Notes

- How does this ADR affect the implementing team? For instance, does it change the algorithms? Does it make testing harder or easier? How will we know when we're "done" implementing it?

- Does this ADR introduce or decommission infrastructure? What does that entail?

- Are cross-cutting concerns like security or observability affected? If so, what effects will that have across the organization?

Time and money are big—be sure to think this one through!

- How will the decision affect your time and budget? Does it introduce costs or save money? Will it take arduous effort to implement or make things easier?

Of course, the ADR might make things simpler and more cost-effective. If so, that's definitely worth highlighting.

- Does the ADR introduce any one-way paths? (For example, using queues means we can't control the order of messages.) If so, elaborate on this.

Collaborating with others is a great way to make sure your assessment is thorough. No matter how hard you think through the consequences of the ADR, you're likely to miss a few things; multiple perspectives will reveal more potential consequences. Here's a sample Consequences section:

Highlight the consequences of the decision for the implementation team.

Consequences

Since we will be using a single representation for all surveys, multiple documents will need to be changed when a common survey question is updated, added, or removed.

The IT team will need to shut down survey functionality during the data migration from the relational database to the document database, causing downtime.

It's important to note consequences that might affect customers or users.

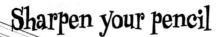 Sharpen your pencil ────────────

Help the Two Many Sneakers team iron out the Consequences section of their ADR. Here are a few things to think about:

➢ A queue introduces a new piece of infrastructure.

➢ The queues themselves will probably need to be highly available.

➢ Queues mean a higher degree of coupling between services.

There are no right or wrong answers, but if you'd like to see how we approached this, glance at the solution at the end of the chapter.

──────────→ Solution on page 120

Brain Power

Think about an architectural decision made in your current project, or one you've worked on in the past. It might be programming language used, the application's structure, or even the choice of database. Can you think of at least two intended consequences and two unintended consequences of that decision?

Writing ADRs: Ensuring governance

Have you ever made a New Year's resolution that fizzled out before the end of February? Maybe you joined a gym, only to end up paying but never working out? Us too. A decision is only good if you act on it, and if you don't accidentally stray away from it in the future.

Sure, you and your team spent a bunch of time analyzing trade-offs and writing an ADR to record the decision. Now what? How do you ensure that the decision is correctly implemented—and that it stays that way?

This is the role of the Governance section, which is vital in any ADR. Here, you outline how you'll ensure that your organization doesn't deviate from the decision—now or in the future. You could use manual techniques like pair programming or code reviews, or automated means like specialized testing frameworks.

> One of your authors has written a book called "Building Evolutionary Architectures" that shows you how to use "fitness functions" for architectural governance. Be sure to pick up a copy. (After you're done with this book, of course!)

> These two sections aren't part of the standard ADR template, but we think they add a lot of value.

> If the word "governance" conjures up ideas of regulatory compliance, well, this isn't that.

Writing ADRs: Closing notes

The Notes section contains metadata about the ADR itself. Here's a list of fields we like to include in our ADRs:

- Original author
- Approval date
- Approved by
- Superseded date
- Last modified date
- Modified by
- Last modification

> This section is handy even if the tool you use to store your ADRs automatically records things like creation and modification dates. Yes, including this information may be repetitive, but making it part of the ADR makes it easier to discover.

Exercise

Let's bring it all together! You've been working piecemeal on the ADR for the Two Many Sneakers team. We'd like you to flip back to the past few exercises and copy your ADR sections onto this page to create a full ADR. We've given you the section titles—all you have to do is fill 'em out. (Assume the status to be "Accepted.") You can find our version at the end of the chapter.

Title

Status

Context

Decision

Consequences

And there you have it: a complete ADR in its full glory.

We'll skip Governance and Notes here since they're not part of the standard template.

They grow up so quickly! :')
We're so proud of you all.

Solution on page 121

there are no Dumb Questions

Q: I really like the ADR template. But where am I supposed to store my ADRs?

A: There are lots of options—it all depends on what you and your team are comfortable with, and who else might be interested in reading or contributing to the ADRs.

One option is to store ADRs in plain-text files (or maybe Markdown or AsciiDoc files) in a version-control system like Git. This way, there's a commit history showing any changes to the ADRs. The downside is that nondevelopers don't always know how to access version-controlled documents. If you do choose to store your ADRs this way, we recommend keeping them in a separate repository (as opposed to stuffing them in with your source code). You'll thank us later.

Alternatively, you could use a wiki. Most wikis use a WYSIWYG ("what you see is what you get") editor, so they're accessible to more people. Just be sure that your choice of wiki can track changes. You wouldn't want someone to edit an ADR accidentally without everyone knowing.

Whatever you choose, make sure it's easy to add, edit, and search for ADRs. We've seen too many honest efforts at recording ADRs die just because no one could find the ADRs again if their lives depended on it.

Q: My whole team loves Markdown. (Plain text for the win!) Any advice on file naming conventions?

A: Recall that ADR titles have a three-digit prefix, followed by a very succinct description of the ADR. If you store your ADRs as plain-text files, we recommend using the title as your filename, including the prefix. For example, an ADR with the title "042: Use queues between the trading and downstream services" should be stored in a file named *042-use-queues-between-the-trading-and-downstream-services.md*. We like using all lowercase letters, which avoids any confusion between different operating systems. Replace spaces with hyphens to avoid whitespace.

This forces you to come up with good titles! And the three-digit prefix means you can simply sort the files in a folder by name to put them in the right order.

Q: Can you recommend any tools that make it easier to write and manage ADRs?

A: Oh, sure! There are many options, from command-line tools to language-specific tools that allow you to record ADRs directly in your source code. You can see a list of available tools at *https://adr.github.io/#decision-capturing-tools*.

Most third-party tools make assumptions about the format of the ADR—perhaps they generate Markdown files or store the files in a specific directory structure. Test-drive a tool a few times to get a feel for it.

Finally, some age-old advice: keep it simple, silly. We suggest you start by writing out ADRs without any complicated tooling or automation. Get a sense of what works best for your team. Then, as your needs grow, go find a tool that fits those needs.

Q: Do ADRs always belong to a single project, or can they affect multiple projects and teams? How about the whole organization?

A: Yes, yes, and yes. ADRs can be as narrow or as broad as you'd like them to be. Some ADRs are project-specific, affecting only one team. Other ADRs affect many or all teams in an organization. At the online retailer Amazon, there's an ADR affectionately referred to as "the Jeff Bezos API mandate." It records a decision that company founder Jeff Bezos once made: that all services within Amazon can only talk to other services via an API. Naturally, this affected the entire organization—no small feat, given Amazon's size.

Most cross-project or cross-team ADRs require a lot of collaboration, and often the blessing of a central architecture review board. Such ADRs tend to affect cross-cutting concerns, like how services should communicate with one another or which data transfer protocol to use. ADRs related to security or regulatory compliance often cut across multiple teams or a whole organization.

The benefits of ADRs

We hope we've convinced you by now that recording your decisions in ADRs need not be a long, arduous process. We really like the format we've shown you in this chapter, but feel free to tweak or modify it.

Is recording architectural decisions really that important? We certainly think so! There are tons of benefits to recording these decisions—not just for you and your team, but for your entire organization. Let's quickly recap.

ADRs are records of a system, including how it's structured and how it works, that anyone can review at any time.

ADRs answer the question "What were we thinking?" even if no one who made the decision is still around.

ADRs can help prevent teams from going down the same road again and again, encouraging new solutions instead.

Bidirectional linking between Superseded and Accepted ADRs is a huge boon here.

Why don't we just use a document store?

Ah! Here's a Superseded ADR—apparently we did at one point.

ADRs are key to building institutional knowledge and memory. Teams can read and learn from each other's ADRs.

⚠️ Watch it! Keep the ADR process as frictionless as possible

It's tempting to add sections to the ADR template in the hope of being comprehensive. While that's a noble goal, it adds work. If you keep "feeding the beast," the documentation process gets harder. That can discourage people, and some might stop writing ADRs altogether.

Focus on concision and brevity. Keep it simple. You'll thank us later.

Two Many Sneakers is a success

The team at Two Many Sneakers is ecstatic. Their customers *love* getting real-time notifications about new offerings in the app, and the improved analytics are giving the security team the information they need to sniff out any and all sneaker scams from a mile away.

> Just got the email from the finance team: they want the trading service to keep the compliance service in the know. That should be an easy change.

> Learning about the two laws of software architecture sure made this easy. Not only do we know we've made the right decision, but we've also captured it in an ADR. I feel so much better.

Grokking the two laws of software architecture will serve you well. Now you know that there are no "best practices" in software architecture—just trade-offs. It's up to you (and your team) to find the most viable and best-fitting option. And don't forget to record your decision in an ADR!

Onward and upward.

Bullet Points

- There is nothing "static" about architecture. It's constantly changing and evolving.

- Requirements and circumstances change. It's up to you to modify your architecture to meet new goals.

- For every decision, you will be faced with multiple solutions. To find the best (or least worst), do a *trade-off analysis*. This collaborative exercise helps you identify the pros and cons of every possible option.

- The **First Law of Software Architecture** is: Everything in software architecture is a trade-off.

- The answer to every question in software architecture is "it depends." To learn which solutions are best for your situation, you'll need to identify the top *priorities and goals*. What are the requirements? What's most important to your stakeholders and customers? Are you in a rush to get to market, or hoping to get things stable in growth mode?

- The product of a trade-off analysis is an *architectural decision*: one of the four dimensions needed to describe any architecture.

- An *architectural decision* involves looking at the pros and cons of every choice in light of other constraints— such as cultural, technical, business, and customer needs—and choosing the option that serves these constraints best.

- Making an architectural decision isn't just about choosing; it's also about *why* you're choosing that particular option.

- The **Second Law of Software Architecture** is: Why is more important than how.

- To formalize the process of capturing architectural decisions, use *architectural decision records* (ADRs). These documents have seven sections: Title, Status, Context, Decision, Consequences, Governance, and Notes.

- Over time, your ADRs will build into a *log* of architectural decisions that will serve as the memory store of your project.

- An ADR's *title* should consist of a three-digit numerical prefix and a noun-heavy, succinct description of the decision being made.

- An ADR can be assigned one of many *statuses*, depending on the kind of ADR and its place in the decision workflow.

- Once all parties involved in the decision sign off on the ADR, its status becomes Accepted.

- If a future decision supplants an Accepted ADR, you should write a new ADR. The supplanted ADR's status is marked as Superseded and the new ADR becomes Accepted.

- The *Context* section of an ADR explains why the decision needed to be made to begin with.

- The *Decision* section documents and justifies the actual decision being made. It always includes the "why."

- The *Consequences* section describes the decision's expected impact, good and bad. This helps ensure that the good outweighs the bad, and aids the team(s) implementing the ADR.

- The *Governance* section lists ways to ensure that the decision is implemented correctly and that future actions do not stray away from the decision.

- The final section is *Notes*, which mostly records metadata about the the ADR itself—like its author and when it was created, approved, and last modified.

- ADRs are important tools for abiding by the Second Law of Software Architecture, because they capture the "why" along with the "what."

- ADRs are necessary for building institutional knowledge and helping teams learn from one another.

"Two Laws" Crossword

Think you've mastered the two laws of software architecture? Why don't you document your knowledge by completing this crossword?

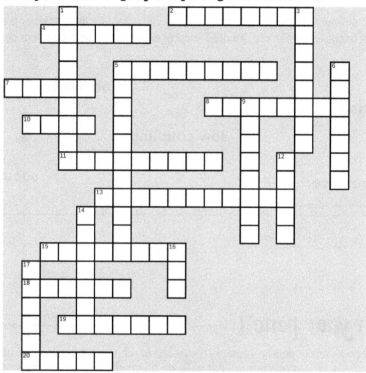

Across

2. Two Many _____
4. Topics use a fire-and-_____ system
5. A new ADR can _____ an old one
7. You can list pros and cons on a _____board
8. You should record every architectural _____ you make
10. Documents made up of seven sections (abbr.)
11. Heterogeneous
13. Important architectural characteristic for a fast-growing business
15. "Everything in software architecture is a trade-off" is the _____ _____ of software architecture (two words)
18. Examples of messaging mechanisms include queues and _____
19. Best tone to use when writing an ADR
20. If you're too excited about a new tool, you might have _____ Object Syndrome

Down

1. Topics can be independently _____
3. An architectural characteristic that's especially important for financial transactions
5. Architects are responsible for making architecturally _____ decisions
6. ADR section that tells you why a decision needed to be made
9. High or low interdependence
12. Short way to say "not at the same time"
14. Two Many Sneakers' mobile app communicates with the trading _____
16. More important than how, according to the Second Law
17. The _____ of an ADR might be Accepted

Solution on page 122

Exercise Solution

From page 85

Which of the following architectural characteristics stand out as important for this particular problem? *Hint: There are no right answers here, because there is a lot we don't know or aren't sure of yet.* Take your best guess—here are our thoughts:

Lots of downstream services need to know about sneaker trades. This sounds important!

modularity

upgradability

Since business is booming, this could be something to look out for.

extensibility

low coupling

performance

security

From page 89

Sharpen your pencil

Spend a few minutes comparing the results of our trade-off analysis. Notice how both options support some characteristics but trade off on others? Now we're going to present you with some requirements—see if you can decide if you'd pick queues or topics to support each one. Here are our answers:

Requirements

"Security is important to us." **Queues** / Topics

"Different downstream services need different kinds of information." **Queues** / Topics

"We'll be adding other downstream services in the future." Queues / **Topics**

From page 91

Sharpen your pencil
Solution

This time, we'd like you to do some trade-off analysis on your own. We chose messaging as the communication protocol between our trading service and its consumers. Messaging is asynchronous. Choosing between asynchronous and synchronous forms of communication comes with its own set of trade-offs! We've given you two whiteboards, one for each form of communication, and we've listed a bunch of "-ilities." We'd like you to consider how each architectural characteristic would work in both contexts. Is this characteristic a pro or a con (or neither) in synchronous communications? What about in asynchronous communications? Place each "-ility" in the appropriate column. *Hint: Not all of them apply to this decision.* You'll find our answers below:

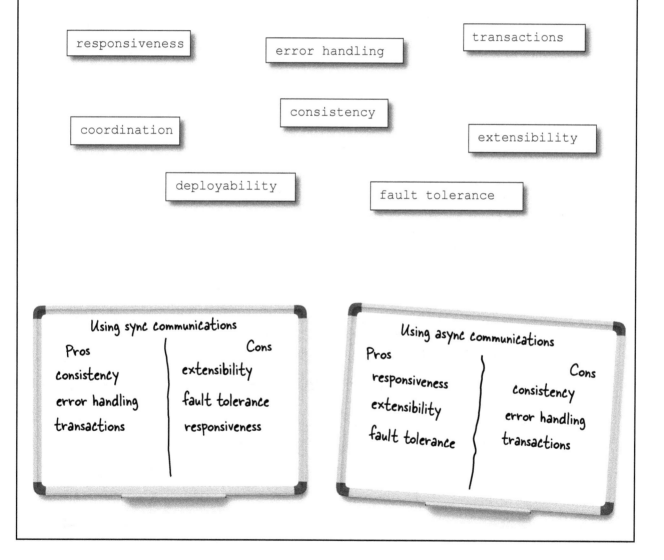

responsiveness

error handling

transactions

consistency

coordination

extensibility

deployability

fault tolerance

Using sync communications

Pros
consistency
error handling
transactions

Cons
extensibility
fault tolerance
responsiveness

Using async communications

Pros
responsiveness
extensibility
fault tolerance

Cons
consistency
error handling
transactions

Exercise Solution

From page 99

In the following exercises, you're going to help the team at Two Many Sneakers write an ADR. They've decided to use asynchronous messaging, with queues between the trading service and downstream services. Assume this is the **12th** ADR the team is writing. What title would you give this ADR? Don't forget to number it! Here's what we came up with:

> 012: Use of queues for asynchronous messaging between order and downstream services

Exercise Solution

From page 102

In the previous exercise, you hashed out the title of Two Many Sneakers' ADR about using queues for messaging. Let's say you get the green light. Write down the title you chose in the space below and give it a status. Here's ours:

Title: 012: Use of queues for asynchronous messaging between order and downstream services

Status: Accepted

Three months later:

Whoops! The requirements have changed. Your latest trade-off analysis reveals that topics would be a better fit. Everyone has signed off on this, so you need to supersede your ADR with a new ADR. This is the 21st ADR your team has worked on. Write down the title and the new status of the old ADR:

Title: 012: Use of queues for asynchronous messaging between order and downstream services

Status: Superseded by 021

Now write down the title and status of the newly introduced ADR. Here's ours:

Title: 021: Use of topics for asynchronous messaging between order and downstream services

Status: Accepted, Supersedes 012

Sharpen your pencil Solution

From page 104

Continue building out the ADR for Two Many Sneakers. Use the space below to write a Context section for the team's decision to use queues for communication between the trading service and other services. Here's our take:

The trading service must inform downstream services (namely the notification and analytics services, for now) about new items available for sale and about all transactions. This can be done through synchronous messaging (using REST) or asynchronous messaging (using queues or topics).

Exercise Solution

From page 106

It's time for you to write the Decision section of the ADR for Two Many Sneakers. Here are the main factors the team considered when making their decision:

- Queues allow for heterogeneous messages.
- Security is an important architectural characteristic for the stakeholders.

We've given you some space to write out a Decision section, including the corresponding justification. This section should answer the question, "Why queues?" *Hint: Be sure to focus on the decision and the "why."* There are no right answers, but here's what we came up with:

We will use queues for asynchronous messaging between the trading and downstream services.

Using queues makes the system more extensible, since each queue can deliver a different kind of message. Furthermore, since the trading service is acutely aware of any and all subscribers, adding a new consumer involves modifying it—which improves the security of the system.

Sharpen your pencil
Solution

From page 108

Help the Two Many Sneakers team iron out the Consequences section of their ADR. Here are a few things to think about:

➢ A queue introduces a new piece of infrastructure.

➢ The queues themselves will probably need to be highly available.

➢ How do queues affect coupling between components?

Queues mean a higher degree of coupling between services.

We will need to provision queuing infrastructure. It will require clustering to provide for high availability.

If additional downstream services (in addition to the ones we know about) need to be notified, we will have to make modifications to the trading service.

Here's our take.

Exercise Solution

From page 110

Let's bring it all together! You've been working piecemeal on the ADR for the Two Many Sneakers team. We'd like you to flip back over the past few exercises and copy your ADR sections onto this page to create a full ADR. We've given you the section titles—all you have to do is fill 'em out. (Assume the status to be "Accepted.") Here's our version:

Title

012: Use of queues for asynchronous messaging between order and downstream services

Status

Accepted

Context

The trading service must inform downstream services (namely the notification and analytics services, for now) about new items available for sale and about all transactions. This can be done through synchronous messaging (using REST) or asynchronous messaging (using queues or topics).

Decision

We will use queues for asynchronous messaging between the trading and downstream services.

Using queues makes the system more extensible, since each queue can deliver a different kind of message. Furthermore, since the trading service is acutely aware of any and all subscribers, adding a new consumer involves modifying it—which improves the security of the system.

Consequences

Queues mean a higher degree of coupling between services.

We will need to provision queuing infrastructure. It will require clustering to provide for high availability.

If additional downstream services (in addition to the ones we know about) need to be notified, we will have to make modifications to the trading service.

And there you have it! A complete ADR in its full glory.

"Two Laws" Crossword Solution

From page 115

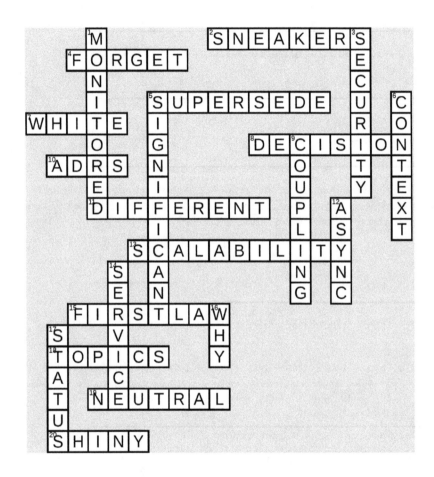

4 logical components
The Building Blocks

Ready to start creating an architecture? It's not as easy as it sounds—and if you don't do it correctly, your software system could come crumbling to the ground, just like a poorly designed skyscraper or bridge.

In this chapter we'll show you several approaches for identifying and creating *logical components*, the functional building blocks of a system that describe how its pieces all fit together. Using the techniques described in this chapter will help you to create a solid architecture—a foundation upon which you can build a successful software system.

Put on your hard hat and gloves, get your tools ready, and let's get started.

Logical components revisited

Logical components are one of the dimensions of software architecture. They
are the functional building blocks of a system that make up what is known as
the *problem domain*. In Chapter 1 you learned a bit about them, and in this
chapter we'll dive deep into what logical components are and how to create
them.

All of these rounded-edge boxes
represent the logical components that
comprise the problem domain.

Remember this example?
It's from Chapter 1.

**Order
Tracking**

**Order
Placement**

**Payment
Processing**

**Order
Shipping**

**Inventory
Management**

Remember that, in most programming languages, logical components are
represented through the *directory structure* of your source code repository. For
example, source code located in the `app/order/tracking` directory would be
contained within a logical component named Order Tracking.

The directory structure
identifies the logical
components and is therefore
part of the architecture.

app ← This is the domain.

order ← This is the subdomain.

This is the logical
component.

tracking ←

**Order
Tracking**

source_code_file

source_code_file

source_code_file

source_code_file

The source code identifies
how the logical component is
implemented and is therefore
part of the design.

This source code implements the
order tracking functionality.

Exercise

Name that component

It's your first week on the job as the new architect, and you've been assigned to an existing project to build a trouble ticket system. You want to understand the logical components of the architecture, but your team doesn't know anything about logical components—they just started coding. To determine the logical architecture, you have to look at the existing directory structure. How many individual logical components can you identify from the codebase below?

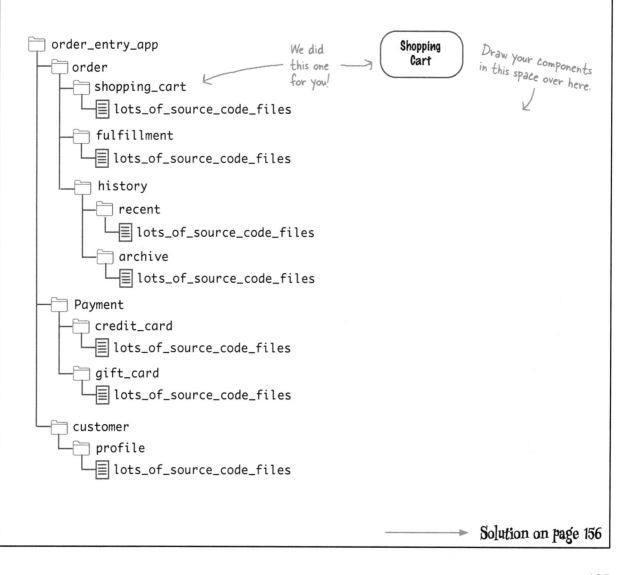

📁 order_entry_app
   └─📁 order
      └─📁 shopping_cart
         └─📄 lots_of_source_code_files
      └─📁 fulfillment
         └─📄 lots_of_source_code_files
      └─📁 history
         └─📁 recent
            └─📄 lots_of_source_code_files
         └─📁 archive
            └─📄 lots_of_source_code_files
   └─📁 Payment
      └─📁 credit_card
         └─📄 lots_of_source_code_files
      └─📁 gift_card
         └─📄 lots_of_source_code_files
   └─📁 customer
      └─📁 profile
         └─📄 lots_of_source_code_files

We did this one for you! →

Shopping Cart

Draw your components in this space over here.

→ Solution on page 156

Adventurous Auctions goes online

Want to go on a safari in Tanzania? Observe wildlife in the Galapagos Islands? Hike to the base camp of Mount Everest? Adventurous Auctions is here to help!

You've probably seen our ads or attended some of our live auctions around the country. These kinds of adventures are hard to come by and can take years to reserve; our company auctions them off at a significant cost savings.

We want more people around the world to be able to access these great trips, so we're taking our adventurous auctions online (in addition to our in-person auctions).

That's where you come in: we need a new system to support the online auctions of our adventurous trips.

Let's go on an adventure!

This is Kate. She wants to bid for an adventure trip.

Here's what the new system needs to do:

● Scale up to meet demand, so hundreds or even thousands of people can participate in each auction.

● Include both in-person and online bids in every auction.

● Allow online users to register with Adventurous Auctions and provide us with their credit card details so they can pay if they win a trip.

● Allow online users to view live video streams of in-person auctions, as well as all bids placed so far, both in person and online.

● Allow online users to bid on trips, just like the people in the room.

● Determine which online bidder bids the asking price first (this is called "winning the bid"). If an online bidder bids at the same time as an in-person bidder, the auctioneer then determines who bid first.

● When the auctioneer announces an online user as the winner, the system charges the winner's credit card, notifies the winner, then moves on to the next trip in the auction.

Pay attention, because we're going to show you how to create a logical architecture for this system.

Logical versus physical architecture

A ***logical architecture*** shows all of the logical building blocks of a system and how they interact with each other (known as ***coupling***). A ***physical architecture***, on the other hand, shows things like the architectural style, services, protocols, databases, user interfaces, API gateways, and so on.

We're going to be talking a lot about component coupling later in this chapter.

The logical architecture of a system is independent of the physical architecture—meaning the logical architecture doesn't care about databases, services, protocols, and so on. Let's look at an example of what we mean by a logical architecture.

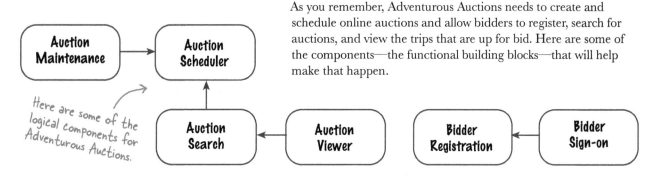

Here are some of the logical components for Adventurous Auctions.

As you remember, Adventurous Auctions needs to create and schedule online auctions and allow bidders to register, search for auctions, and view the trips that are up for bid. Here are some of the components—the functional building blocks—that will help make that happen.

This physical architecture shows some of the services and databases.

See how the logical architecture *doesn't* include the various components of physical architecture mentioned above? It's a different view of the system. To see what we mean, compare the diagram above with the following physical architecture diagram. Notice how the physical architecture associates services with components from the logical architecture, and also shows the services and databases for the system.

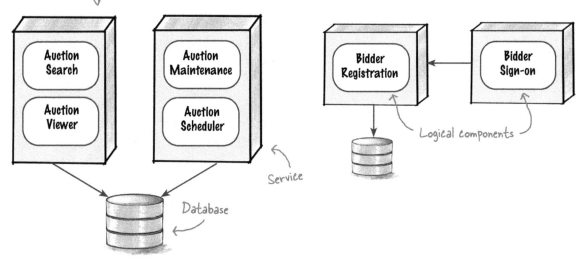

Who Does What?

We had our logical and physical architecture responsibilities all figured out, but somehow they got all mixed up. Can you help us figure out who does what? Be careful—some responsibilities may not have a match (they aren't part of a logical or physical architecture).

Be sure to check the answers (located at the end of this chapter) before moving on.

Shows which programming language is used for each component

Maps components to services

Logical architecture

Shows the logical components within the system and how they communicate with each other

Shows how many databases there are in the system and which services access them

We did this one for you.

Shows communication between services and the protocol they use (like REST)

Physical architecture

Shows the source code files used to implement a component

Shows the components and their interactions within the user interface

Shows the API gateways and load balancers used in the system

Solution on page 157

Creating a logical architecture

Identifying logical components isn't as easy as it sounds. To help, we've created this flowchart. Don't worry—we'll be covering all of these steps in detail in the following pages.

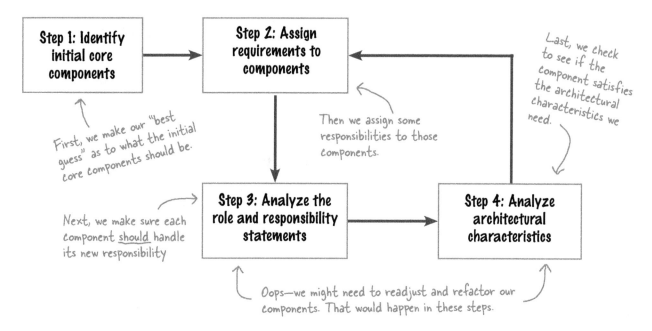

Step 1: Identify initial core components

Step 2: Assign requirements to components

Step 3: Analyze the role and responsibility statements

Step 4: Analyze architectural characteristics

First, we make our "best guess" as to what the initial core components should be.

Next, we make sure each component <u>should</u> handle its new responsibility

Then we assign some responsibilities to those components.

Last, we check to see if the component satisfies the architectural characteristics we need.

Oops—we might need to readjust and refactor our components. That would happen in these steps.

This flow continues as long as the system is alive.

This flowchart shows a series of steps to begin *greenfield applications* (new systems created from scratch) and perform ongoing maintenance on existing ones.

Ever wonder why it's so common for a well-designed system to end up as an unmaintainable mess in no time? It's because teams don't pay enough attention to the logical architecture of their systems.

Anytime you make a change or add a new feature to the system, you should always go through each of these steps to ensure that the logical components are the right size and are doing what they are meant to do.

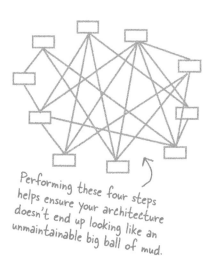

Performing these four steps helps ensure your architecture doesn't end up looking like an unmaintainable big ball of mud.

Step 1: Identifying initial core components

The first step in creating a logical architecture is identifying the ***initial core components***. Many times this is purely a guessing game, and you'll likely refactor the components you initially identify into others. So don't spend a lot of time worrying about how big or small your components are—we'll get to that. First, let's show you what we mean by a "guessing game."

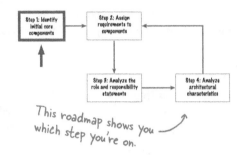

This roadmap shows you which step you're on.

This is Frank, the CIO of Adventurous Auctions.

> The auction flow is pretty simple. Participants join a live auction, view the auction, and bid on a trip they are interested in.

Given this simple description, you can start out by creating three logical components, one for each of the three major things the system does.

| Live Auction Session | Video Streamer | Bid Capture |

Don't forget—these are components, not services.

This component represents a live auction taking place and allows participants to join the auction.

This component is responsible for streaming the live auction to online participants.

This component is responsible for capturing bids.

These components aren't really doing anything yet. You see, we've *identified* the initial components, but we haven't assigned them any responsibility yet. You could think of them as empty jars. They represent our initial best guess, based on a major action that takes place in the system. That's why we call them *initial* core components.

This jar exists but is empty, just like the initial core components you identify.

Live Auction Session

Creating a logical architecture is all a "guessing game"? That's the most ridiculous thing I've ever heard. Isn't there some way to take the guesswork out of identifying logical components?

Yes, there is! In fact, you can use several approaches to remove some of the guesswork.

You don't know a lot of details about the system or its requirements yet, and the components you initially identify are likely to change as you learn more. That's why we say it's a guessing game at this stage—and that's perfectly okay!

We'll show you two common approaches for identifying initial core components: the *workflow approach* and the *actor/action approach*.

There are other approaches that may seem like good ideas initially but that can lead you down a very bad path. We'll discuss those after we show you the good stuff.

Workflow approach

The **workflow approach** is an effective way to identify an initial set of core components by thinking about the major workflows of the system—in other words, the journey a user might take through the system. Don't worry about capturing every step; start out with the major processing steps, and then work your way down to more details.

You can model different workflows to create even more initial components.

Let's use the workflow approach to identify some initial core components for the Adventurous Auctions architecture.

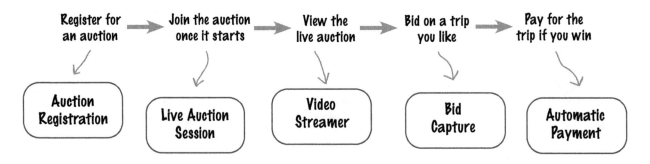

| Register for an auction | → | Join the auction once it starts | → | View the live auction | → | Bid on a trip you like | → | Pay for the trip if you win |

| Auction Registration | Live Auction Session | Video Streamer | Bid Capture | Automatic Payment |

there are no Dumb Questions

Q: You identified "Video Streamer" as a logical component, but what if our team decides to use a third-party library or service to stream the auction?

A: Great question! Even though you might not develop the functionality yourself, it's still part of the logical architecture.

Q: Is each step in a workflow always mapped to a single logical component?

A: Not always. You might have several steps in a workflow that point to the same logical component, particularly if their functionalities are closely related.

Names matter.

Pay close attention to how you name your initial core components. A good name should *succinctly describe* what that component does.

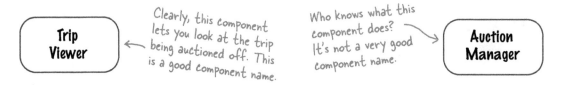

Trip Viewer

Clearly, this component lets you look at the trip being auctioned off. This is a good component name.

Who knows what this component does? It's not a very good component name.

Auction Manager

Sharpen your pencil

Your company wants a new system to assign workers to construction sites, and it's your job as the software architect to identify its initial core components. Using the workflow approach, identify as many core components as you can, matching each to its associated workflow step. Remember, a workflow step can have multiple components, and not every workflow step has to have a unique component.

Step 1: Maintain a list of all construction workers, their skills, and their locations

Step 2: Create a new construction project and specify the work site

Step 3: Create a schedule for when various construction projects start and end

Step 4: When a new project starts, assign workers based on their skills and locations

Step 5: When the project completes, free up workers so they can be reassigned

Draw your logical components in this space. Remember to give them good descriptive names.

Solution on page 158

Actor/action approach

The ***actor/action approach*** is particularly helpful if you have multiple actors (users) in the system. You start by identifying the various actors. Then, you identify some of the primary actions they might take and assign each action to a new or existing component.

Remember Kate? She wants to go on a trip, so she'll be a bidder.

Returning to our Adventurous Auctions example, let's use the actor/action approach to identify some initial core components.

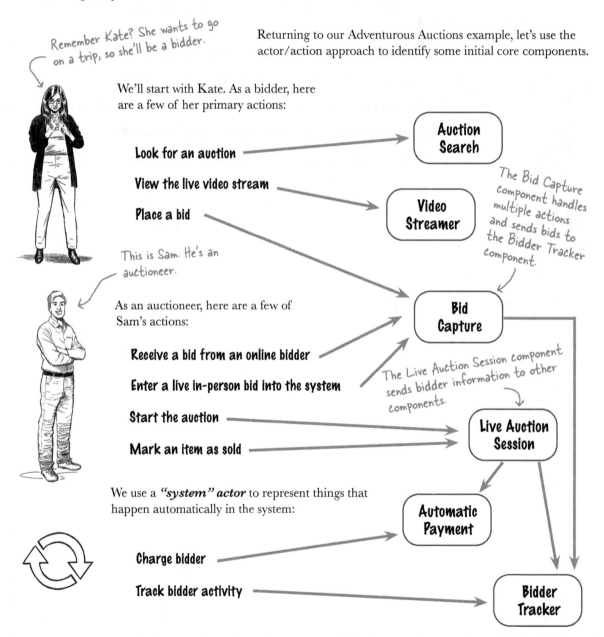

We'll start with Kate. As a bidder, here are a few of her primary actions:

Look for an auction — **Auction Search**

View the live video stream

Place a bid — **Video Streamer**

The Bid Capture component handles multiple actions and sends bids to the Bidder Tracker component.

This is Sam. He's an auctioneer.

As an auctioneer, here are a few of Sam's actions:

Receive a bid from an online bidder

Enter a live in-person bid into the system — **Bid Capture**

Start the auction

Mark an item as sold

The Live Auction Session component sends bidder information to other components.

Live Auction Session

We use a *"system" actor* to represent things that happen automatically in the system:

Charge bidder — **Automatic Payment**

Track bidder activity — **Bidder Tracker**

Exercise

You have a bakery that is ready to expand operations, and you would like a new system that lets customers view, order, and pay for bakery items online for pickup. Orders are sent to the bakery coordinator, who purchases ingredients and schedules orders. The baker receives the schedule of items to bake each morning and tells the system when the items are baked. The system then emails the customers to let them know their items are ready for pickup.

Using the actor/action approach, identify what actions each actor might take. Then draw as many logical components as you can for the new bakery system, matching the actions you identified to the components.

We started this exercise for you and filled in some of the components.

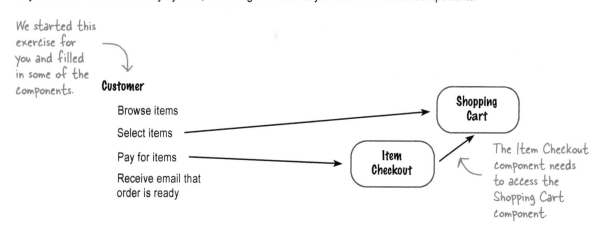

Customer

Browse items

Select items

Pay for items

Receive email that order is ready

Shopping Cart

Item Checkout

The Item Checkout component needs to access the Shopping Cart component.

Solution on page 159

The entity trap

Okay, so if I identify lots of actions that have to do with bids, then should I put all of them together in a single component called the Bid Manager?

Welcome to the entity trap.

We call this approach the *entity trap* because it's very easy to fall into it when identifying the initial core logical components, and you'll run into lots of issues if you do this.

First of all, the name "Bid Manager" is too vague. Can you tell what the component does just by looking at the name? Neither can we. A name like this doesn't tell us enough about the component's role and responsibilities.

Second, the component has too many responsibilities. All too often, components in the entity trap become convenient dumping grounds for all functionality related to those entities. As a result, they take on too much responsibility and become too big and difficult to maintain, scale, and make fault tolerant.

This component will be hard to scale because it's doing too much.

Bid Manager

These are all the things the component does.

- Accept a bid
- Display all winning bids
- Track bids for auditing purposes
- Determine bid winner
- Notify auctioneer of online bid
- Generate bid reports

Pro Tip

Watch out for words like *manager* or *supervisor* when naming your logical components—those are good indicators that you might be in the entity trap.

Sharpen your pencil

What other words besides *manager* can you list that, if they appeared in a component name, might indicate that you've fallen into the entity trap?

We did this one for you. → **supervisor**

Solution on page 160

Exercise

Can you select the most appropriate approach to identifying initial core components in the following scenarios? In some cases, more than one approach may be appropriate.

The system has only one type of user	☐ Workflow	☐ Actor/Action
The system has well-defined entities	☐ Workflow	☐ Actor/Action
You have minimal functional requirements	☐ Workflow	☐ Actor/Action
The system has many complex user journeys	☐ Workflow	☐ Actor/Action
The system has many types of users	☐ Workflow	☐ Actor/Action

⟶ Solution on page 160

there are no Dumb Questions

Q: The actor/action approach reminds me a lot of event storming. Are they the same thing?

A: Great observation, and we're glad you saw the similarities. Event storming is a workshop-based approach that is part of *domain-driven design* (DDD). With this approach, you analyze the business domain to identify domain events. While both approaches have the final goal of identifying actions performed within the system, event storming takes identifying components much further than the actor/action approach does. You could say that the actor/action approach identifies the *domain event* and *actor* elements of event storming, but doesn't continue with other elements such as *command*, *aggregate*, and *view*. You can learn more about event storming at *https://en.wikipedia.org/wiki/Event_storming*.

Q: Can you combine the workflow approach and actor/action approach, or do you have to choose between them?

A: You can combine them, and in most cases this is a good idea. If you start with the actor/action approach to identify actions, you can then use the workflow approach to arrange them in the order in which they are likely to occur.

Q: Are you telling me I should never use the words *manager*, *supervisor*, and so on as part of my component names?

A: Not necessarily—there is no hard and fast rule to the entity trap. Sometimes it's hard to come up with a name for something that does a general task. Take, for example, a component that manages all of the reference data in your application—name/value pairs like country codes, store codes, color codes, and so on. A good name for such a component would be "Reference Data Manager." However, names like "Order Manager" or "Response Handler" are too broad and don't describe what those components actually do.

Q: When using the actor/action approach, how many actions should you identify for each actor?

A: That's a tough question. The purpose of identifying actions is to tease out likely logical components and what they might be responsible for. We usually look at the *primary* actions an actor might take, rather than diving into too many details.

Step 2: Assign requirements

Once you've identified some initial core components, it's time to move on to the next step: ***assigning requirements*** to those logical components.

In this step, you'll take functional user stories or requirements and figure out which component should be responsible for each one. Remember, each component is represented by a directory structure. Your source code resides in that directory, so it contains that requirement.

Let's go back to the initial set of components we defined based on what Frank (the CIO) said about the basic workflow of Adventurous Auctions. Now it's time to assign some responsibilities to these components.

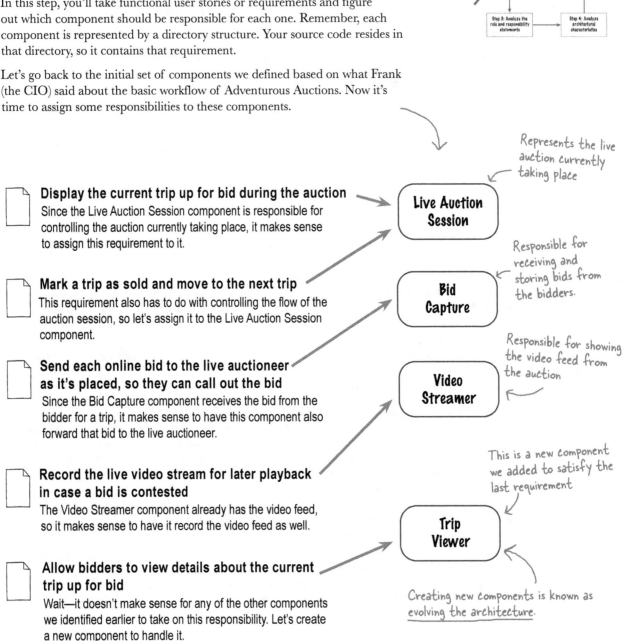

Display the current trip up for bid during the auction
Since the Live Auction Session component is responsible for controlling the auction currently taking place, it makes sense to assign this requirement to it.

Mark a trip as sold and move to the next trip
This requirement also has to do with controlling the flow of the auction session, so let's assign it to the Live Auction Session component.

Send each online bid to the live auctioneer as it's placed, so they can call out the bid
Since the Bid Capture component receives the bid from the bidder for a trip, it makes sense to have this component also forward that bid to the live auctioneer.

Record the live video stream for later playback in case a bid is contested
The Video Streamer component already has the video feed, so it makes sense to have it record the video feed as well.

Allow bidders to view details about the current trip up for bid
Wait—it doesn't make sense for any of the other components we identified earlier to take on this responsibility. Let's create a new component to handle it.

Live Auction Session — *Represents the live auction currently taking place*

Bid Capture — *Responsible for receiving and storing bids from the bidders.*

Video Streamer — *Responsible for showing the video feed from the auction*

Trip Viewer — *This is a new component we added to satisfy the last requirement*

Creating new components is known as evolving the architecture.

Sharpen your pencil

Your company, Going Green Corporation, wants a system to support its new electronics recycling program, where customers can send in their old electronic devices (like cell phones) and get money. We've already identified some of the initial core components. Your job is to figure out which component should be responsible for each of the functionalities listed below, or if a new component is needed. You'll also need to come up with names for any new components.

Device Receiving — Physically receive the device from the customer.

Device Assessment — Assess the device's condition

Device Recycling — Recycle or resell the old device.

Locate the nearest safe disposal facility for destroying the device

☐ Device Receiving ☐ Device Assessment ☐ Device Recycling ☐ Other: _____

Capture and store customer information (name, address, etc.)

☐ Device Receiving ☐ Device Assessment ☐ Device Recycling ☐ Other: _____

Post the device on a third-party site to resell it on the secondary market

☐ Device Receiving ☐ Device Assessment ☐ Device Recycling ☐ Other: _____

Pay the customer for their recycled device

☐ Device Receiving ☐ Device Assessment ☐ Device Recycling ☐ Other: _____

Record that the device has been received and is ready for assessment and valuation

☐ Device Receiving ☐ Device Assessment ☐ Device Recycling ☐ Other: _____

Determine the value (if any) of the recycled device

☐ Device Receiving ☐ Device Assessment ☐ Device Recycling ☐ Other: _____

Determine the monthly profit and loss for recycled and resold devices

☐ Device Receiving ☐ Device Assessment ☐ Device Recycling ☐ Other: _____

Going Green Corp. needs to make a profit, after all.

Solution on page 161

Step 3: Analyze roles and responsibilities

As you start assigning **functionality** (in other words, user stories or requirements) to logical components, the roles and responsibilities of each component will start to naturally grow. The purpose of this step is to make sure that the component to which you are assigning functionality **should** actually be responsible for that functionality and that it doesn't end up doing too much.

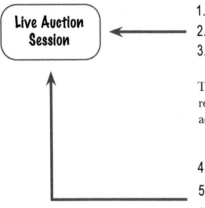

Let's say we create a component called *Live Auction Session* that has the following responsibilities during a live auction:

Live Auction Session

1. Start and stop the auction
2. Show the current trip up for bid
3. Mark a trip as sold and move to the next trip

This is a well-designed component and has just the right amount of responsibility. However, as iterations move forward, the development team adds some new requirements to the Live Auction Session component:

4. Display the details of each trip in this auction
5. Keep track of all the bidders currently in the auction
6. Keep track of each winning bidder for the auction
7. Notify the bidder that they won the trip

Hey, component, can you wash my car too?

If you've ever had too much on your plate at work, you likely gave some of that work to others. Do the same with components—offload some of the responsibility to someone else.

With this added functionality, this component is now taking on too much responsibility. This is a common situation, so don't be surprised if it happens to you. When it does, don't panic—that's what this step is here for. Let's see if we can fix this situation by moving some of the responsibility of the Live Auction Session component to other components.

Geek Note

Have you ever created a class file called `Utility`? What did it do? Chances are it contained a bunch of unrelated functions that you'd had a hard time placing. The same thing can happen with logical components within software architecture. Try to avoid components that contain lots of unrelated functions.

Sticking to cohesion

When you analyze a component's role and responsibility statement or set of operations, check to see if the functionality is closely related. This is known as **cohesion**: the degree and manner to which the operations of a component are interrelated. Cohesion is a useful tool for making sure a component has the right responsibilities.

When analyzing the role and responsibilities of a component, it's common to find an *outlier* (an odd piece of functionality) or a component that is doing too much. In these cases, it's usually a good idea to shift some of the responsibility to other components.

Now it's your turn to fix the Live Auction Session component.

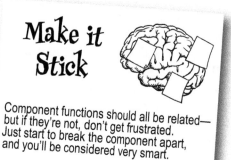

Make it Stick

Component functions should all be related—but if they're not, don't get frustrated. Just start to break the component apart, and you'll be considered very smart.

Exercise

See if you can offload some of the responsibility of the Live Auction Session component to others by creating new components to handle the additional functionality. Keep the first three original requirements associated with the Live Auction Session.

We did this one for you.

Live Auction Session

Draw your new components in this space here.

1. Start and stop the auction
2. Show the current trip up for bid
3. Mark a trip as sold and move to the next trip

4. Display the details of each trip in this auction

5. Keep track of all the bidders currently in the auction

6. Keep track of each winning bidder for the auction

7. Notify the bidder that they won the trip

Hint: You might consider combining a few of these requirements when creating new components.

Solution on page 162

Step 4: Analyze characteristics

The final step in identifying initial core components is to verify that each component aligns with the ***driving architectural characteristics*** that are critical for success. In most cases this involves breaking apart a component for better scalability, elasticity, or availability, but it could also involve putting components together if their functionalities are tightly coupled.

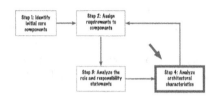

Let's look once again at our Adventurous Auctions example. We previously identified a Bid Capture component that is responsible for *accepting bids*, *storing all bids in a Bid Tracker database*, and *forwarding the highest bid to the auctioneer*. Here is the overall flow for the Bid Capture component:

This architecture looks good, but just to be sure, we should make sure the Bid Capture component supports the system's critical architectural characteristics (those that are important for success).

We know the system has to support thousands of bidders per second—that's *scalability*. We also know the system must be up and running while auctions are taking place—that's *availability*. Finally, the system must accept a bid and get it to the auctioneer as fast as possible—that's *performance*.

Now it's your turn to analyze the Bid Capture component against these critical architectural characteristics.

BE the architect

Your job is to play architect and analyze the Bid Capture component on the previous page to see if it should be modified based on the critical architectural characteristics we identified. Our solution is on the next page.

These are the critical architectural characteristics for Adventurous Auctions:

Scalability: The system has to support thousands of bidders per second

Availability: The system must be up and running while the auctions are taking place

Performance: The system must accept a bid and get it to the auctioneer as fast as possible.

Hints (things to consider):

- What if the database goes down?
- Can the database keep up with the volume of inserts based on the bids coming in?
- Will inserts into the database be fast enough to get the bids to the auctioneer?
- Consider the actions the Bid Capture component has to take upon receiving a bid.

Use this area to draw how you might change the Bid Capture component based on the critical architectural characteristics and considerations above.

The Bid Capture component

Let's work through this exercise by reviewing the current responsibilities of the Bid Capture component:

1. Accept bids from online bidders and from the auctioneer for live bidders.
2. Determine which online bid is the highest.
3. Write all bids to a Bid Tracker database for tracking purposes.
4. Notify the auctioneer of the highest bid.

It makes sense for the Bid Capture component to write the bids to the database, since it has them. But database connections and throughput are limited, so having Bid Capture do this significantly impacts *scalability*. It also impacts *performance* by adding wait time for writing the data to the database, as well as *availability* if the database were ever to go down.

This is what we mean by analyzing characteristics.

If we assign the last requirement to a *new* component called Bid Tracker, we can significantly increase the scalability, performance, and availability of the Bid Capture component. That lets the system process more bids faster and get the highest bid to the auctioneer as quickly as possible. The Bid Capture component can send the bids to the Bid Tracker and won't have to wait for the bid to be written to the database.

You might break apart or combine components in this step, based on the architectural characteristics needed.

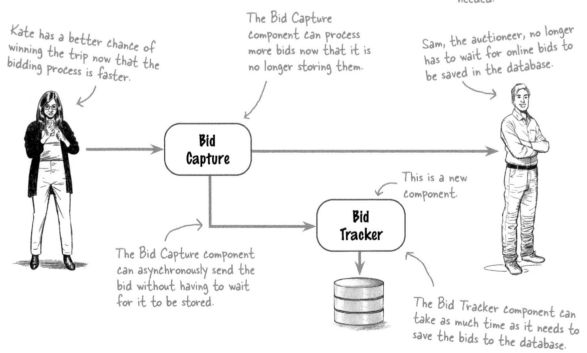

Kate has a better chance of winning the trip now that the bidding process is faster.

The Bid Capture component can process more bids now that it is no longer storing them.

Sam, the auctioneer, no longer has to wait for online bids to be saved in the database.

Bid Capture

This is a new component.

Bid Tracker

The Bid Capture component can asynchronously send the bid without having to wait for it to be stored.

The Bid Tracker component can take as much time as it needs to save the bids to the database.

Component coupling

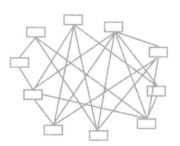

I should probably start thinking about how the logical components interact with and depend on each other, right?

Yes, and this is the right time to do it.

As you identify the initial core components, it's important to determine how they interact. This is known as ***component coupling***: the degree to which components know about and rely on each other. The more the components interact, the more tightly coupled the system is and the harder it will be to maintain.

Remember this diagram from several pages ago? It's called a "big ball of mud" because there are so many component interactions and dependencies that the diagram starts to look like a ball of mud (or maybe like a bowl of spaghetti).

That's why it's so important to pay attention to how components interact and what dependencies exist between them.

You need to be concerned about two types of coupling when creating logical components: ***afferent coupling*** and ***efferent coupling***. Don't be concerned if you've never heard these formal terms before—we're going to explain them in the following pages.

Afferent coupling

Children depend on their parents for a lot of things, like making sure they have plenty of food to eat and a safe place to live, driving them to soccer practice, or even giving them an allowance so they can buy candy or a really cool comic book. As it turns out, parents are *afferently* coupled to their children, and even to the family dog, because all of them depend on the parents for something.

Afferent coupling is the degree and manner to which other components are dependent on some target component (in this case, Mom). It's sometimes referred to as *fan-in*, or *incoming*, coupling. In most code analysis tools, it's simply denoted as *CA*.

Everyone is dependent on Mom.

Mom is afferently coupled to the family.

Responsible for allowing bidders to sign up for an auction

Responsible for managing all of the information about a bidder

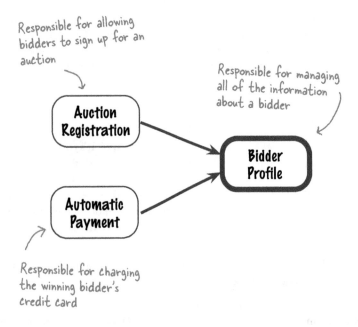

Responsible for charging the winning bidder's credit card

To see how afferent coupling works, look at the interaction between three of the logical components within the Adventurous Auctions logical architecture on the left.

Both the Auction Registration component and the Automatic Payment component depend on the Bidder Profile component to return bidder profile information. In this scenario, the Bidder Profile component has an afferent coupling level of 2, because two components depend on it to complete their work.

Geek Note

Did you know that the odd-sounding word *afferent* means "carrying toward"? It gets its roots from the Latin words *ad* (meaning "to" or "toward") and *ferre* ("to carry"). In the medical field, the word *afferent* refers to nerves that carry impulses to the brain (your *afferent nerves*).

Efferent coupling

Now let's look at things from a young child's point of view. As a child, you might have been dependent not only on your parents, but also your teachers, friends, classmates, and so on. Being dependent on others is known as *efferent coupling*.

Efferent coupling is exactly the opposite of afferent coupling, and it's measured by the number of components on which a target component depends. It's also known as *fan-out coupling* or *outgoing coupling*. In static source code analysis tools, it's usually denoted as *CE*.

This is Josh.

These are Josh's parents.

Josh is dependent on these people, which means he's efferently coupled to them.

This is Josh's teacher.

So, what does efferent coupling look like with logical components? Let's take a look at Adventurous Auctions again, this time considering the process of accepting a bid from Kate for a trip.

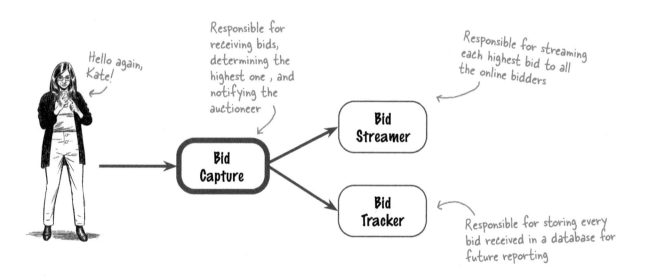

Hello again, Kate!

Responsible for receiving bids, determining the highest one, and notifying the auctioneer

Responsible for streaming each highest bid to all the online bidders

Bid Capture

Bid Streamer

Bid Tracker

Responsible for storing every bid received in a database for future reporting

Because the Bid Capture component depends on the Bid Streamer and Bid Tracker components to process a bid, it is *efferently coupled* to these components. It has an efferent coupling level of 2 (in other words, it's dependent on two other components).

Measuring coupling

You can measure a particular component's amount of coupling in three ways: by considering its **total afferent coupling** (CA), its **total efferent coupling** (CE), and its **total coupling** (CT), or the sum of the total afferent and efferent coupling. These measurements tell you which components have the highest and lowest coupling, as well as the entire system's overall coupling level.

This logical architecture has a total coupling (CT) level of 6.

$$CA + CE = CT$$

You can use this information to track whether things are getting more or less coupled over time.

CA=0   CE=1   CA=1   CE=2

Bid Placer   CT=1   **Bid Capture**   CT=3

CA=1   CE=0

Bid Streamer   CT=1

CA=1   CE=0

Bid Tracker   CT=1

Sharpen your pencil

Given the components below, can you identify the total afferent coupling (CA), total efferent coupling (CE), and total coupling (CT) for each component? Also, what is the total coupling level for this logical architecture? Does the CT for this architecture seem high or low to you?

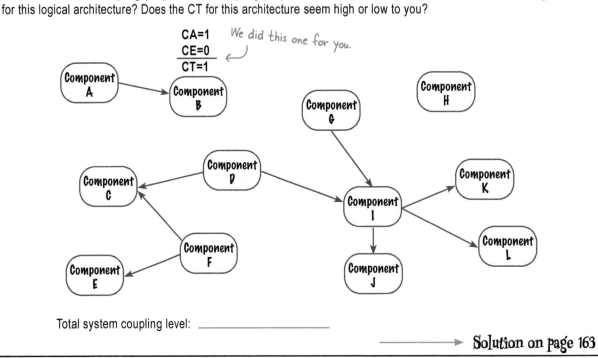

CA=1
CE=0
————
CT=1   *We did this one for you.*

Total system coupling level: _____

Solution on page 163

> Okay, now I get coupling and how to measure it. But how do I reduce component coupling to create loosely coupled systems?

Great question. Developers are taught to strive for loosely coupled systems, but not *how* to do it. We'll show you how by introducing a technique called the ***Law of Demeter***.

The Law of Demeter, also known as the Principle of Least Knowledge, is named after Demeter, the Greek goddess of agriculture. She produced all grain for mortals to use, but she had no knowledge of what they did with the grain. Because of this, Demeter was *loosely coupled* to the mortal world.

Logical components work in the same way. The more knowledge a component has about other components and what needs to happen in the system, the more coupled it is to those components. By reducing its *knowledge* of other components, we reduce that component's level of coupling.

On the next few pages, we'll show you more about the Law of Demeter and how it can be used to decouple systems.

A tightly coupled system

Let's see how the Law of Demeter can be used to decouple systems by taking a look at the logical architecture of a typical order entry system.

The components in this architecture are well defined in terms of their individual responsibilities.

The Order Placement component sure does know a lot about placing an order.

CA=1
CE=4
CT=5

Place an order → **Order Placement**

Decrement inventory → CT=1 **Inventory Management**

Stock low? Order more

Notify the customer

Stock low? Raise the price *Now that's not nice.*

CT=1 → **Email Notification**

CT=1 → **Item Pricing**

CT=1 → **Supplier Ordering**

Total System Coupling = 9

Brain Power

What possible issues do you see with the logical architecture above? We've provided some (but not all) potential problems. Check off the ones you think might be an issue, and write down any other possible issues you see with this logical architecture.

☐ **The customer might not be available to get their email when it's sent.**

☐ **The supplier might not have stock on hand.**

☐ **The Order Placement component knows too much about the steps involved in placing an order.**

☐ _____

☐ _____

☐ _____

Applying the Law of Demeter

The total system coupling level didn't bother us that much. What *does* bother us is how tightly coupled the Order Placement component is (CT=5), how unbalanced the component coupling is, and how much knowledge the Order Placement component has about the order placement process.

The Order Placement component is taking charge.

Let's apply the Law of Demeter to fix these problems by moving the "low stock" knowledge to the Inventory Management component.

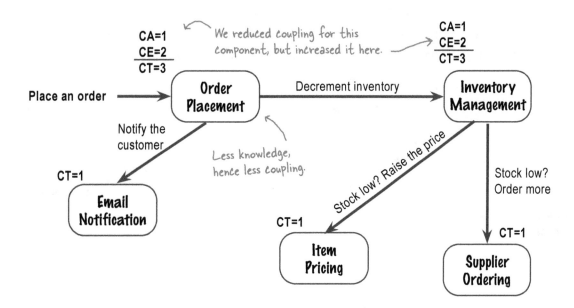

CA=1
CE=2
CT=3

We reduced coupling for this component, but increased it here.

CA=1
CE=2
CT=3

Place an order → **Order Placement** — Decrement inventory → **Inventory Management**

Notify the customer

Less knowledge, hence less coupling.

CT=1

Email Notification

Stock low? Raise the price

Stock low? Order more

CT=1

Item Pricing

CT=1

Supplier Ordering

Total System Coupling = 9

By moving the *knowledge of actions to take for a "low stock" condition* to Inventory Management, we reduced the amount of knowledge about the system, and hence the coupling, of the Order Placement component However, we *increased* the knowledge of the Inventory Management component, and thus increased its coupling. This is what the Law of Demeter is all about—less knowledge, less coupling; more knowledge, more coupling.

Coupling is all about how much knowledge components have about the rest of the system.

Geek Note

Did you notice that while we reduced the coupling of the Order Placement component, the total system coupling level remained the same? That's because we didn't *remove* the knowledge from the system, we just *moved* it to another component—Inventory Management.

Test Drive

Now it's time to take the Law of Demeter for a test drive to see if you can decouple a logical architecture. Below is a logical architecture for a system where customers who have purchased a support plan with an electronic item can submit a trouble ticket and have an expert come out to fix the item. Here's how it currently works:

1 A customer creates a ticket.

2 The ticket gets assigned to an available expert in the field.

3 The ticket is uploaded to an app on the expert's mobile device (that's Ticket Routing).

4 The customer is notified that the expert is on their way to fix the problem.

5 Once the expert fixes the problem, they mark the ticket as completed.

Keeping the components the same, how can you make this architecture more loosely coupled?

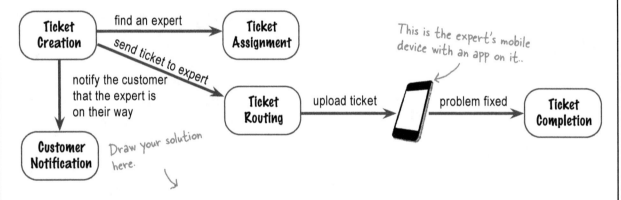

Solution on page 164

A balancing act

Do you remember the *First Law of Software Architecture*? Here it is again (because it's so important):

Everything in software architecture is a trade-off.

Loose coupling is no exception. Let's compare the two architectures we've just seen and analyze their trade-offs.

Tightly coupled

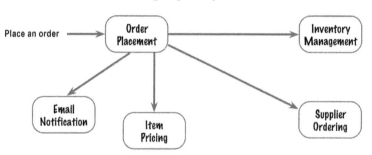

Centralized workflow, but more risk with each change

With the *tightly* coupled architecture, if you want to know what happens when a customer places an order, you only have to look at the Order Placement component to understand the workflow.

However, in this case, the Order Placement component is dependent on four other components. If any one of those components changes, it could break the Order Placement component.

These are the trade-offs for tight coupling.

With *loose* coupling, you distribute the knowledge about what needs to happen, so that no one component knows all the steps. If you want to understand the workflow of placing an order, you have to go to multiple components to get the full picture.

However, changing the Item Pricing and Supplier Ordering components will no longer affect the Order Placement component.

Loosely coupled

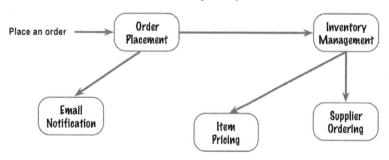

Distributed workflow, but less risk with each change

These are the trade-offs for tight coupling.

This is a good rule to remember.

Two components are coupled *if a change in one component might cause a change in the other component.*

Some final words about components

Congratulations! Now that you can identify logical components and the dependencies between them, you're on your way to creating a software architecture. We know this was a long chapter, but it's also an important one. Thinking about a system as a collection of logical components helps you, as an architect, better understand its overall structure and how it works.

In the next part of your software architectural journey, you'll be focusing on the technical details of the system—things like architecture styles, services, databases, and communication protocols. But before you go, review the following bullet points to make sure you fully understand everything about logical components.

Bullet Points

- *Logical components* are the functional building blocks of a system.

- A logical component is represented by a *directory structure*—the folder where you put your source code.

- When naming a component, be sure to provide a descriptive name to clearly identify what the component does.

- Creating a logical architecture involves four continuous steps: identify components, assign requirements, analyze component responsibilities, and analyze architectural characteristics.

- You can use the *workflow approach* to identify initial core logical components by assigning the steps in a primary customer journey to components.

- You can use the *actor/action approach* to identify initial core logical components by identifying the actors in the system and assigning their actions to components.

- The *entity trap* is an approach that models components after major entities in the system. Avoid using this approach, because it creates ambiguous components that are too large and have too much responsibility.

- When assigning requirements to components, review each component's role and responsibilities to make sure it should be performing that function.

- *Coupling* happens when components depend on one other to perform a business function.

- *Afferent coupling*, also known as incoming coupling, occurs when other components are dependent on a target component.

- *Efferent coupling*, also known as outgoing coupling, occurs when a target component is dependent on other components.

- Components having too much knowledge about what needs to happen in the system increases component coupling.

- The *Law of Demeter* states that services or components should have limited knowledge of other services or components. This law is useful for creating loosely coupled systems.

- While loose coupling reduces dependencies between components, it also distributes workflow *knowledge*, making it harder to manage and control that knowledge.

- Determining the total coupling (CT) of a logical architecture involves adding the afferent and efferent coupling levels for each component (CA + CE).

Logical Components Crossword

Now's your chance to have a little fun and see how much knowledge you've gained. See if you can fill in this crossword puzzle with clues about logical components.

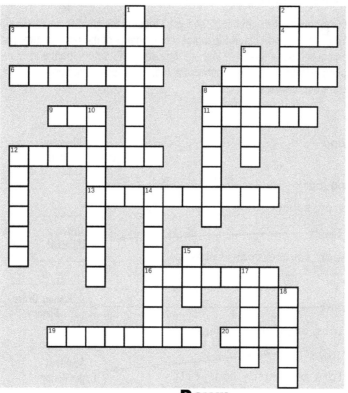

Across

3. Each component performs a _____
4. _____ gateways appear in a physical architecture but not a logical one
6. A physical architecture associates _____ with components
7. One system component might be a live video _____
9. Avoid building a big ball of _____
11. Be sure to avoid the _____ trap
12. Coupling might be _____ or efferent
13. Logical _____ are the functional building blocks of a system
16. Early on, you'll identify _____ core components
19. A user's journey through the system is called their _____
20. Each logical component has a _____ and a responsibility

→ Solution on page 165

Down

1. A component's _____ is about how interrelated its operations are
2. Give each component a descriptive _____
5. Afferent and efferent coupling are both forms of _____ coupling
8. The Principle of Least Knowledge is also called the Law of _____
10. A good place to look for components is the codebase's _____ structure
12. Step 2 is to _____ requirements to logical components
14. An architecture diagram can show the logical or _____ architecture
15. Adventurous Auctions lets users _____ on trips
17. You can identify components with an _____/action approach
18. Identifying logical components may involve taking your best _____

Exercise Solution

From page 125

Name that component

It's your first week on the job as the new architect, and you've been assigned to an existing project to build a trouble ticket system. You want to understand the logical components of the architecture, but your team doesn't know anything about logical components—they just started coding. To determine the logical architecture, you have to look at the existing directory structure. How many individual logical components can you identify from the codebase below? Here are our answers.

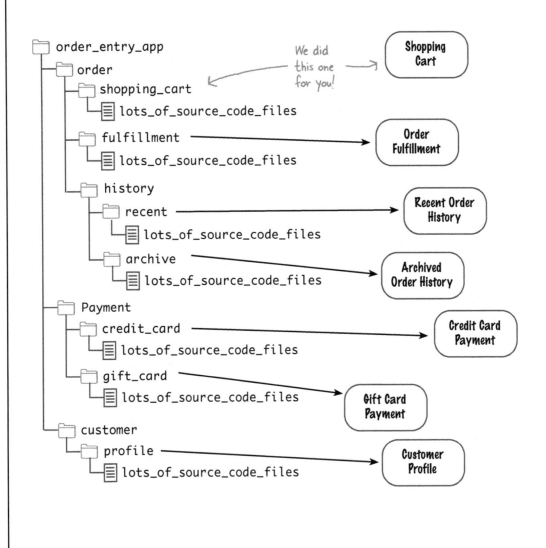

Who Does What **?**
Solution

From page 128

We had our logical and physical architecture responsibilities all figured out, but somehow they got all mixed up. Can you help us figure out who does what? Be careful—some responsibilities may not have a match (they aren't part of a logical or physical architecture).

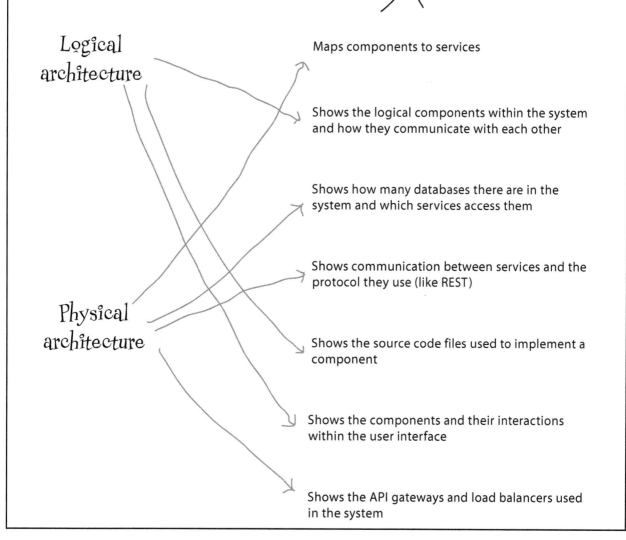

This is part of implementation, not architecture. ⟶ Shows which programming language is used for each component

Logical architecture

Maps components to services

Shows the logical components within the system and how they communicate with each other

Shows how many databases there are in the system and which services access them

Shows communication between services and the protocol they use (like REST)

Physical architecture

Shows the source code files used to implement a component

Shows the components and their interactions within the user interface

Shows the API gateways and load balancers used in the system

Sharpen your pencil
Solution

From page 133

Your company wants a new system to assign workers to construction sites, and it's your job as the software architect to identify its initial core components. Using the workflow approach, identify as many core components as you can, matching each to its associated workflow step. Remember, a workflow step can have multiple components, and not every workflow step has to have a unique component.

Step 1: Maintain a list of all construction workers, their skills, and their locations

Step 2: Create a new construction project and specify the work site

Step 3: Create a schedule for when various construction projects start and end

Step 4: When a new project starts, assign workers based on their skills and locations

Step 5: When the project completes, free up workers so they can be reassigned

Draw your logical components in this space. Remember to give them good descriptive names.

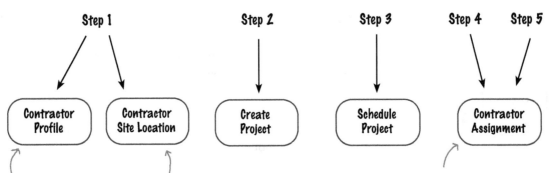

It makes sense to have two components because the profile is relatively static, whereas the location changes a lot.

The Contractor Assignment component can handle both assigning contractors (step 4) and unassigning them (step 5).

Exercise Solution

From page 135

You have a bakery that is ready to expand operations, and you would like a new system that lets customers view, order, and pay for bakery items online for pickup. Orders are sent to the bakery coordinator, who purchases ingredients and schedules orders. The baker receives the schedule of items to bake each morning, and tells the system when the items are baked. The system then emails the customers to let them know their items are ready for pickup.

Using the actor/action approach, identify what actions each actor might take, then draw as many logical components as you can for the new bakery system, matching the actions you identified to the components.

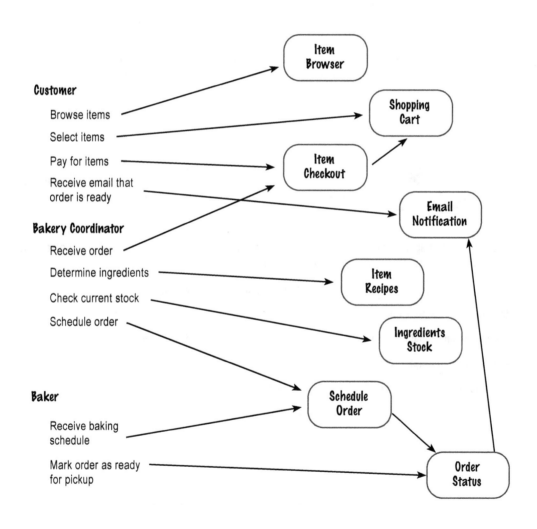

exercise *solutions*

Sharpen your pencil Solution

What other words besides **manager** can you list that, if they appeared in a component name, might indicate that you've fallen into the entity trap?

We did this one for you. → **supervisor**

handler

agent

Add the word "Order" to the front of these words and you'll see what we mean.

controller   **service**

utility

engine

worker   **mediator**   **orchestrator**

coordinator   **processor**

Exercise Solution

From page 137

Can you select the most appropriate approach to identifying initial core components in the following scenarios? In some cases, more than one approach may be appropriate.

The system has only one type of user — ☒ Workflow   ☐ Actor/Action

The system has well-defined entities — ☒ Workflow   ☒ Actor/Action ←

You have minimal functional requirements — ☒ Workflow   ☒ Actor/Action

The system has many complex user journeys — ☒ Workflow   ☐ Actor/Action

The system has many types of users — ☐ Workflow   ☒ Actor/Action

Remember to avoid the entity trap, even if the system has well-defined entities.

Neither approach requires lots of functionality to create initial logical components.

From page 139

Sharpen your pencil
Solution

Your company, Going Green Corporation, wants a system to support its new electronics recycling program, where customers can send in their old electronic devices (like cell phones) and get money. We've already identified some of the initial core components. Your job is to figure out which component should be responsible for each of the functionalities listed below, or if a new component is needed. You'll also need to come up with names for any new components.

Device Receiving — *Physically receive the device from the customer.*

Device Assessment — *Assess the device's condition*

Device Recycling — *Recycle or resell the old device.*

Locate the nearest safe disposal facility for destroying the device
☐ Device Receiving ☐ Device Assessment ☒ Device Recycling ☐ Other: _____

Capture and store the customer information (name, address, etc.)
☐ Device Receiving ☐ Device Assessment ☐ Device Recycling ☒ Other: Customer Profile

Post the device on a third-party site to resell it on the secondary market
☐ Device Receiving ☐ Device Assessment ☒ Device Recycling ☐ Other: _____

Pay the customer for their recycled device
☐ Device Receiving ☐ Device Assessment ☐ Device Recycling ☒ Other: Accounts Payable

Record that the device has been received and is ready for assessment and valuation
☒ Device Receiving ☐ Device Assessment ☐ Device Recycling ☐ Other: _____

Determine the value (if any) of the recycled device
☐ Device Receiving ☒ Device Assessment ☐ Device Recycling ☐ Other: _____

Determine the monthly profit and loss for recycled and resold devices
☐ Device Receiving ☐ Device Assessment ☐ Device Recycling ☒ Other: Financial Reporting

Going Green Corp. needs to make a profit, after all.

Exercise Solution

From page 141

See if you can offload some of the responsibility of the Live Auction Session component to others by creating new components to handle the additional functionality. Keep the first three original requirements associated with the Live Auction Session.

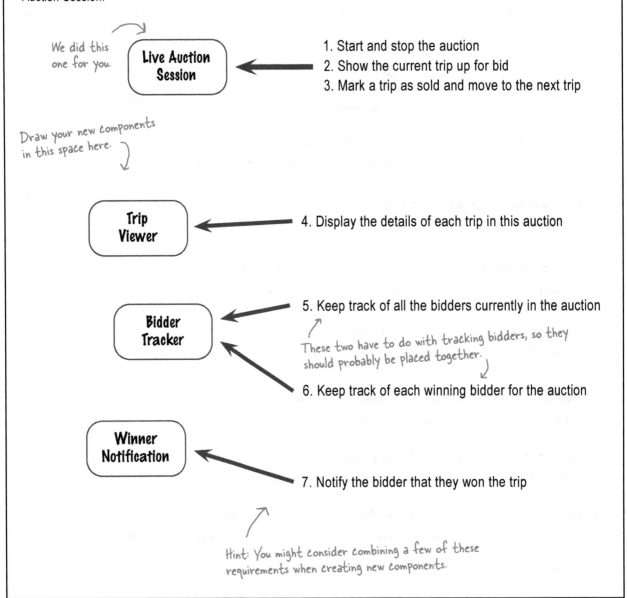

We did this one for you.

Live Auction Session

1. Start and stop the auction
2. Show the current trip up for bid
3. Mark a trip as sold and move to the next trip

Draw your new components in this space here.

Trip Viewer

4. Display the details of each trip in this auction

Bidder Tracker

5. Keep track of all the bidders currently in the auction

These two have to do with tracking bidders, so they should probably be placed together.

6. Keep track of each winning bidder for the auction

Winner Notification

7. Notify the bidder that they won the trip

Hint: You might consider combining a few of these requirements when creating new components.

From page 148

Sharpen your pencil
Solution

Given the components below, can you identify the total afferent coupling (CA), total efferent coupling (CE), and total coupling (CT) for each component? Also, what is the total coupling level for this logical architecture? Does the CT for this architecture seem high or low to you?

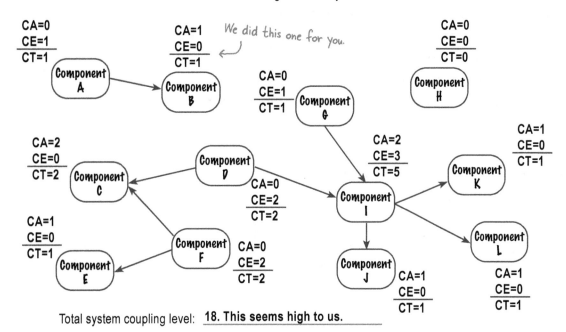

Total system coupling level: __18. This seems high to us.__

Test Drive Solution

From page 152

It's time to take the Law of Demeter for a test drive to see if you can decouple a logical architecture. Below is a logical architecture for a system where customers who have purchased a support plan with an electronic item can submit a trouble ticket and have an expert come out to fix the item. Here's how it currently works:

❶ A customer creates a ticket.

❷ The ticket gets assigned to an available expert in the field.

❸ The ticket is uploaded to an app on the expert's mobile device (that's Ticket Routing).

❹ The customer is notified that the expert is on their way to fix the problem.

❺ Once the expert fixes the problem, they mark the ticket as completed.

Keeping the components the same, how can you make this architecture more loosely coupled?

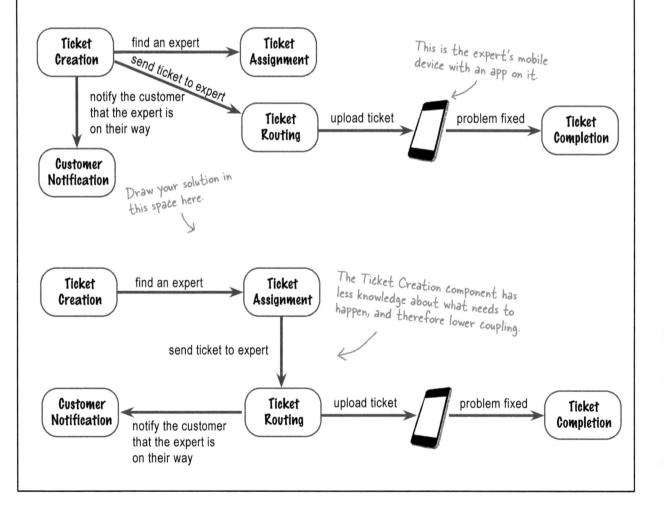

Logical Components Crossword Solution

From page 155

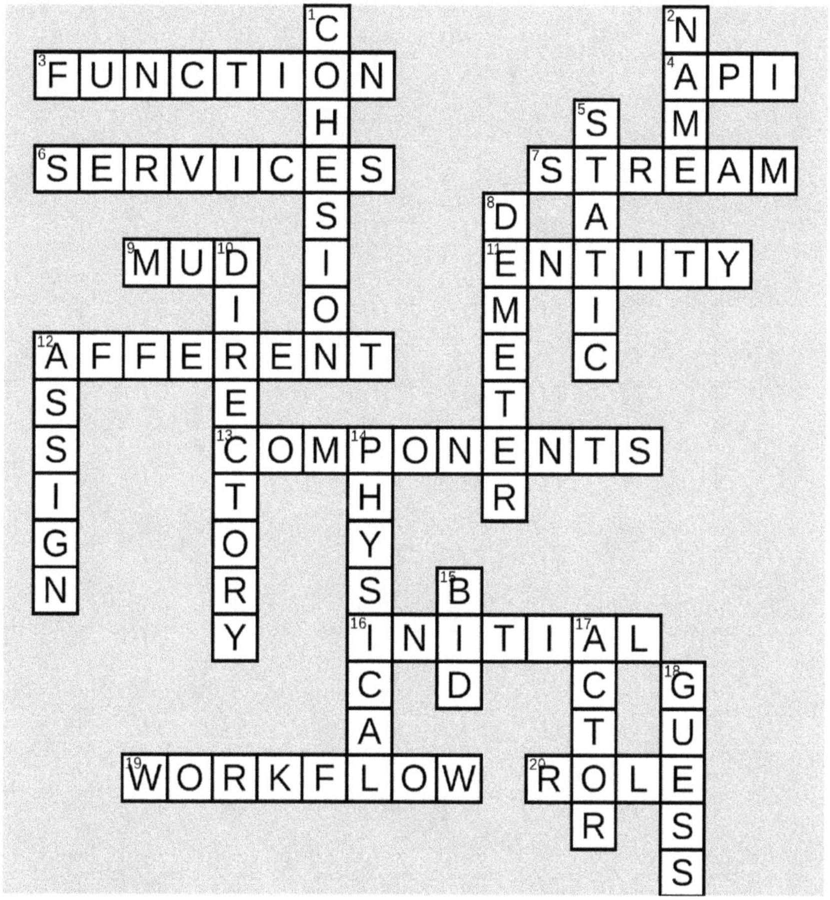
1 COHESION
2 NAME
3 FUNCTION
4 API
5 STATIC
6 SERVICES
7 STREAM
8 DEMETER
9 MUD
10 DIRECTORY
11 ENTITY
12 AFFERENT
12 ASSIGN
13 COMPONENTS
14 PHYSICAL
15 BID
16 INITIAL
17 ACTOR
18 GUESS
19 WORKFLOW
20 ROLE

5 architectural styles

Categorization and Philosophies

There are lots of different architectural styles out there. Each one exists for a reason and has its own philosophy about how and when it should be used. Understanding a style's philosophy will help you judge whether it's the right one for your domain. This chapter gives you a framework for the different kinds of architectural styles (which we'll be diving into for the remainder of this book), to help you make sense of these and all the other architectural styles you'll encounter as a software architect.

Let's fill in that final piece of the puzzle, shall we?

There are lots of architectural styles

You've learned a lot about software architecture so far, but there's *one* thing we still haven't talked about: ***architectural styles***. That's what we'll do in this chapter—in fact, the *rest* of this book is dedicated to architectural styles!

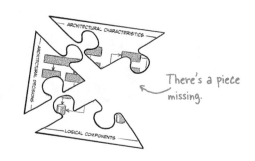

There's a piece missing.

Before we get started: look around your neighborhood, then watch a show or movie set in a different part of the world. How many styles of homes do you see? There are literally hundreds—all influenced by the locale, weather, and the owners' personal preferences. New styles are created every day.

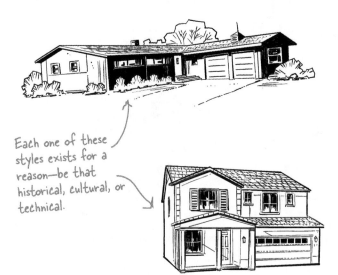

Each one of these styles exists for a reason—be that historical, cultural, or technical.

That's true for architectural styles in software, too. There are so many out there that even in a book this big, try as we might, we'll barely scratch the surface of all the available styles.

This chapter will give you a framework for thinking about architecture and architectural styles in general. Then, in the chapters that follow, we'll dive deep into a handful of specific architectural styles and examine their philosophies, using what you learn in this chapter. Understanding a few crucial styles will leave you with a good foundation to understand others as you encounter them.

Let's do this.

And there's our missing piece!

The world of architectural styles

If you've done software development for any length of time, you may have heard about different architectural styles, like monoliths and microservices. To help us think systematically about them, we place them into two categories. The first deals with how the code is divided: either by technical concerns or by domain (business) concerns. The second category is about how the system is deployed: is all the code in the system delivered as one unit, or as multiple units?

Recall from Chapter 2 that the domain is "the thing you're writing software about."

We'll describe these axes in the following pages. For now, just let it wash over you.

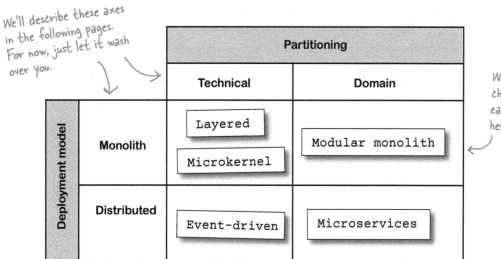

We have entire chapters dedicated to each style mentioned here.

As you can see, there are multiple ways to slice and dice architectural styles. This doesn't cover everything, of course—there are domain-specific architectures that are built explicitly for certain problems—but a book can only be so long.

We won't spend time on domain-specific architectures in this book. Let's just say they don't appeal to a broad audience.

Each category reveals some of the architectural characteristics of its styles. For example, architectural styles delivered as one unit are easier to understand, but those delivered as multiple units tend to scale better.

Let's examine each category.

Partitioning: Technical versus domain

Think back to the last time you had dinner at a fancy restaurant. When you walked in, a *host* probably greeted you and escorted you to a table. A *server* offered you drinks and menus and explained the specials. The *chef* and other cooks prepared your food for you. When you finished your meal, a *busser* cleaned and reset the table.

These restaurant workers' duties are separated by **technical concern**. A busser's role isn't to welcome you, and you probably don't want the server cooking your food.

Now, think back to the last application you worked on. Did it have a controller layer? Did it have services? How about a persistence tier? If so, congratulations: you've already worked on a technically partitioned architecture.

In a **technically partitioned architecture**, code is divvied up by technical concerns—there might be a presentation tier, a business (services) layer, and so on. The principle at play here is separation by concern—which most people think about in horizontal layers.

Another analogy that might help is a burger, with two halves of a bun, condiments, veggies, and a patty—each layer has a distinct and separate role.

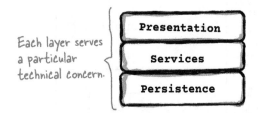

Each layer serves a particular technical concern.

On the other hand, imagine a food court. It has lots of restaurants, each specializing in a particular kind of food: pizza, salads, stir-fry, burgers. In other words, each restaurant has a specific *domain*.

Each of these restaurants might have servers and bussers. But at a high level, the restaurant specializes in a particular kind of food.

In **domain-partitioned architectures**, the structure of the system is aligned with the domain. Rather than by roles, the code (and systems) are separated in ways that align with the problem you're attempting to solve.

We'll dive into a lot of these details in future chapters.

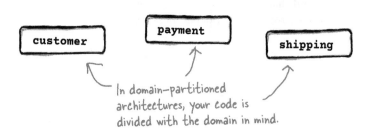

In domain-partitioned architectures, your code is divided with the domain in mind.

there are no
Dumb Questions

Q: In a domain-partitioned architecture, where do the presentation and services layers reside?

A: In a domain-partitioned architecture, you are making the domain the "first-class citizen," leaving the technical implementation as just that: implementation. The logical components that make up your architecture are organized around the *domain*, as opposed to the role they perform.

A technically partitioned architecture's components might be organized in namespaces like `app.presentation.customer` or `app.services.customer`. Note how the customer domain appears *within* the technical partition. However, in a domain-partitioned architecture, you'll have namespaces like `app.customer.presentation` and `app.customer.services`.

Q: Domain partitioning is pretty logical. Frankly, it sounds better. So why would anyone use technical partitioning?

A: We prefer not to use value judgments such as "better" and "best" when discussing architectural styles. (You're going to get tired of us saying this!) Your choice of architectural style will always be driven by a variety of factors, as you know, including the domain and the required architectural characteristics.

Technical partitioning is great if your teams tend to specialize—say, if you have teams of frontend experts, backend developers, and database administrators. But domain partitioning better aligns your system with the actual problem at hand.

Exercise

A short-order cook pretty much does everything. They can cook everything on the menu, from fries to sandwiches, as well as blending smoothies and plating desserts. Often, they also serve food, take payments, and even clean tables after customers leave. Would you categorize a short-order cook's work as partitioned technically or by domain? Why? Jot down your thoughts here.

Solution on page 182

Deployment model: Monolithic versus distributed

Let's play a game—we say a word, and you respond with the first thing that pops into your mind. Ready? *Monolith*.

We don't know about you, but this word makes us think of something like a boulder or a glacier—something *big*. That's exactly what monolithic architectures represent.

In a ***monolithic architecture***, you deploy all the logical components that make up your application as *one unit*. This also means that your entire applications runs as one process.

This would be like packaging and deploying your entire application as a single WAR or JAR file in the Java ecosystem, or as an executable in the .NET world.

This is a monolithic application, containing all the logical components in one deployment unit.

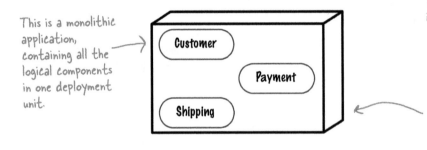

Recall that architectural characteristics influence the structure of the application.

In a ***distributed architecture***, by contrast, you split up the logical components that make up the application across many (usually smaller) units. These units each run in their own process and communicate with each other over the network.

Distributed architectures deploy lots of smaller units.

There's a lot to this distinction, so let's talk about the pros and cons of both types.

Exercise

Take a moment and consider your smartphone. It does it all—it lets you take pictures and videos, browse the web, post to your favorite social networking site, track your fitness activity, and navigate via GPS. And somewhere, embedded deep within the settings, there's even a phone! As you can see, your phone is a monolithic system. We'd like you to jot down the pros and cons of such a system. Think in terms of architectural characteristics, like availability, upgradability, cost, and ease of use.

Monolithic

Pros   **Cons**

Just a few years ago, people used separate devices for all those functions your phone performs today. Phones were, well, just *phones*, maybe with text messaging. We used laptop or desktop computers to browse the web and post to social networking sites; we could buy fitness trackers to help track workouts and GPS devices to install in cars for navigation help. Each of these "services" was deployed separately.

Just like you did above, jot down the pros and cons of such a system. Again, think in terms of architectural characteristics.

Distributed

Pros   **Cons**

Solution on page 183

Monolithic deployment models: The pros

In Chapter 2, you learned that architectural characteristics always influence some *structural aspect* of the design. Monoliths support some characteristics better than distributed systems, and knowing where they shine can help you decide when to use them.

Because monolithic systems run in one process, they make development easier— at least initially. And since they're deployed as one unit, tracing errors is a lot easier.

Let's take a look at the pros and cons of both deployment models, starting with monoliths. Here are the pros:

simplicity

Typically, monolithic applications have a single codebase, which makes them easier to develop and to understand.

feasibility

Rushing to market? Monoliths are simple and relatively cheap, freeing you to experiment and deliver systems faster.

cost

Monoliths are cheaper to build and operate because they tend to be simpler and require less infrastructure.

These are just a few of the many things monoliths are good at.

debuggability

If you spot a bug or get an error stack trace, debugging is easy, since all the code is in one place.

reliability

A monolith is an island. It makes few or no network calls, which usually means more reliable applications.

Keep an eye out for this point when we discuss cons on the next page.

Now for the cons...

Monolithic: The cons

Some of monoliths' strengths can become problematic as an application grows. Many of the operational characteristics we discussed in Chapter 2, like scalability and reliability, suffer as a monolithic application grows bigger and more complex.

scalability

If you ever need to scale one part of the application independently of the others, well, you're in trouble. It's all or nothing with monoliths.

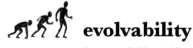

evolvability

As monolithic applications grow, making changes becomes harder. Furthermore, since the whole application is one codebase, you can't adapt different technology stacks to different domains if you need to.

Again, this isn't the entire list—just a few cons we thought we'd point out.

reliability

Because monolithic applications deploy as a single unit, any bug that degrades the service will affect the whole monolith.

There's reliability again!

deployability

Implementing any change will require redeploying the whole application, which could introduce a lot of risk.

Next, we'll look at the pros and cons of distributed architectures.

Brain Power

Spend a few minutes thinking about your industry. Does your organization have any special regulatory, security, or compliance needs? How might using a monolithic architecture help or hurt its ability to achieve the architectural characteristics that address those needs? List any ways you can think of here:

Pros	Cons

Hint: Think about things like auditability, reportability, the "right to be forgotten," etc.

Distributed deployment models: The pros

With distributed architectures, you deploy your logical components as separate units. This makes it easy to scale some parts of your application separately from others. And since logical components are physically separate, distributed architectures encourage *low coupling*.

So, what architectural characteristics are distributed architectures good for? Here's a sampling:

scalability

Distributed architectures deploy different logical components separately from one another. Need to scale one? Go ahead!

testability

Each deployment only serves a select group of logical components. This makes testing a lot easier—even as the application grows.

Distributed architectures are a lot more testable than monolithic applications.

modularity

Distributed architectures encourage a high degree of modularity because their logical components must be loosely coupled.

deployability

Distributed architectures encourage lots of small units. They evolved after modern engineering principles like continuous integration, continuous deployments, and automated testing became the norm.

Having lots of small units with good testability reduces the risk associated with deploying changes.

fault tolerance

Even if one piece of the system fails, the rest of the system can continue functioning.

As you might have noticed, distributed architectures do better on many of monolithic architectures' weak points. But is the opposite true? Let's find out.

Distributed deployment models: The cons

Can't have pros without cons. Trade-offs, right? It's all about trade-offs.

 performance
Distributed architectures involve lots of small services that communicate with each other over the network to do their work. This can affect performance, and although there are ways to improve this, it's certainly something you should keep in mind.

 cost
Deploying multiple units means more servers. Not to mention, these services need to talk to one another—which entails setting up and maintaining network infrastructure.

Debugging distributed systems involves thinking deeply about logging, and usually requires aggregating logs. This also adds to the cost.

 simplicity
Distributed systems are the ***opposite*** of simple. Everything from understanding how they work to debugging errors becomes challenging.

We cannot emphasize enough how complex distributed architectures can be!

 debuggability
Errors could happen in any service involved in servicing a request. Since logical components are deployed in separate units, tracing errors can get very tricky.

Distributed architectures make some things easy, while making others very hard.

 It's easy to underestimate how hard distributed computing is!
For all their benefits, distributed architectures depend on the network. Software architects often underestimate the complexities that arise from this dependency. Look up "The Fallacies of Distributed Computing," a list compiled in the 1990s by L. Peter Deutsch and others at Sun Microsystems, to get a sense of what to watch out for.

Brain Power

Let's repeat the exercise you did earlier, this time for distributed architecture. Does your organization have any special regulatory, security, or compliance needs? How might using a distributed architecture help or hurt your organization's ability to achieve the architectural characteristics that address those needs? List any ways you can think of here:

Pros	Cons

Fireside Chats

Tonight's talk: **Monolithic and distributed** architectures answer the question: **"Who's more relevant?"**

Monolithic Architecture

Distributed Architecture

It's a good thing I'm still around. Boy, do you make things complicated.

I don't like that attitude. Sure, you might be "simpler" to develop, but you can't keep up. Businesses need to move fast, and you just don't deliver the goods.

I might be simple, but I'm also faster to develop. I can't imagine anyone building a minimum viable product with you—they'd never launch!

I might give you that—but I'll make sure they make it to the finish line. And if their product is a smash hit, will you help or just get in the way? I can ensure success even at scale.

Oh! And I'm way cheaper. You realize that most businesses don't want to waste money, right? I can't imagine anyone using you to create a proof of concept.

Monolithic Architecture

Distributed Architecture

Businesses also like *making* money. Once their applications grow, you're just a money pit. I personify agility—I help teams and organizations scale as they grow.

I also make testing easier, while *you* just rack up the technical debt.

It's a good thing you can be tested easily—ever seen a useful error stack trace? Of course you haven't. You're all over the place. Good luck trying to trace why and where an error actually happened.

At least when I get an error, you get a nice, clear stack trace.

Riiiight. And when you fail, you just topple over. I provide a high degree of fault tolerance. Need a service to scale? Just scale that service. Scaling *you* is arduous.

At least I'm just one process. No unnecessary network traffic here. You're all talk, man—so *much* chatter. All your services are constantly talking to one another.

And that's only if the network is always reliable, because without it, you have nothing! Heaven help you if the network should fail.

Plus, with me, you don't need a whole bunch of network infrastructure. Do you know how expensive that stuff is to maintain?!

Hey, that's the cost of doing business at scale. Teams might *start* with you, but if they want to keep growing, they'll come to me—and leave you in the rearview mirror.

What? Are you saying I'm old news? Well, the next time a team needs to get to market quickly, don't call me—and then we'll see how tough you really are.

Feeling's mutual, bud. Don't call *me* when your team's minimum viable product is a success and their architecture can't handle all the attention.

And that's a wrap!

Now you know how to categorize the tons of architectural styles out there. Having a framework can help you make sense of them. And remember—each quadrant of the framework represents both the pros *and* cons of those architectural styles.

In the next chapter, we'll start our deep dive into individual styles.

Bullet Points

- There are a lot of architectural styles—in fact, too many to count.

- There are multiple ways to categorize architectural styles. One is by their *partitioning style*. Architectural styles can be either technically partitioned or domain partitioned.

- In *technically partitioned* architectural styles, the code is split up by technical concern. For example, there might be a presentation layer and a services layer.

- In *domain-partitioned* architectural styles, the code is instead split up by problem domain.

- Another way to categorize architectural styles is by their *deployment model*. *Monolithic* architectural styles deploy all the logical components that make up an application as a single unit. *Distributed* architectural styles deploy the logical components separately from one another, as multiple units.

- Monolithic architectures are easier to understand and debug and are often cheaper to build (at least initially). This makes them great candidates if there is a rush to bring a product to market.

- As monolithic applications grow, scaling them up can become arduous. It's an all-or-nothing scenario: you either scale up the whole application or nothing at all.

- Monolithic applications can also be unreliable—a bug can make the entire application unusable.

- Distributed architectures are highly scalable since their logical components are deployed separately, allowing different parts of the application to scale independently of one another.

- Distributed architectures encourage a high degree of modularity, which means testing them is easier.

- Distributed architectures are extremely expensive to develop, maintain, and debug.

- Distributed architectures use the network so that different services can talk to one another to complete work. This introduces even more complexity.

Stylin' Architectures Crossword

Now that you can make sense of architectural styles,
see if you can make sense of this crossword.

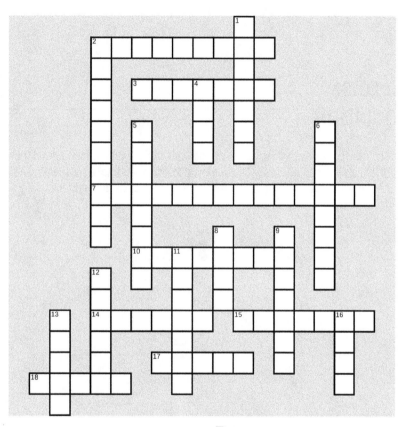

Across

2. You can _____ systems technically or by domain
3. L. Peter _____ helped compile "The Fallacies of Distributed Computing"
7. Monoliths are good for creating a _____
10. Regardless of the physical architecture, a _____ system provides more confidence in correct outcomes
14. Distributed and monolithic are both deployment _____
15. Minimum viable _____
17. Monolithic systems are easier to _____
18. Monolithic architectures have _____ deployment units

Solution on page 184

Down

1. Layers are separated by _____
2. Each architectural style has its own _____
4. Monolithic architectures tend to have a fast _____ to market
5. A system deployed as one big unit
6. If you change anything in a monolith, you'll need to _____
8. An architecture's organization is reflected in its _____ spaces
9. Services in a distributed architecture use this to communicate
11. Distributed systems consist of many _____ deployment units
12. Nothing about distributed deployment models is _____
13. Architectures often have more than one _____
16. Distributed systems usually _____ more than monolithic ones do

Exercise
Solution

From page 171

A short-order cook pretty much does everything. They can cook everything on the menu, from fries to sandwiches, as well as blending smoothies and plating desserts. Often, they also serve food, take payments, and even clean tables after customers leave. Would you categorize a short-order cook's work as partitioned technically or by domain? Why? Jot down your thoughts here.

Because a short-order cook does everything needed to get customers their meals, from setting the tables to prepping and cooking to cleaning up, they own the whole "domain" of food preparation. This makes their job domain-partitioned.

Exercise Solution

From page 173

Take a moment and consider your smartphone. It does it all—it lets you take pictures and videos, browse the web, post to your favorite social networking site, track your fitness activity, and navigate via GPS. And somewhere, embedded deep within the settings, there's even a phone! As you can see, your phone is a monolithic system. We'd like you to jot down the pros and cons of such a system. Think in terms of architectural characteristics, like availability, upgradability, cost, and ease of use.

Monolithic

Pros	Cons
Convenience—I only need to carry one device.	Availability—If my phone dies or is damaged, I can't do any of these functions.
Upgradability—I don't have to deal with patching and upgrading multiple devices.	Cost—Smartphones can be expensive to replace.
Ease of use—If I'm in a rush or going on a trip, I only need to carry one device.	Portability—I can only use apps that work on my phone's operating system.

Just a few years ago, people used separate devices for all those functions your phone performs today. Phones were, well, just *phones*, maybe with text messaging. We used laptop or desktop computers to browse the web and post to social networking sites; we could buy fitness trackers to help track workouts and GPS devices to install in cars for navigation help. Each of these "services" was deployed separately.

Just like you did above, jot down the pros and cons of such a system. Again, think in terms of architectural characteristics.

Distributed

Pros	Cons
Coupling—If my phone's camera breaks, I can still make calls or track my workout.	Upgradability—Everything has to be managed separately, like upgrading.
Modularity—Each device does one thing and one thing only, so it's easier to test.	Complexity—There's much more to manage (I need multiple batteries, chargers, and so on).
Evolvability—I can buy an SLR camera if I want to take really nice pictures.	Reliability—Network connectivity can be unreliable; devices might drop connections or have spotty connections.

Stylin' Architectures Crossword Solution

From page 181

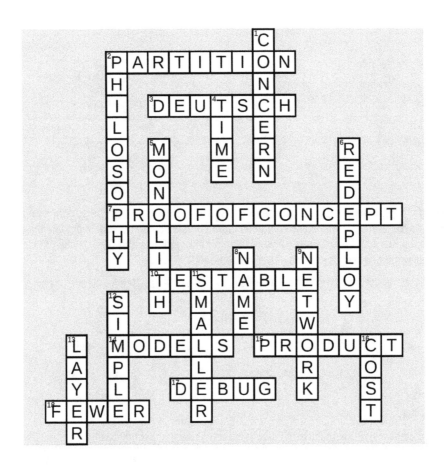

6 layered architecture

Separating Concerns

What if your problem is simple and time is of the essence? Should you even bother with architecture? It depends on how long you want to keep what you build. If it's disposable, throw caution to the wind. If not, then choose the simplest architecture that still provides some measurable organization and benefit, without imposing many constraints on speed of delivery. The *layered architecture* has become that architecture because it's easy to understand and implement, leveraging design patterns developers already know. Let's peel back the layers of this architecture.

Naan & Pop: Gathering requirements

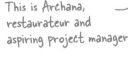

Sangita likes simple meals, so she created an Indian-inspired mom-and-pop restaurant called Naan & Pop, specializing in flatbread sandwiches and sodas.

The restaurant needs a website where customers can place orders online. Since Naan & Pop is a startup with a small budget, it needs to be simple and created quickly.

Sangita has some specific requirements.

This is Archana, restaurateur and aspiring project manager.

Time to market

The restaurant is already open. The faster they can get the site online, the faster they can start making money. The site should be simple.

Separation of responsibilities

The company has part-time help with specialized skills, such as user interface (UI) specialists and database administrators (DBAs). Thus, it would help to keep each part of the system separate.

Simple, yet extensible

While this is Sangita's first foray into software architecture, she would like to keep building on the company's online presence and find ways to extend and reuse parts of the system.

Sangita has some software development experience and realizes that many of these goals require a good separation of responsibilities. She passes these requirements to the development team she's hired for this project. You're a part of that team, so pay close attention.

Cubicle conversation

Alex

Mara

Sam

Alex: Our project manager just sent the requirements and goals for Naan & Pop's web application. It's so simple. Couldn't we just find an existing framework or library to handle most of it?

Mara: That would solve the simplicity goal. But Sangita also wants extensibility, and existing frameworks tend to be a bit rigid.

Sam: What kind of extensibility does she want?

Mara: If the restaurant is a success, we might want the site to support different kinds of user interfaces, or we could build integration points for delivery services.

Alex: Yeah—existing simple applications might not handle the separation of responsibilities Sangita would need for that kind of extensibility.

Sam: But we don't have time to build a fancy architecture!

Alex: This seems impossible—how can we build a proper architecture with specializations under these time constraints?

Sam: Fortunately, we've already worked with other team members to define the architectural characteristics (for the application's capabilities) and domain design (for its behavior). We just need to choose the appropriate architecture.

Mara: Those are some serious trade-offs and conflicting goals. We need a simple architectural style that lets us separate responsibilities around technical areas, such as user interface, data, business logic, and so on. That way, adding a new user interface will only affect one layer.

Alex: "Separate responsibilities..." I just read that phrase in the book *Head First Design Patterns*! I was reading about the Model-View-Controller design pattern.

Sam: Yeah, but that's a design pattern—how would you translate that to architecture?

Mara: Lots of design patterns end up in architecture, because often their goals overlap. But, while design patterns can focus just on design elements, architecture has to account for real-world constraints. Let's crack open the book and see if we can map Model-View-Controller into architecture.

Design patterns redux

To illustrate the concept of design patterns, the influential book *Head First Design Patterns* uses the **Model-View-Controller** (MVC) design pattern, which separates capabilities based on their purpose.

A "design pattern" is a contextualized solution to a common problem in software design.

In MVC, the **model** represents business logic and entities in the application; the **view** represents the user interface; and the **controller** handles the workflow, stitching model elements together to provide the application's functionality, as shown here:

O'REILLY

Head First

Design Patterns

Building Extensible & Maintainable Object-Oriented Software

Eric Freeman & Elisabeth Robson
with Kathy Sierra & Bert Bates

A Brain-Friendly Guide

Second Edition

You can learn more about design patterns from this book.

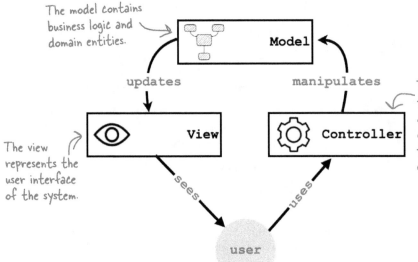

The model contains business logic and domain entities.

The controller represents the workflow of the application, combining model elements and facilitating their translation into view elements.

The view represents the user interface of the system.

The user interacts with the application through the user interface, using the workflow defined by the controller to manipulate the model elements.

Brain Power

The MVC design pattern separates *logical* responsibilities, but software architecture must also deal with *physical* systems, like browsers and databases. How would you split the responsibilities covered by MVC within the constraints of software architecture, while maintaining the overall goal of separating responsibilities and concerns?

Layering MVC

Design patterns represent logical solutions to problems, but architecture must deal with real-world constraints like databases, user interfaces, and other implementation details.

Typical layered architecture

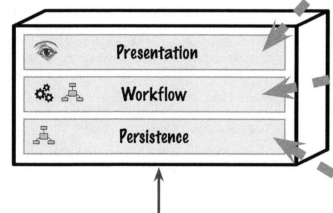

Presentation

The V for "view" in MVC concerns the UI and how the user interacts with the system. In a layered architecture, UI elements appear in the ***presentation layer***.

Workflow

The ***workflow layer*** contains most of the application's code. Business logic, workflows, validations, and other domain activities reside in this layer.

Like most layers, this one is optional, depending on the application's requirements.

Persistence

Many teams use a special ***persistence layer*** in their architecture to map code-based hierarchies (such as object-oriented languages) into set-based relational databases.

This dotted box represents the monolith.

"Monolith" implies that this is a single deployment unit.

Database

While it's optional, the "model" from MVC usually maps to a database or other persistence mechanism.

Not all applications use a database, but they may persist information elsewhere: a file system, the cloud, and so on.

Layered Monolith

The monolithic deployment model, discussed in Chapter 5, is often combined with layered architectures. While it's common for different teams to work on the code and on the database, a monolithic architecture releases both database and code changes ***together***.

Today's Interview

Layering it on with an architecture star:
the Layer

Head First: Welcome, Layer, to our luxurious studio. I know you have a busy schedule, so thanks for making the time.

Layer: You're welcome. As you say, I'm a pretty big deal. They even named an architecture after me!

Head First: Let's dig into that, Layer. Why base a whole architecture on you?

Layer: Great question. I make everything nice and understandable in an application's architecture, since each layer has a specific responsibility.

Head First: So, this architecture is just for neat freaks?

Layer: No! Putting all the similar functionality in separate layers makes it easier to find it again to make changes. For example, if the team needs to add a different database, they only have to change the persistence layer.

Head First: Ah. So organizing everything allows for easier discovery and updating. Seems like a good reason for an architecture.

Layer: While unified organization is nice, it's not the only reason to base an architecture on me.

Head First: What do you mean?

Layer: I hate to brag, but us layers are quite flexible—we can be used for all sorts of things!

Head First: Well, I know you often show up for user interfaces and provide a place to put all the business logic.

Layer: Sure, we do the heavy lifting for those. But teams can mold us into all kinds of UIs. For instance, a services layer can provide an interface to other applications that need to interact with this one.

Head First: Do you have a good example of how teams have leveraged you, Layer?

Layer: You bet! I worked with a team that handled loyalty programs for a hotel. Every purchase a user made could qualify for bonus points, depending on their membership status, years of membership, and a bunch of other complicated stuff. The team successfully used a bonus layer to keep all the calculations in a single place.

Head First: OK, that sounds useful. Can you address the recent controversy about your chilly relationship with Domain-Driven Design?

Layer: What kind of interview is this? There's no credence to those rumors that we can't get along. Well, as you know, I specialize in *technical* separation. My friend DDD focuses more on *domain* or business separation. I'm happy to host a domain in my architecture, but it'll likely have to split across the layers.

Head First: Isn't it true that you're older than other architectural styles?

Layer: The idea of layers in architecture predates just about any other concept. And is that really surprising? When architects start thinking about how to organize things, I just make sense.

Head First: We're nearly out of time, but can you tell us about your cozy relationship with the monolith? You seem to be hosted by it a lot.

Layer: No comment.

But I still don't understand how it <u>works.</u> How does a user request fit into the layered structure we've been building?

Great question. Requests and responses flow through the layers.

In a layered monolithic architecture, when a user asks the system to do something, the user interface initiates the request. Then that request flows through each layer in the architecture. If the database is involved in persisting something, then the request goes from top to bottom and back.

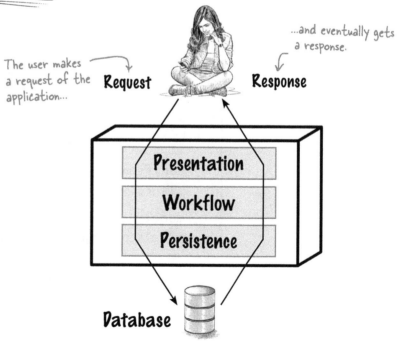

The user makes a request of the application...

Request

...and eventually gets a response.

Response

Presentation

Workflow

Persistence

Database

Layering it on

For an application like the Naan & Pop site, your team will build logical components to match the problem. But how will you implement those components?

Layers, in this type of architecture, are created with packages or namespaces, just like domain components. However, to maintain the separation of concerns, the layers' package structures typically reflect their place within the partitioning:

```
com.naanpop.orderapp.presentation

com.naanpop.orderapp.workflow

com.naanpop.orderapp.model

com.naanpop.orderapp.persistence
```

The fully qualified names of these layers will appear as packages in Java, namespaces in .NET, or whatever namespacing mechanism your language of choice uses.

Like the logical components, the architectural layers use the component implementation of the underlying platform, which often maps to the underlying filesystem:

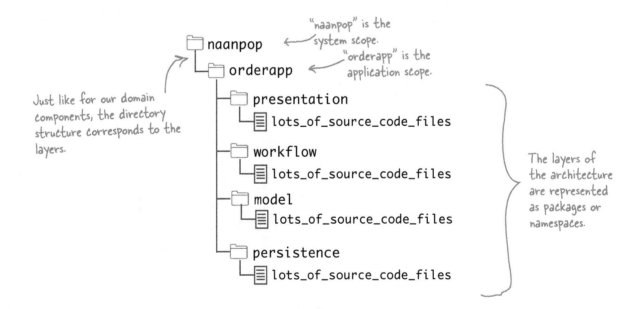

"naanpop" is the system scope.

"orderapp" is the application scope.

Just like for our domain components, the directory structure corresponds to the layers.

The layers of the architecture are represented as packages or namespaces.

Translating layers into code

Once your team has built the component packages (or namespaces), you'll need to assist the developers in implementing the architecture. Here's an example in Python-like pseudocode to illustrate how the layers translate to code.

The **user interface layer**, or **presentation layer**, is the topmost layer. It's responsible for interacting with the user, serving the same purpose as the *view* part of MVC.

```
def UI_layer(request):
    data = request.get_data()
    return business_logic_layer(data)
```

Get the request from the user.

Pass the request to the workflow layer.

The **workflow layer** (sometimes called the **business rules layer**) is responsible for processing each request from the UI layer and returning a response.

```
def business_logic_layer(data):
    processed_data = process_data(data)
    return data_access_layer(processed_data)
```

Process the data from the UI layer.

Pass the processed data to the data access layer.

The **persistence layer** (or **data access layer**) is responsible for accessing the data from the database and returning it to the workflow layer.

```
def data_access_layer(data):
    retrieved_data = retrieve_data(data)
    return retrieved_data
```

Access the data in the database.

Return the retrieved data to the workflow layer.

---

there are no Dumb Questions

Q: You said in Chapter 5 that every architectural style has a category and a philosophy. Where does the layered architecture fit in?

A: We're glad you're thinking about that. As we said in Chapter 5, understanding the categories reveals a lot about what characteristics a particular architectural style will support.

The layered architecture is a *technically partitioned* architectural style, typically deployed as a *monolith*. (We say *typically* because we'll discuss some variations on this model soon.)

Wait. We went through a logical component analysis to determine the application's behavior. Where do those components reside within the layers of this architecture?

This is an important point—the domain behavior lives *across* the layers in this architecture.

The *domain*, as you'll recall, represents logical components based on the problem you're trying to solve. However, the layers in this architecture represent *technical* capabilities—user interface, business logic, and so on.

The domain maps onto the layered architecture, sometimes spreading between layers.

there are no
Dumb Questions

Q: Why these particular layers—presentation, workflow, and persistence?

A: These are common layers, but they are by no means required. Most applications have at least some of this separation: for instance, the UI is often distinct from the core logic of the system, which in turn is separate from the database development.

Q: Was the layered architecture inspired by the Model-View-Controller design pattern?

A: The opposite is likely true. Layered architectures, which have existed as long as people have been building software from different parts, may well have inspired the design pattern. Design patterns are often harvested from observations of common occurrences, and the layered architecture has been around for quite some time in many forms.

Domains, components, and layers

In a simple restaurant ordering system like Naan & Pop's, we might come up with the following components based on the problem domain:

"Place order" includes concepts like payment.

But there's a problem. These components are based on the logical *behavior* of the domain, but the layered architecture splits things by *capabilities*. So, we need to separate the logical components (which include workflows and entities) into components that match what we need for the layered architecture:

Once we've split the logical components into workflow and entities, we can overlay the components over the layers in this architecture:

The concept of an "order" cuts across physical layers.

Domains are typically smeared across physical layers in layered architectures.

This is an important point, so take a moment and let it soak in. We'll come back to this at the end of the chapter.

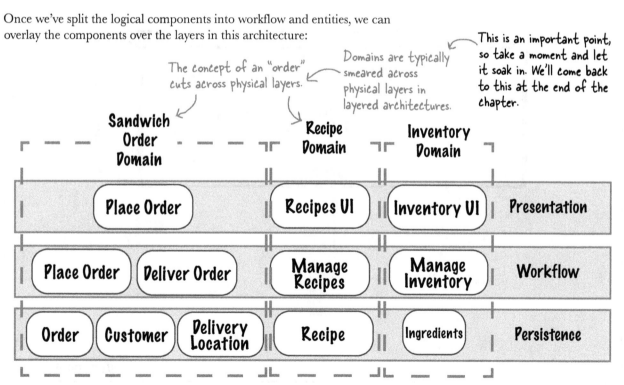

Sharpen your pencil

Naan & Pop's lead architects have designed a layered architecture. Today, though, they're off at a daylong breadmaking seminar to learn more about their problem domain, leaving you to sort out which components go where. Can you decide in which layer (or layers) each component should reside? Draw the components below on the layer(s) to which they should map.

Hint: Some components may end up in several layers.

Components

Delivery Address

Billing Address

Sales Promotion

Blacklisted Customers

Frequent Diner Rewards

Presentation

Employee Information

Workflow

Persistence

The typical implementation of this architecture assumes that anything in the persistence layer ends up in the database.

We did one for you. Employee information, like drivers' details, may be needed by workflows and persisted, yet not be part of the presentation layer.

Solution on page 210

It seems like every architecture provides some benefits but also imposes some restrictions. If only I could have an architecture that maps perfectly to my problem domain, without any pesky trade-offs! But that's only a dream...

there are no Dumb Questions

Q: Why go to the trouble of identifying logical components if we have to break them apart to fit them into this architecture?

A: The logical components represent the problem you're trying to solve. Mapping that to any architecture means applying real-world constraints (and trade-offs). We'll show you a more direct domain-to-architecture mapping in the next chapter, but it has trade-offs, too.

Q: Why is the layered architecture so popular?

A: This architecture shows up a lot. First, it's simple, without many moving parts. Second, as you've seen, it maps closely to the MVC design pattern, making it easy to understand. Third, it's so common that teams can build simple projects quickly in this style. Fourth, many companies separate their employees by skill set, which facilitates an architecture with similar partitions.

Drivers for layered architecture

We've put together a list of the things the layered architecture is really good at—that is, the things that might drive us toward picking this particular architectural style.

Specialization

Using a layered architecture allows organizations to split teams into specialists, sharing their capabilities between different projects.

The ability to specialize makes this architecture popular in organizations that need to share special skills across multiple projects.

Ease of (technical) reuse

Splitting the architecture by technical capabilities allows better opportunities to reuse code. For example, if all persistence code resides in a single layer, it's easier for developers to find, update, and reuse it.

The ability to reuse components within a layer is one of the key advantages of this architecture for many organizations.

Matches physical separation

The layered architecture typically separates the logical components to match the physical separation. For example, it's common for teams to implement different layers in different technology stacks (such as JavaScript, Java, and MySQL).

Often, the real world prevents architects from designing what they want, instead forcing them to design with what they have.

Conceptual twin of MVC

Simplicity and concerns about feasibility are driving forces in many architectures. Developers find it easier to understand and work within an architecture that matches familiar design patterns, such as MVC.

Feasibility and simplicity for the win!

Layers, meet the real world: Physical architectures

The layered monolith describes a logical architecture, but architects may implement that logical architecture in a variety of physical architectures.

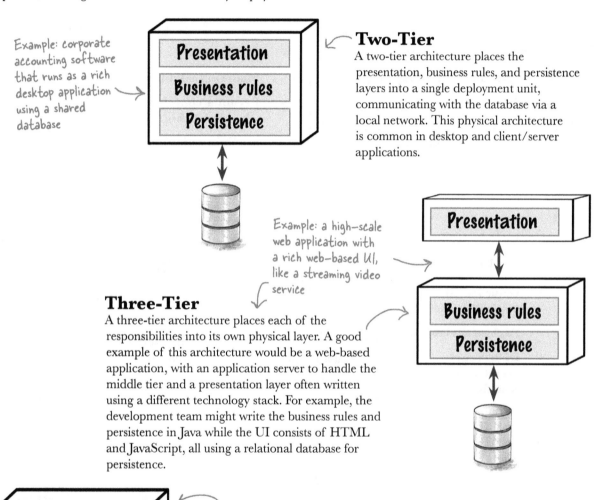

Example: corporate accounting software that runs as a rich desktop application using a shared database

Two-Tier

A two-tier architecture places the presentation, business rules, and persistence layers into a single deployment unit, communicating with the database via a local network. This physical architecture is common in desktop and client/server applications.

Example: a high-scale web application with a rich web-based UI, like a streaming video service

Three-Tier

A three-tier architecture places each of the responsibilities into its own physical layer. A good example of this architecture would be a web-based application, with an application server to handle the middle tier and a presentation layer often written using a different technology stack. For example, the development team might write the business rules and persistence in Java while the UI consists of HTML and JavaScript, all using a relational database for persistence.

Embedded/Mobile

Often, because of physical constraints, all the logical layers end up in a single physical deployment. This physical architecture commonly appears in embedded systems and mobile applications, where a network connection may not be consistent or even possible.

Examples: a mobile game or soda-machine software

Physical architecture trade-offs

Which physical architecture should you choose? Well, they all have trade-offs, like everything in software architecture.

Two-Tier

Pros

+ **Rich user interface**

+ **High performance**

+ **Simple**

These architectures are simple because everything can typically be implemented as a single project.

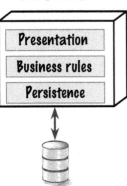

Cons

- **Medium scalability**

- **Becomes complex when it gets big**

- **Medium reliability**

Reliability is only medium, because this architecture relies on the network for data access.

Three-Tier

Pros

+ **Detached UI (typically web)**

+ **Highest scalability**

+ **Distributed architecture benefits**

Distributed architectures offer higher scalability and similar benefits.

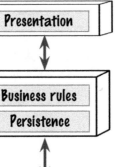

Cons

- **Least reliability**

- **More complex**

- **Distributed architecture headaches**

More complex because it has the most moving parts

Distributed architectures are more complex, with more moving parts and failure modes.

While a single stack is nice, it isn't always portable to other platforms.

Embedded/Mobile

Pros

+ **Self-contained**

+ **Single tech stack**

+ **Highly tunable to hardware devices**

A single tech stack can be an advantage for simplicity.

Cons

- **Least scalable**

- **Resource-constrained**

- **Often tied to implementation platform**

Exercise

Generic trade-offs are one thing, but software architecture is always based on a real system. The architects at Naan & Pop need some help evaluating the trade-offs for each physical architecture as they decide which one to use. Can you help them figure out which specific trade-offs the Naan & Pop application will face for each physical architecture?

Two-Tier

Pros   We'll help you get   **Cons**
                          started.

Simplicity   Scalability

_____   _____

_____   _____

_____   _____

Three-Tier

Pros   **Cons**

_____   _____

_____   _____

_____   _____

Embedded/Mobile

Pros   **Cons**

_____   _____

_____   _____

_____   _____

Solution on page 211

Cubicle conversation

Alex: Is Naan & Pop generic enough to only use the standard layers? When do teams add layers?

Sam: Why add layers to the architecture?

Mara: Each layer in a layered architecture has a specific responsibility within the system, so when they're needed, we add layers.

Sam: What kinds of layers?

Alex: It's common to add a ***services layer,*** which provides access for business-to-business integration, or ***integration layers*** for other internal systems. Each request goes through each layer, so layers need to be things that happen to every request.

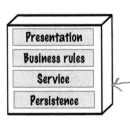

No need to be stingy with layers—you can have as many as you need, as long as each layer applies to each request.

Mara: That's right—architects can add whatever layers we need to support some new behavior. For example, the site needs integration with third-party delivery services, so maybe we should add an integration layer. Here, let me draw what I have in mind for our layered architecture on the whiteboard...

The integration layers allow interaction with third-party delivery services.

Alex: Adding an integration layer for our delivery hooks would make things easier, wouldn't it? It looks like all the code pertaining to that integration lives in the same place, which would make it easy to find and update.

Mara: Yes, and that's true for the user interface layer, too. In fact, one of the next requirements we have to implement is an additional UI to support mobile.

Sam: So, if we add a separate mobile UI, we'd only have to change one layer?

Mara: That's one of the best things about layered architecture!

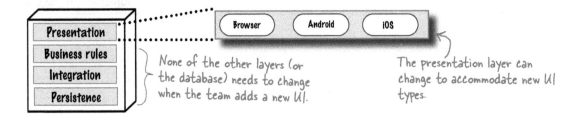

None of the other layers (or the database) needs to change when the team adds a new UI.

The presentation layer can change to accommodate new UI types.

One final caveat about domain changes

One of the primary advantages of a layered architecture is that it lets us group similar technical things together. For example, in the Naan & Pop application, separating the UI into its own set of components allows the team to add new UI types without affecting the other layers.

Let's pause for a second and think about this—what about changes to the problem domain? If Naan & Pop wanted to add something other than sandwiches to the menu, like pizza, would *every layer* have to change?

The power to change things in isolation is the layered architecture's superpower, but it's not a silver bullet. This architectural style's big trade-off is that **the problem domain is smeared across the layers** in the architecture. For example, the *Place Order* logical component in the Naan & Pop architecture requires a UI (presentation), code to implement the workflow (workflow), and a data schema (persistence).

That means that *technical* capabilities are easy to change and enhance, but *domain* changes can create side effects that ripple through the layers.

We alluded to this earlier in the chapter.

Layered architectures facilitate technical changes but make domain changes more difficult.

So, what to do? Well, there's a reason why we started this book by showing you how to identify the architectural characteristics your application needs to support. If **continual, significant domain changes** are expected or suddenly become a higher priority, there are other architectural styles to consider.

Take a deep breath. The next chapter will introduce you to an architectural style that is better suited to accommodating domain changes. Oh, the suspense!

All that said, let's quickly summarize the good and bad of the layered architecture.

---

there are no
Dumb Questions

Q: That's a rather large caveat. Why would I even consider the layered architectural style?

A: Remember the First Law of Software Architecture—everything's a trade-off. Sure, other architectural styles might allow for easier changes to the domain, but they have their own caveats. Align the strengths and weaknesses of every architectural style with your requirements, and then choose. There's no one right choice, just the choice that works best for *your* particular set of circumstances.

Layered architecture superpowers

Layered architectures have been demonstrating their powers for many, many years—this is one of the oldest recognizable architectural styles.

If your whole company runs on investment dollars, feasibility is especially important.

Feasibility

If time and budget are overwhelmingly important, the simplicity of this architecture is quite appealing.

Technical partitioning

Architects design components around technical capabilities, making it easier for them to reuse common capabilities. For example, if several teams need the same data functionality, they could implement it once in a persistence layer and then share it across teams.

Performance

Well-designed layered monoliths can demonstrate high performance—making no network calls and processing data in a single place (the monolithic database) means there's no need for network calls that could decrease performance.

Quick to build

Simplicity plus a single work/deployment unit means that teams can build small systems quite rapidly.

Data-intensive

Systems that do a lot of data-level processing may benefit from a layered architecture because it isolates data processing in a single database that's optimized for the task.

In general, the less a system needs to access data over the network, the more efficient it can be.

Lean and mean

Keeping these systems small helps avoid some of the kryptonite on the next page.

Layered architecture kryptonite

This architecture is pervasive and popular, but it can be overused and even abused. While feasibility may be a superpower, many teams default to this architecture because of its simplicity, long history, and widespread use, without considering if it's really the most suitable option.

Scalability

Probably the biggest problem with monoliths is that when you only have one bucket and you keep adding things to it, it will eventually fill up. The same is true for monoliths generally, which eventually become constrained by some resource (memory bandwidth, and so on).

Elasticity

A single process has a harder time dealing with sudden bursts of users.

Deployability

As monolithic systems get bigger, deployments tend to become more complex—especially when developers keep adding behavior.

Testability

High coupling and a large codebase make testing harder and harder over time.

Big ball of mud

Because everything is connected to everything else, this architecture can become a highly coupled mess without careful governance.

Layered architecture star ratings

The Naan & Pop architecture team decides to use a rating chart they found in the book *Fundamentals of Software Architecture* (O'Reilly), written by two of your authors, that describes the layered architecture in a convenient way. One star means that the architectural characteristic is not well supported; five stars means the architectural characteristic is very well supported.

Just like movie reviews.

Testing isn't especially easy, but the team has been dealing with layered architectures so long that they've built up many techniques.

Layered architectures are nice and simple.

Monoliths in general don't handle scalability and elasticity well, and layered ones even less so.

Well-designed layered architectures can boast quite high performance.

Simplicity, in this case, leads to affordability.

Architectural Characteristic	Star Rating
Maintainability	★
Testability	★ ★
Deployability	★
Simplicity	★ ★ ★ ★ ★
Evolvability	★
Performance	★ ★ ★
Scalability	★
Elasticity	★
Fault Tolerance	★
Overall Cost	$

Exercise

Which of the following systems might be well suited for the layered monolithic architectural style, and why? *Hint: Take into account its superpowers, its kryptonite, and the nature of the system.*

An online auction system where users can bid on items

Why? _____

_____

_____

☐ Well suited for layered monolith

☐ Might be a fit for layered monolith

☐ Not well suited for layered monolith

A large backend financial system for processing and settling international wire transfers overnight

Why? _____

_____

_____

☐ Well suited for layered monolith

☐ Might be a fit for layered monolith

☐ Not well suited for layered monolith

A company entering a new line of business that expects constant changes to its system

Why? _____

_____

_____

☐ Well suited for layered monolith

☐ Might be a fit for layered monolith

☐ Not well suited for layered monolith

A small bakery that wants to start taking online orders

Why? _____

_____

_____

☐ Well suited for layered monolith

☐ Might be a fit for layered monolith

☐ Not well suited for layered monolith

A trouble ticket system for electronics purchased with a support plan, in which field technicians come to customers to fix problems

Why? _____

_____

_____

☐ Well suited for layered monolith

☐ Might be a fit for layered monolith

☐ Not well suited for layered monolith

Solution on page 212

Wrapping it up

Congratulations! The Naan & Pop team looked at several architectural styles, but after considering the business's priorities, you chose a layered architecture. This paid off handsomely, allowing the business to grow without any problems.

Bullet Points

- A layered architecture is *monolithic*: the entire system (code and database) is deployed as a single unit.

- The layers are separated by technical capabilities. Typical layers in this architecture include *presentation* (for the user interface), *business rules* (for the workflow and logic of the application), and *persistence* (facilities to support databases for systems that need persistent data).

- The layered architecture supports feasibility well; it is easy to understand and it lets you build simple systems fast.

- The layered architecture supports excellent separation of technical concerns, making it easy to add new capabilities like user interfaces or databases.

- The layered architecture mimics some of the same concerns as the Model-View-Controller design pattern, but translated into physical layers and subject to real-world constraints.

- User requests flow through the user interface and through each layer before a response is returned to the user.

- Each request in this architecture goes through each layer.

- A layered architecture's capabilities degrade over time if teams continue to add functionality due to eventual resource limits (for example, they run out of capacity).

- The layered architecture provides excellent support for specialization (user interface designers, coders, database experts, and so on).

- Logical components represent the problem domain, yet layers focus on technical capabilities, requiring translation between the domain and architecture layers.

- A layered architecture may manifest in several physical architectures, including *two-tier* (also known as *client/server*), *three-tier* (web), and *embedded/mobile*.

- Changing and adding to the technical capabilities represented in layers is easy; the layered architecture facilitates this.

- Changing the problem domain requires coordination across the layers of the architecture, making domain changes more difficult.

Layered Architecture Crossword

Ready to add learning on top of learning by solving the layers of this crossword?

Across

3. Layered architectures use familiar design _____
5. Kind of layered architecture often found in smartphone apps
6. Type of architecture covered in this chapter
8. _____ can be confined to one layer
9. Namespaces and packages correspond to the directory _____
11. Too much coupling can lead to a big ball of _____
14. Layer that maps object models to relational models for databases
17. Depending on the network for data access makes an architecture _____ reliable
19. Kind of database often used for persistence
21. Layered architectures might have two or more _____

Solution on page 213

Down

1. The integration layer lets the system _____ with third parties
2. Layered architectures facilitate _____
4. The _____ domain spreads across all of the layers
7. Logical and _____ components are usually separated in the same way
10. Logical _____ reside in layers
12. Domain-driven _____
13. Layer that applies business rules
15. The user _____ is part of the presentation layer
16. The MVC pattern and layered architecture both _____ responsibilities
18. A user's request and its response _____ through the layers
20. Model-_____-Controller design pattern

From page 196

Sharpen your pencil
Solution

Naan & Pop's lead architects have designed a layered architecture. Today, though, they're off at a daylong breadmaking seminar to learn more about their problem domain, leaving you to sort out which components go where. Can you decide in which layer (or layers) each component should reside? Draw the components below on the layer(s) to which they should map.

Hint: Some components may end up in several layers.

Components

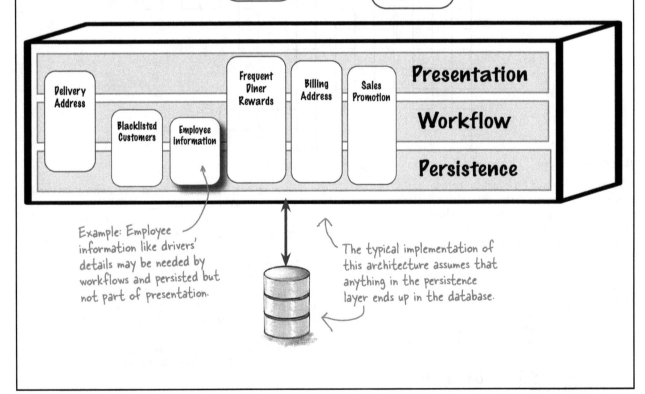

Delivery Address   Billing Address   Sales Promotion

Blacklisted Customers   Frequent Diner Rewards

Delivery Address   Blacklisted Customers   Employee Information   Frequent Diner Rewards   Billing Address   Sales Promotion

Presentation

Workflow

Persistence

Example: Employee information like drivers' details may be needed by workflows and persisted but not part of presentation.

The typical implementation of this architecture assumes that anything in the persistence layer ends up in the database.

Exercise
Solution

From page 201

Generic trade-offs are one thing, but software architecture is always based on a real system. The architects at Naan & Pop need some help evaluating the trade-offs for each physical architecture as they decide which one to use. Can you help them figure out which specific trade-offs the Naan & Pop application will face for each physical architecture?

Two-Tier

Pros

Simplicity

Performance

Simplicity facilitates short time to market.

While performance isn't a driving concern, fewer tiers tends to lead to better performance.

Cons

Scalability

Fewer tiers tends to result in poorer scalability.

Three-Tier

Separation supports one of the driving goals.

Pros

Architectural separation

Scalability

Better scalability supports more users.

More tiers creates more parts to the architecture, complicating dependencies and communication...

Cons

Complexity

Slower time to market

...which leads to...

Embedded/mobile

Pros

Self-contained

A pure monolith has the fewest parts.

It's hard to make a self-contained monolith with high scalability and/or performance.

Cons

Less extensible

Scalability

Performance

It's hard to extend an embedded system, counter to one of the stated goals.

Exercise Solution

From page 207

Which of the following systems might be well suited for the layered monolithic architectural style, and why?
Hint: Take into account its superpowers, its kryptonite, and the nature of the system.

An online auction system where users can bid on items

Why? *An online auction will require more scalability and performance than most layered architectures can support.*

☐ Well suited for layered monolith
☐ Might be a fit for layered monolith
☒ Not well suited for layered monolith

A large backend financial system for processing and settling international wire transfers overnight

Why? *This system requires high throughput and high availability, both difficult for layered monoliths.*

☐ Well suited for layered monolith
☐ Might be a fit for layered monolith
☒ Not well suited for layered monolith

A company entering a new line of business that expects constant changes to its system

Why? *Layered architectures separate concerns by technical capabilities, making some changes easier.*

☐ Well suited for layered monolith
☒ Might be a fit for layered monolith
☐ Not well suited for layered monolith

A small bakery that wants to start taking online orders

Why? *A small bakery has a simple problem and small scale, well suited for a simple architecture.*

☒ Well suited for layered monolith
☐ Might be a fit for layered monolith
☐ Not well suited for layered monolith

A trouble ticket system for electronics purchased with a support plan, in which field technicians come to customers to fix problems

Why? *A trouble ticket system will need to support different architectural characteristics (for users and technicians, for example), which is difficult in monolithic architectures.*

☐ Well suited for layered monolith
☐ Might be a fit for layered monolith
☒ Not well suited for layered monolith

Layered Architecture Crossword Solution

From page 209

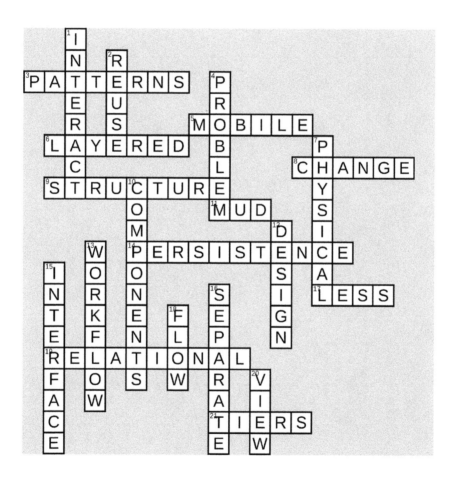

7 modular monoliths

Driven by the Domain

There's more than one way to build a monolith. So far, you've encountered the layered architecture, which aligns things *technically*. You can go a long way with a layered monolith, but when changes begin to involve lots of communication and coordination between different teams, you might need a little more horsepower under the hood—and perhaps even a different architectural style.

This chapter looks at the *modular monolith* architectural style, which divides applications up by *business concerns* as opposed to technical concerns. You'll learn what this means, what to look out for, and all the trade-offs associated with this style. Let's take the modular monolith for a spin, shall we?

Remember Archana, founder of
Naan & Pop and aspiring project
manager from Chapter 6?

As a reminder, Naan & Pop's sandwich shop has a small development team, and its requirements haven't changed a whole lot since the team built their layered application in Chapter 6. The competition is stiff, and time to market remains a concern. The system should remain simple.

Be sure to review
Chapter 6 if you need
to refresh your memory.

Exercise

Cast your mind back to the layered architecture we built for Naan & Pop in Chapter 6. The following diagram shows its layers and logical components. Adding a new category to the menu (say, pizza) means changing a bunch of moving parts. Grab a marker and put a triangle (▲) next to everything this new requirement will affect.

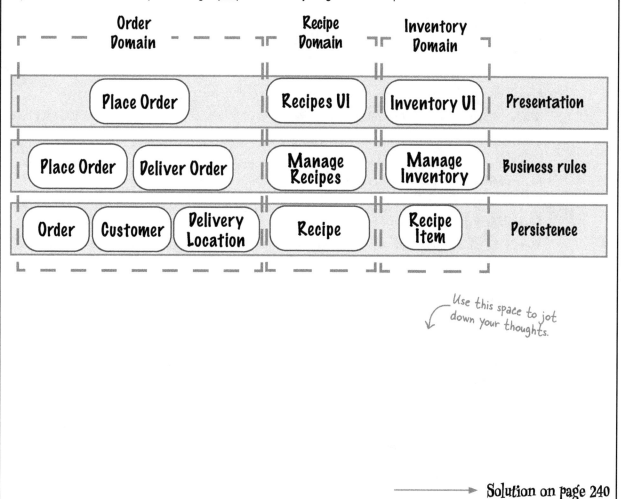

Use this space to jot down your thoughts.

Solution on page 240

Cubicle conversation

Alex: Pfft! This is *easy*. We've already delivered a working and extensible system. Let's get to it.

Mara: Hold your horses. This might be our first rodeo with such a change, but I doubt it'll be our last.

Sam: So what? We've built an extensible system. Why are you being so reticent?

Mara: Let's think this through—we have to add pizzas to the menu. Not only will we have to add new recipes and ingredients, but we'll also need to allow patrons to order pizzas online. So where will we have to make changes?

Sam: Lots of places! It'll at least affect ordering and recipe management. I still don't see a concern.

Alex: I think I do. We've built a layered architecture, and we have specialists working on each layer. A change like this means coordinating changes across *all* of those folks.

Mara: Bingo! The layered architecture *smears* the domain across all the layers. So, implementing anything that changes the domain can be arduous.

Alex: You're telling me that choosing the layered architecture was a mistake?

Mara: The layered architecture was simple and quick to build. It allowed us to launch quickly. But now we need to think about ***maturing*** the architecture to support modularity, so changes like these will be easier in the future.

Alex: So where do we start?

Mara: Allow me to introduce you to the modular monolith. Rather than partitioning by technical concern, we'll partition by ***business domain***, using modules—hence the word *modular*. I'll show you what this looks like as I explain it.

Sam: Ooh, I'm so excited. Let's do it!

Modular monolith?

A modular monolithic architecture, like a layered architecture, is deployed as a single unit, usually with its own database.

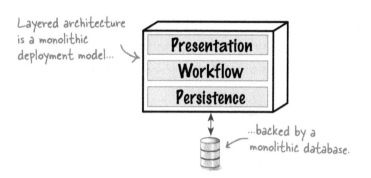

Layered architecture is a monolithic deployment model...

Presentation
Workflow
Persistence

...backed by a monolithic database.

Think back to Chapter 5. Architectural styles can be separated by how the code is partitioned and by deployment model.

That's where the similarity ends. In a modular monolith, rather than partitioning your application by technical concerns, you partition it by *functionality*. Every business operates within a certain domain—like banking, education, or retail. Online stores usually have several *subdomains*, like Order Placement, Payment, and Inventory Management. Together, they make up the Online Store domain. You organize your application according to these subdomains, separating them into modules.

Heads up—you'll find the terms domain and <u>subdomain</u> used interchangeably. As long as you understand that both terms represent business concerns, you're good.

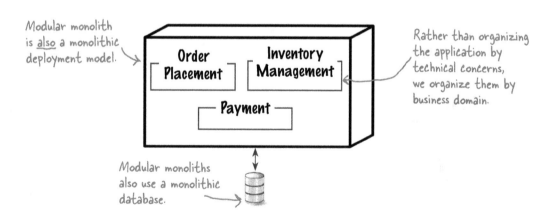

Modular monolith is <u>also</u> a monolithic deployment model.

Order Placement
Inventory Management
Payment

Rather than organizing the application by technical concerns, we organize them by business domain.

Modular monoliths also use a monolithic database.

What is a *module*? At a high level, it's just how you organize your code. In some languages, you might have support like packages or namespaces. But it doesn't start or stop there.

Partitioning your code using modules has implications for how you'll go about separating concerns between modules and how modules will interact with each other. We have a lot more to say about this, so stay tuned. For now, we just want you to be able to distinguish between the layered and modular monolith architectural styles.

Q: Can you explain more about what you mean when you say *module*?

A: A *module* is a software design element representing an independent unit that fulfills one piece of functionality. Technically, every layer in a layered architecture is a module—these modules just happen to be divided by technical concern.

In a modular monolith, on the other hand, each module represents a particular piece of the domain—that is, a *subdomain*. Each module contains all the business functionality needed for that particular subdomain.

Who Does What?

Identifying which components should belong to a particular module can be tricky. In this game of "Who Does What?"—or rather, "What Goes Where?"—we'd like you to match each component to the module where it fits best. Multiple components can belong to one module.

| Shopping Cart |

| Credit Card Form |

| Primary Email Preference |

| Fulfillment Workflow |

| Order History |

┌─ Order ─┐

┌─ Payment ─┐

┌─ Customer ─┐

Solution on page 241

Domain ~~pains~~ changes

Naan & Pop wants to add a new food category (pizza) to the menu. Which parts of the architecture need to change to make this happen? Let's take a look.

▲ Components That Change

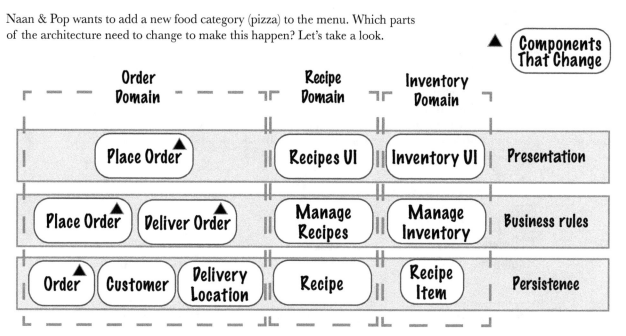

Introducing a new menu category primarily affects the Order domain. The menu needs to allow customers to order pizzas and customize their toppings. That might require changing or adding new business rules to support customization and perhaps delivery, since pizzas need to be delivered hot. It could also change how the system stores orders (since customers may ask for customizations.)

As you can see, introducing new menu items can affect multiple components across multiple layers. This is because, as mentioned in the previous chapter, in a technically partitioned architecture the business domain gets "smeared" across multiple layers. This is great if you're implementing a technical change, like changing the view technology or swapping out the database. But it's not so great if the change affects the domain—you'll have to round up folks from multiple teams to figure out how to implement it.

No one ever woke up and said, "How can I add yet another meeting to my calendar?"

This is where modular monoliths can really help.

 Geek Note

It's not unusual for teams to start with a layered architecture, then refactor it into a modular monolith over time as the application grows.

Why modular monoliths?

When you eat a burger (or a veggie burger!), do you take a bite of the top bun first, then bite into the gooey cheese, then take a bite of the patty? Or do you take one bite that slices vertically through every layer of the burger? The latter, right?

Every layer in a burger serves a specific purpose—so it tastes best if you bite through all the layers together.

Yum!

That's exactly how you can think of a modular monolith. You don't organize the application in horizontal layers separated by technical concern, but in vertical slices scoped by business concern. Each vertical slice aligns with a piece of the domain and is encapsulated in a module. Every module contains a set of business functions—for example, order placement, order completion, and order delivery would all be part of the Order Placement module.

Individual domains make up the modules of your application.

Order domain	Recipe domain	Inventory domain
Order placement	**Recipe management**	**Inventory management**
Presentation	Presentation	Presentation
Business rules	Business rules	Business rules
Persistence	Persistence	Persistence

These "slices" represent a particular set of business functions within a domain.

What does this mean? Changes to the domain that affect many or all layers require lots of coordination between different teams. You'll need to ensure that everybody's changes work with everybody else's.

Now, rather than having teams that specialize in the presentation layer or the persistence layer, you have ***cross-functional teams***, each specializing in a *domain*. The result? It's far easier to coordinate domain changes when one team takes full ownership.

This isn't business-word bingo! It's not always easy to build out cross-functional teams that work in multiple different technical stacks.

Hold up. I still see layers in each module. Is this some kind of Jedi mind trick? How is this any different from a layered architecture?

How astute of you! You're absolutely right that each module here still consists of layers—but they don't have to. The important thing is that your application is organized by domain.

Your system still needs to process and respond to each request, though. So you'll need an entry point (presentation layer), some business processing (workflow layer), and maybe a data store to write to (persistence layer). Even within a modular architecture, it makes sense to separate those responsibilities, much like the layered architecture does.

However, if you zoom out and look at the whole architecture, you'll see that the application is carved up into subdomains. The fact that each module is composed of a bunch of technically partitioned layers becomes an implementation detail, as opposed to an architectural concern. In other words, ***how a module is laid out internally isn't how the architecture is partitioned***. Modular monoliths are domain-partitioned.

Let's get a bit more concrete by seeing what this looks like in code.

Show me the code!

You've probably recognized that modular monoliths solve the problem you are working on differently from a layered architecture, by organizing applications by domain rather than technical concern. But how does this translate to your code?

Let's first talk about the modules themselves. They represent parts of the domain. Naan & Pop's namespaces look like this:

com.naanpop.orderapp.order

com.naanpop.orderapp.recipe

com.naanpop.orderapp.inventory

Flip back to page 192 in the previous chapter and compare these to the namespaces for the layered architecture.

Remember, we're still working with a monolith—that is, it's still one deployment. Typically, one deployment would translate to one codebase, with the code organized in different namespaces. Each namespace represents a separate module, like so:

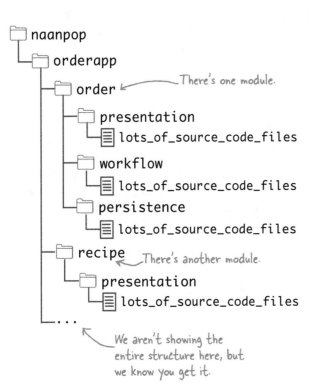

Ah, I see! The layers are an implementation detail, not an architectural concern.

 Exercise

A critical piece of successfully developing modular monoliths is understanding the domain well enough that you can break it into individual modules. One way to do that (and there are many) is to really *listen* to your business experts.

Say you are working for a startup that's creating an expense-tracking app for small to medium-sized businesses. Here are the business requirements:

- There are users and auditors. Users add expenses, and auditors review expense reports to ensure they align with policy guidelines.

- When a user adds an expense, it is recorded in the database for that user.

- The app creates an audit trail that the auditors can use to ensure that everything is in order.

   Can you identify the subdomains that should make up this application? *Hint: Not everything your business users say will translate into a module.*

Solution on page 242

Cubicle conversation, continued...

Alex: I get it. We're increasing the modularity of the codebase because our application is divided up by modules.

Sam: That sounds great in theory, but it's not like they can all work independently of each other. Doesn't the ordering side of things need to know what ingredients we have in our inventory? God forbid the kitchen should run out of mushrooms!

Mara: You're both right. Splitting the application up by business concern means we're increasing its modularity. But on the flip side, different parts of the application might also need to talk to each other.

Alex: But it's one codebase. I can just have the ordering side make an API call to the inventory module, right?

Sam: Oh, brilliant. I can already see the big ball of mud forming! Soon every module will be talking to every other module, and then there goes our modularity.

Mara: Right. If you just start making calls between modules willy-nilly, soon enough there won't be *any* boundaries left. Everything will just start referencing everything else. And that would be, well, a big ball of mud.

Alex: So how do we maintain separate modules, but still have them talk to one another?

Mara: Let me show you.

Keeping modules modular

Modular monoliths are, well, monoliths, so they're generally contained in one codebase. That makes it easy for someone working in one module to inadvertently reach into another module and end up coupling the two modules together.

The auto-import feature in your IDE is not your friend here! It's way too easy to accidentally reference another module without realizing it.

These arrows represent calls from one layer in a module to a layer in another module.

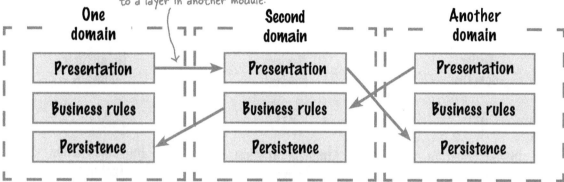

If left unchecked, each module's code becomes more closely coupled with the other modules' code, and their boundaries start to disappear.

The *philosophy* of the modular monolith centers on **partitioning by domain within a monolithic deployment model**. Your objective should be to create loosely coupled modules so that changing one doesn't affect others. So how do you avoid the big ball of mud? Read on.

You got it! Callback to Chapter 5.

Brain Power

Can you think of any mechanisms to help you ensure that one part of your application won't accidentally access another? For example, does your favorite programming language provide any support at compile time to keep modules separate? Jot down any ideas that come to mind here. You can see some of our ideas at the end of the chapter.

Solution on page 242

Keeping modules modular (continued)

From a code design perspective, it's best to *think of each module as a separate service.* Just to be clear, though, they aren't *really* separate—they all still constitute one monolithic deployment. Each "service" exposes a public API while shielding its internal implementation from the other modules.

Calls to any module happen only to their respective APIs.

Order domain	Recipe domain	Inventory domain
API	**API**	**API**
Implementation (private)	**Implementation (private)**	**Implementation (private)**

As long as modules *only* talk to one another through their public APIs, you can safely change one module without affecting others—thereby reducing their coupling.

Of course, this sounds like a great idea *in theory*. But how can you maintain module boundaries so well that you can sleep peacefully at night? Let's look at a few possibilities.

---

there are no
Dumb Questions

Q: **Dividing my application into modules sure seems like a lot of trouble. Are modular monoliths really the better option?**

A: We've said this before, and we'll say it again—we don't like words like *better*. It's always about trade-offs. So far, we've tried to highlight some of the benefits of modular monoliths (and we aren't done yet), while also pointing out some of the challenges.

Do modular monoliths require more thought and discipline, and maybe even more tooling (as we'll see in a minute)? Absolutely.

But the trade-off is a much more modular architecture that allows cross-functional teams to work independently and thus move faster.

Keeping modules modular (last time!)

Keeping your modules modular isn't as easy as it seems, but don't lose hope just yet. You have options, depending on your technical stack—especially if you apply some creative thinking and elbow grease.

Some languages, like Java, have built-in support to build modules. The Java Platform Module System (JPMS) allows you to build modules that are isolated from one another. The .NET platform, meanwhile, offers namespaces that use the `internal` keyword for this purpose.

Gradle, the Java build tool, supports subprojects.

Another approach is to break up your project code so that each module is a separate folder in your repository. These **subprojects** (or, as many build systems call them, *multimodule projects*) force isolation by virtue of being different projects. You might even consider creating different repositories to contain individual modules, then stitching the complete application together at build time.

Of course, you are still deploying a monolith, so you'll probably need to bring all the modules together using your build tool of choice. A monolithic deployment model doesn't have to mean a monolithic codebase!

Architectural governance tools, like ArchUnit for Java projects and ArchUnitNET for the .NET platform, can help maintain module boundaries as a project grows.

Check out ts-arch for TypeScript and JavaScript projects!

And none of these options needs to stand alone: you can use one or more together.

---

there are no
Dumb Questions

Q: Am I way off base here, or could these techniques be useful even for layered architectures?

A: Give us a moment to wipe away the tears—you've grown up so fast! Absolutely; they can be useful whether your project is partitioned technically or by domain. It's a great idea to use tools (like ArchUnit) and language features (like JPMS) to enforce module boundaries, regardless of architectural style.

You've given me some great ideas for how to modularize the code by business concern. But if all modules share the same database, aren't they still coupled at the data level? Should I think about modularizing the database too?

That would be the logical end of modularization, wouldn't it? Modularizing the code may not be enough. If all your data is still intertwined, then you've just moved your ball of mud into the database!

Before we go further, a caveat: most developers are not used to thinking vertically along business concern lines or breaking up their code into separate modules. Extending that modularity all the way to the database sounds like a great idea—*it is*—but it may be too much to take on all at once. Feel free to evolve your architecture over time when needed, rather than trying to get it all right the first time around.

Put all the lessons you've learned in this book at work. Do your architectural characteristics push you to pick the modular monolith architecture? If so, start by modularizing your code first. Once your team gets the hang of thinking modularly, then see if it helps to take that approach all the way into the database.

Next, let's see what modularizing your database might look like.

Taking modularity all the way to the database

The modular monolith is still a monolithic deployment, typically with a monolithic database backing it. There is a lot of power here: having a single database can make things a *lot* simpler. You don't have to worry about transactions or eventual consistency, and most developers are very comfortable working with just one database. However, if you intend to maintain modularity at all levels, then you should consider modularizing your data.

The rule is simple: every module should access only its own tables. Here's how you'd accomplish this for Naan & Pop:

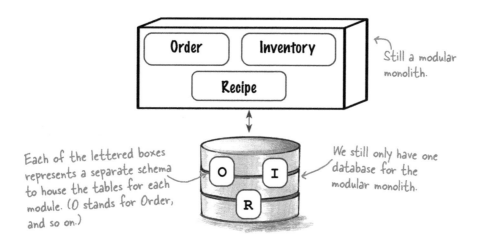

Still a modular monolith.

Each of the lettered boxes represents a separate schema to house the tables for each module. (O stands for Order, and so on.)

We still only have one database for the modular monolith.

For every module in your application, you define a schema and a set of tables. Any and all data that belongs to a particular module will reside *only* in the tables for that module.

As you can see, you can extend modularity all the way to the database by separating data that belongs to different modules into different tables (and maybe even different schemas).

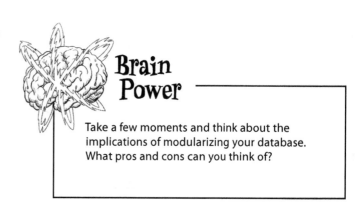

Brain Power

Take a few moments and think about the implications of modularizing your database. What pros and cons can you think of?

Sharpen your pencil

Take a look at the following table names and see if you can identify which tables belong to the schemas we've identified for the Naan & Pop database. Draw an arrow from each table to its schema.

⌐ This is a table.

customers

order_history

recipes

ingredients

delivery_addresses

order_schema	recipe_schema	inventory_schema

These are the schemas we've identified.

Solution on page 243

Beware of joins

Keeping different tables, perhaps even in different schemas, does partition the data belonging to different modules—but it's easy to slip up and accidentally perform a SQL join across tables that belong to different modules. Then you're back to tight coupling!

It's OK to store the IDs of records that belong to one module in another module's tables. For example, the Naan & Pop Order domain is allowed to store "recipe item" IDs in its tables within the order_schema. If it ever needs more information about a particular item, it calls the Recipe module's API and provides it with the recipe item's ID.

Read that again! This is not a foreign key reference.

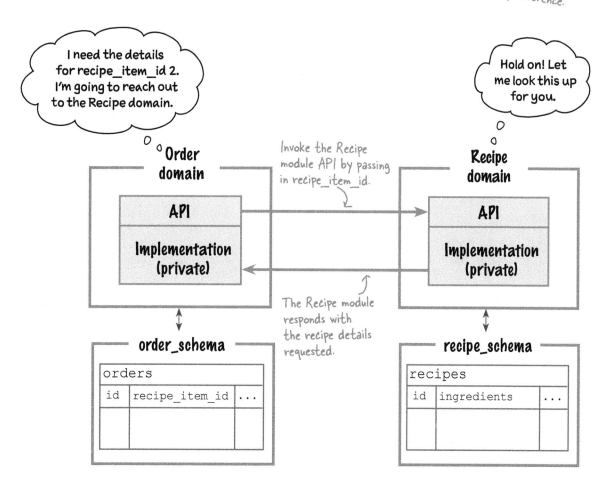

And there you have it. Now, as we've done before, we'll show you some of the strengths and weaknesses of modular monoliths, followed by our star rating chart.

Modular monolith superpowers

Here are some good reasons to use modular monoliths:

Domain partitioning

Architects can design components around domain concerns, then build teams that specialize in one or more of these domains (as opposed to a technical specialization). Domain partitioning is the key superpower of this architectural style.

Domain-based alignment

Modular monoliths encourage cross-functional teams, which are better aligned with the domain than the technically partitioned teams used in layered architectures.

Performance

Performance is usually very good, like for most monolithic architectures. There are no network calls between modules, and all data processing happens in a single place.

Maintainability

Modular monoliths separate business concerns from one another, with cross-functional teams each specializing in a subdomain. This makes it easier to maintain the code, as long as changes don't cross into other domains.

Testability

Since the scope of changes is limited to one module, testing is much easier. And since a cross-functional team's members understand their subdomain really well, they can build out an entire testing suite, including integration, smoke, and end-to-end tests.

Modular monolith kryptonite

Of course, there are always trade-offs. Here are some reasons not to use a modular monolith architecture:

Hard to reuse

Modular organization makes it hard to reuse logic and utilities across modules. For example, you can't share common functionality between modules without extracting it as a dependency, increasing the coupling between the modules.

(Still) a single set of architectural characteristics

Even though modular monoliths are organized by modules, you still get a single set of architectural characteristics for the entire application—even if one business concern has a different set of needs than others.

Modularity can be fragile

It's easy to dilute module boundaries accidentally. Avoiding the big ball of mud takes a lot of governance—and the database is even harder to govern.

It's particularly hard to avoid joins in SQL via tooling.

Operational characteristics

Despite its focus on business concerns, a modular monolith is still, well, a monolith. And as with any monolith, operational characteristics like elasticity and fault tolerance tend to be hard to attain.

Modular monolith star ratings

We've created a star rating chart for modular monoliths, just like the one we showed you for layered architectures in the previous chapter. One star means that the architectural characteristic is not well supported; five stars means it's very well supported.

Just like movie reviews.

Architectural Characteristic	Star Rating
Maintainability	★ ★ ★
Testability	★ ★ ★
Deployability	★ ★ ★
Simplicity	★ ★ ★ ★
Evolvability	★ ★ ★
Performance	★ ★ ★
Scalability	★
Elasticity	★
Fault Tolerance	★
Overall Cost	$ $

These fare better than in the layered architectural style.

Most monolithic architectures perform well, especially if well designed.

Overall, more expensive than layered architectures. Modular monoliths require more planning, thought, and long-term maintainance.

You'll notice that our ratings for modular monoliths' operational characteristics aren't all that different from those for layered architectures. From a process perspective (that is, in terms of maintainability, testability, and deployability), however, the modular monolith does a lot better than the layered architecture. That's because changes to a particular module only affect *that* module and can be tested in isolation, which reduces the risks involved in deploying software.

Modular monoliths cost a little more than layered architectures because they require the team to be vigilant. They also involve additional governance and tooling to maintain module boundaries.

Exercise

Which of the following systems might be well suited for the modular monolith architectural style, and why? *Hint: Take into account its superpowers, its kryptonite, and the problem domain.*

An online auction system where users can bid on items

Why? _____

_____

_____

☐ Well suited for modular monoliths
☐ Might be a fit for modular monoliths
☐ Not well suited for modular monoliths

A large backend financial system for processing and settling international wire transfers overnight

Why? _____

_____

_____

☐ Well suited for modular monoliths
☐ Might be a fit for modular monoliths
☐ Not well suited for modular monoliths

A company entering a new line of business that expects constant changes to its system

Why? _____

_____

_____

☐ Well suited for modular monoliths
☐ Might be a fit for modular monoliths
☐ Not well suited for modular monoliths

A small bakery that wants to start taking online orders

Why? _____

_____

_____

☐ Well suited for modular monoliths
☐ Might be a fit for modular monoliths
☐ Not well suited for modular monoliths

A trouble ticket system for electronics purchased with a support plan, in which field technicians come to customers to fix problems

Why? _____

_____

_____

☐ Well suited for modular monoliths
☐ Might be a fit for modular monoliths
☐ Not well suited for modular monoliths

⟶ Solution on page 244

Naan & Pop is delivering pizza!

The development team has finally grokked modular monoliths! With a modular codebase *and* a modular database, they now feel ready for any other big changes to Naan & Pop's menu. Rumor has it that the owners plan to introduce a full Mediterranean menu next. We can't wait, and we wish them a lot of luck!

⌐ Bullet Points ──────────

- A *modular monolith* is a monolithic architectural style that is partitioned by domains and subdomains that reflect business concerns, not technical concerns.

- Each *subdomain* makes up one *module* of the application. Each module can contain multiple business use cases.

- Each module can be made up of layers to provide better organization. A module may be technically partitioned as a means to organize its functionality.

- Avoid having code in one module directly access any functionality in other modules. Allowing this can reduce or eliminate the boundaries between modules.

- Each module should have a public API that communicates with other modules while shielding the module's internal implementation from the rest of the world.

- Avoiding intermodule communication allows modules to change internally without affecting other modules.

- It takes time and effort to ensure that the modules in a modular monolith remain separate and distinct.

- You can govern a modular monolith using a variety of techniques. Some languages have built-in support for building modules.

- Another approach is to physically break up the codebase into separate subprojects or even different repositories. This usually involves using a build tool to bring all the modules back together when you build the monolith.

- Third-party tools can also help with architectural governance.

- You may choose to use several techniques in combination to ensure the boundaries of individual modules are maintained.

- You can extend modularity all the way to the database, keeping the data for each module separate.

- Watch that you don't accidentally couple modules when inserting or fetching data (for example, when using a SQL join statement across tables that belong to different modules).

Modular Monolith Crossword

Modular monoliths are about separating business concerns. Take a look at these separate clues and test your knowledge about this architectural style.

Across

1. Java _____ Module System
6. _____ to one module don't require _____ to the others
8. The Recipes _____ interface is part of the Recipes domain
9. Each module exposes a public _____
10. Modular monoliths are good when many teams need to _____ their work
13. Monoliths generally have one big _____base
15. Highly rated characteristic in most monolithic architectures
18. Each domain in this style represents a _____ concern
19. With a modular monolith, _____ are often cross-functional
20. Smaller bits of functionality can reside in their own _____ domains
21. It's important to maintain _____ between modules
22. Style of monolithic architecture first used in this system
23. Databases can show modularity by representing an entity via a _____

Down

1. The latest addition to Naan and Pop's menu
2. In a domain-partitioned architecture, each domain gets its own _____
3. If something is an implementation _____, it's not an architectural concern
4. If technical concerns are like horizontal "slices" of a monolith, business concerns are _____ slices
5. "Spaghetti code" is too closely _____
7. This system is for _____ & Pop
11. A challenging kind of architectural characteristic for monoliths
12. Modules use ID references in _____ to look things up
14. Monolithic and distributed are two kinds of deployment _____
16. Example of a language that supports creating modules
17. Modules communicate indirectly, through their _____ APIs
19. Databases build schemas from related _____

→ Solution on page 242

Exercise Solution

From page 217

Cast your mind back to the layered architecture we built for Naan & Pop in Chapter 6. The following diagram shows its layers and logical components. Adding a new category to the menu (say, pizza) means changing a bunch of moving parts. Grab a marker and put a triangle (▲) next to everything this new requirement will affect.

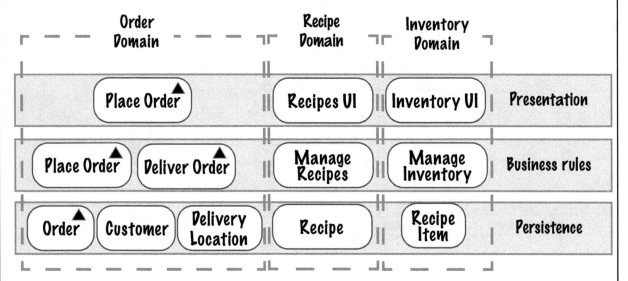

Here's some space for you to explain your thought process:

Offering pizzas probably means the menu will need a new listing. We might need to allow for customized toppings, which would affect the presentation layer and the associated pricing and could introduce new rules. There might be time constraints on deliveries (no one wants a cold pizza). The customizations might also affect how we persist pizza orders (as opposed to other kinds of orders).

However, the recipe and inventory domains won't be affected. A recipe is a recipe is a recipe—a list of ingredients with a set of steps to follow. And while there may be new ingredients, the inventory domain will manage them just like it would any other ingredients.

From page 220

Who Does What? Solution

Identifying which components should belong to a particular module can be tricky. In this game of "Who Does What?"—or rather, "What Goes Where?"—we'd like you to match each component to the module where it fits best. Multiple components can belong to one module.

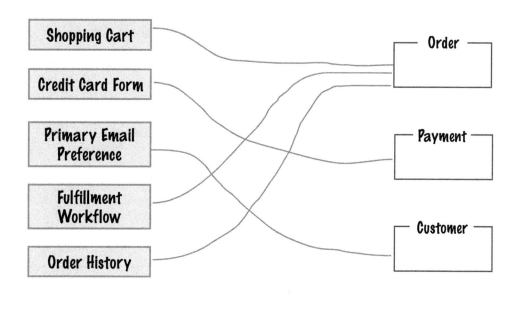

Exercise Solution

From page 225

A critical piece of successfully developing modular monoliths is understanding the domain well enough that you can break it into individual modules. One way to do that (and there are many) is to really *listen* to your business experts.

Say you are working for a startup that's creating an expense-tracking app for small to medium-sized businesses. Here are the business requirements:

- There are users and auditors. Users add expenses, and auditors review expense reports to ensure they align with policy guidelines.

- When a user adds an expense, it is recorded in the database for that user.

- The app creates an audit trail that the auditors can use to ensure that everything is in order.

Can you identify the subdomains that should make up this application? *Hint: Not everything your business users say will translate into a module.*

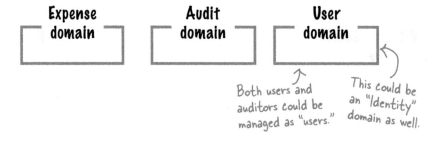

Expense domain

Audit domain

User domain

Both users and auditors could be managed as "users."

This could be an "Identity" domain as well.

Brain Power

From page 227

Can you think of any mechanisms to help you ensure that one part of your application won't accidentally access another? For example, does your favorite programming language provide any support at compile time to keep modules separate? Jot down any ideas that come to mind here.

- •<insert your favorite programming language> feature
- • Repository structure
- • Build tool capabilities
- •Third-party libraries and governance frameworks

From page 232

Sharpen your pencil
Solution

Take a look at the following table names and see if you can identify which tables belong to the schemas we've identified for the Naan & Pop database. Draw an arrow from each table to its schema.

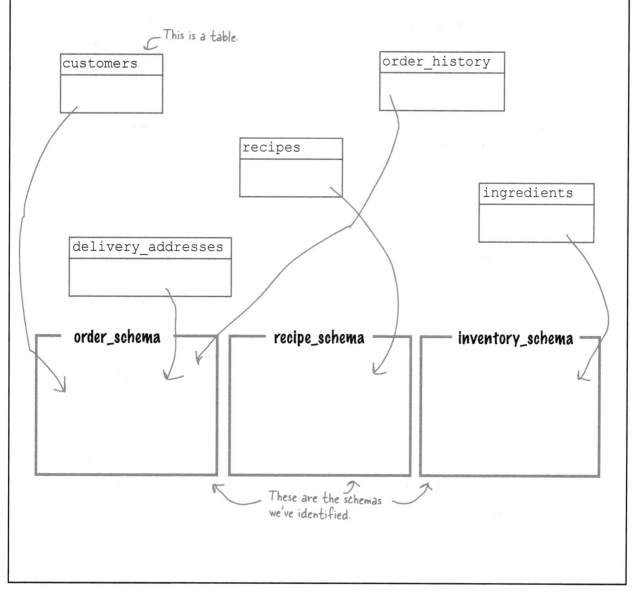

This is a table.

customers

order_history

recipes

ingredients

delivery_addresses

order_schema

recipe_schema

inventory_schema

These are the schemas we've identified.

Exercise Solution

From page 237

Which of the following systems might be well suited for the modular monolith architectural style, and why? *Hint: Take into account its superpowers, its kryptonite, and the problem domain.*

An online auction system where users can bid on items

Why? <u>This system probably needs high degrees</u> <u>of scaling and elasticity. Monoliths aren't</u> <u>ideal for such systems.</u>

☐ Well suited for modular monoliths
☐ Might be a fit for modular monoliths
☒ Not well suited for modular monoliths

A large backend financial system for processing and settling international wire transfers overnight

Why? <u>Financial systems have rich domains;</u> <u>scalability and elasticity don't sound like</u> <u>concerns here.</u>

☒ Well suited for modular monoliths
☐ Might be a fit for modular monoliths
☐ Not well suited for modular monoliths

A company entering a new line of business that expects constant changes to its system

Why? <u>A high degree of modularity is good for</u> <u>handling changes, but it certainly depends</u> <u>on what kinds of changes are expected.</u>

☐ Well suited for modular monoliths
☒ Might be a fit for modular monoliths
☐ Not well suited for modular monoliths

A small bakery that wants to start taking online orders

Why? <u>Ha! We kinda gave this one away, didn't we?</u>

☒ Well suited for modular monoliths
☐ Might be a fit for modular monoliths
☐ Not well suited for modular monoliths

A trouble ticket system for electronics purchased with a support plan, in which field technicians come to customers to fix problems

Why? <u>Lots of moving parts; this system probably</u> <u>needs high degrees of elasticity and</u> <u>scalability.</u>

☐ Well suited for modular monoliths
☐ Might be a fit for modular monoliths
☒ Not well suited for modular monoliths

Modular Monolith Crossword Solution

From page 239

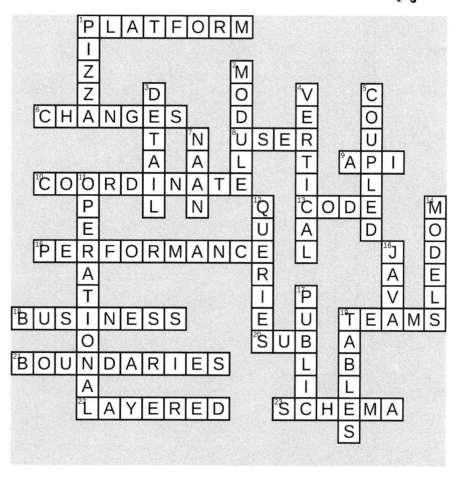

8

microkernel architecture

Crafting Customizations

You can craft custom experiences, one capability at a time. Some architectural styles are particularly well suited for some capabilities, and the microkernel architecture is the world champion at customization. But it's also useful for a bewildering range of applications. Once you understand this architectural style, you'll start seeing it everywhere!

Let's dig into an architecture that lets your users have it *their* way.

The benefits of Going Green

What does everyone have lying around? Old electronics! Going Green is a fast-moving startup that plans to capitalize on the market for buying and recycling old cell phones, music players, and other small electronics.

After analyzing the architectural characteristics required, the architects have designed a three-part system, and each part of which needs different capabilities. They'd like your help. Ready? Here's the system so far:

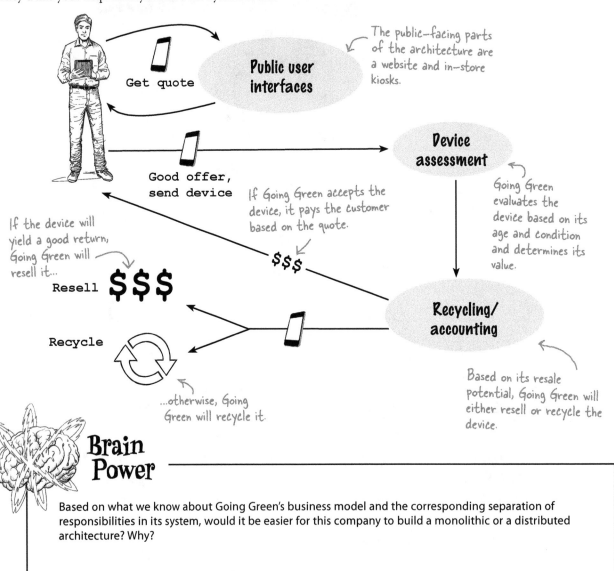

Brain Power

Based on what we know about Going Green's business model and the corresponding separation of responsibilities in its system, would it be easier for this company to build a monolithic or a distributed architecture? Why?

BE the architect

Architects just can't stop analyzing stuff. Can you determine three important architectural characteristics for each of the three services in the new Going Green architecture?

Public user interfaces

Architectural characteristics

Scalability

_____

_____

_____

Fill in some architectural characteristics for each service.

Architectural characteristics

_____

_____

_____

Device assessment

Architectural characteristics

Recycling/ accounting

_____

_____

_____

Solution on page 272

Cubicle conversation

Mara: We need to split up the architecture work for the Going Green application. Mara, you and Alex should work on the device assessment service.

Alex: Great! That's the service that assesses the devices users send us to determine value, right? Seems like one of the more interesting parts of the application.

Sam: How often will we need to add new device configurations to the assessment service?

Mara: At least a few times a month, sometimes even a few times a week. This is especially important, because how fast we can update the device assessment service directly affects the company's profitability.

Sam: Why such a direct connection?

Mara: Going Green makes a profit when it resells the highest-value electronics it receives. Generally, newer devices are in better shape and are worth more. The faster we can add new device assessments, the more money the company makes.

Alex: Wow, so rapid change is a BIG deal for this service.

Mara: It is! And don't forget, we have to make sure that supporting new devices won't affect the system's support for the existing ones. Are y'all up for it?

Sam and Alex: You bet!

Mara: I think we should consider using a microkernel architecture. That style makes it easier to design and add new capabilities using plugins.

The two parts of microkernel architectures

The *microkernel* architecture derives its name from operating system design. The **kernel**, or core, of an operating system is very small, offering only the most basic capabilities. A microkernel architecture consists of two primary parts: its *core* and its *plugins* (any number of them).

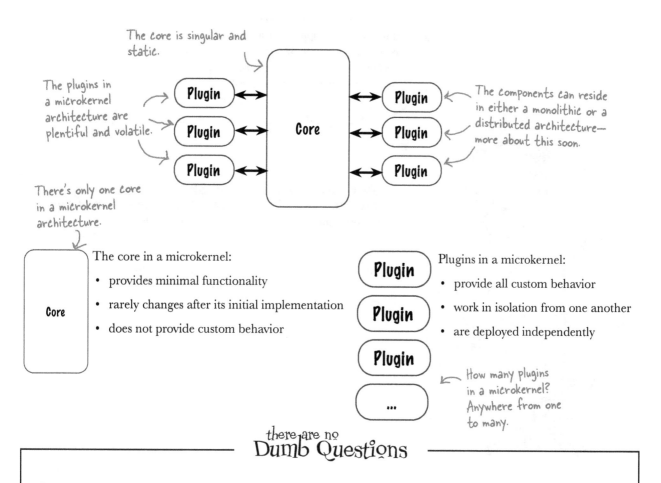

The core is singular and static.

The plugins in a microkernel architecture are plentiful and volatile.

The components can reside in either a monolithic or a distributed architecture—more about this soon.

There's only one core in a microkernel architecture.

The core in a microkernel:

- provides minimal functionality
- rarely changes after its initial implementation
- does not provide custom behavior

Plugins in a microkernel:

- provide all custom behavior
- work in isolation from one another
- are deployed independently

How many plugins in a microkernel? Anywhere from one to many.

there are no

Dumb Questions

Q: Is the microkernel architecture technically or domain-partitioned?

A: Flashback to Chapter 5! Most microkernel architectures are technically partitioned. You *could* divide the core into layers—perhaps one for presentation, another for business or workflow logic, and so on. However, microkernel is one of those strange architectural styles that can also be domain-partitioned, depending on how you design your plugins.

As for deployment models, microkernel architectures are usually monolithic. As you'll see in this chapter, however, in some scenarios a distributed model might make more sense.

Wait a minute. Just about all the software I use supports plugins one way or another. Are you telling me that **all** those systems use the microkernel architectural style?

Not quite. Every microkernel has plugins, but not all plugins belong to microkernels.

Unfortunately, there is no definitive dividing line between microkernel systems and systems that support plugins. Mostly, we evaluate how "microkernel-y" an architecture is (let's call that "microkern-ality") by how functional its core is without any plugins and how *volatile* its core is (how often it needs to change).

The spectrum of "microkern-ality"

Lots of software supports plugins: IDEs, web browsers, build tools, you name it. But simply supporting plugins doesn't make a system a microkernel—it's all about the core. In extreme microkernels, the core can do very little useful work without plugins installed.

A browser is perfectly useful without any plugins, so it's not much of a microkernel.

Eclipse IDE

The Eclipse IDE is designed as a "pure" microkernel, facilitating different languages and tools via plugins.

Insurance application

An insurance application has standard rules for each policy yet allows customization for unique local rules and regulations, so it has a medium level of functionality without plugins.

Web browser

Web browsers support plugins but don't rely on them to function.

less functional	Degree of "microkern-ality" Functionality/volatility of core	more functional

Linter

Linters are tools that use plugins to parse source code and apply style and syntax rules to it. Most programming languages have linters; for example, JavaScript has esLint.

Continuous integration tool (like Jenkins)

Jenkins works as a standalone continuous integration (CI) tool, but it supports a number of plugins for extensibility.

Insurance claims processing system

These systems are a common example of customization. They usually handle most claims in a standard way but allow developers to build custom rules for specific situations.

there are no Dumb Questions

Q: Is every system that supports plugins a microkernel?

A: Not at all. Lots of systems support plugins. How much of a microkernel it is (and no one is actually grading you on this) depends on the volatility and functionality of its core.

Q: Is this architectural style only useful for software development tools?

A: A lot of development tools use this architecture because it lets them offer programmatic customization, but many business and other applications use it too. It works for any problem domain that requires customization and in which each change acts in isolation.

Q: Are microkernel and microservices the same thing?

A: No, the similarity in the names is just a coincidence. Microkernel's name comes from operating system design, whereas microservices is named for its relatively small and separate deployment units in a distributed architecture.

Exercise

The microkernel architectural style shows up in lots of places. See if you can place the specific tools and categories below in the correct place on the spectrum, by determining how much of a microkernel each one is. *Hint: Each system's degree of "microkern-ality" depends on how useful it is* without *plugins.*

We did one for you. Eclipse is an example of a product defined by its "microkern-ality."

Not familiar with the BFF pattern? Check out https://samnewman.io/patterns/architectural/bff/.

IDE with plugin support (not Eclipse)

Backend for Frontend (BFF) design pattern

Eclipse IDE

Web browser

Mobile device operating system

Device assessment service for a recyling business

| less functional | Functionality/volatility of core | more functional |

Degree of "microkern-ality"

Solution on page 273

Device assessment service core

You and your team all agree to use a microkernel architecture for the new device assessment service.

The core system includes the criteria needed to assess a device, like its age, condition, and model number. For each type of device, it defers to a device-specific plugin that executes the rules to determine how the system will assess the device's resale value.

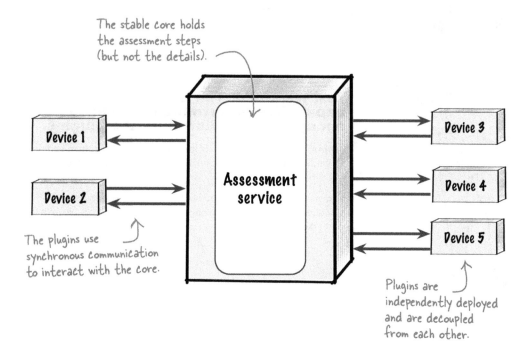

The stable core holds the assessment steps (but not the details).

The plugins use synchronous communication to interact with the core.

Plugins are independently deployed and are decoupled from each other.

You decide to use a distributed physical architecture for the plugins, for better scalability. This also gives Going Green the option to add plugins in other languages in the future.

Finally, you decide on synchronous communication, because the service is sufficiently responsive that there's no need to add the complexity of asynchronous communication.

Let's dig into those decisions a little further.

I can see that it's common to implement plugins as components within a monolithic architecture. But doesn't having everything in one deployment make it harder to hot-deploy plugins? It would be easier if they were distributed. Could we build distributed plugins?

Yes, we could! The architecture's capabilities determine whether to encapsulate or distribute the plugins.

Some microkernel architectures include both the core system and the plugins in a single monolithic architecture; others are distributed, as you might recall from Chapter 5.

The microkernel style exists in the shadowy netherworld between monolithic and distributed architectures. Architects can implement it with either deployment model.

there are no
Dumb Questions

Q: Does a microkernel architecture's core system have to be a monolith?

A: Not necessarily—microkernels often feature in hybrid architectures. When it makes sense (such as for a desktop application), you might implement the core as a single system; other times, you might distribute parts of the core as well as the plugins.

Q: How do I implement plugins?

A: You can implement your own plugin designs using interfaces, but virtually all platforms and technology stacks have libraries and frameworks to help out.

Q: Can I implement plugins in different tech stacks than the stack in which the core is written?

A: One of the advantages of using distributed plugins is that you can write them using any platform you can call via a network connection.

Encapsulated versus distributed plugins

The core system in a microkernel is where the plugins, well, plug in. Generally, we implement that connection via an ***interface***. The plugin implements the interface, while the core system supports that component via that interface.

If we design a microkernel as a monolithic architecture, we'll implement each plugin as a component that connects to the core through the interface.

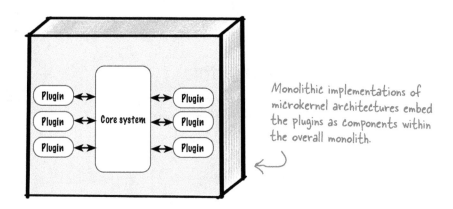

Monolithic implementations of microkernel architectures embed the plugins as components within the overall monolith.

In other implementations of microkernel architectures, plugins are distributed: web endpoints, event queues, and so on. In addition, we can decide whether to call the plugins synchronously or asynchronously. (We'll cover this in much more depth in Chapter 11.)

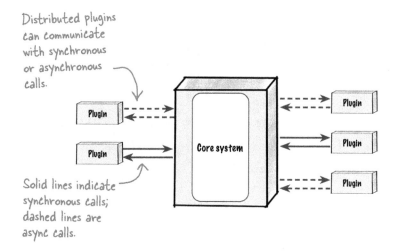

Distributed plugins can communicate with synchronous or asynchronous calls.

Solid lines indicate synchronous calls; dashed lines are async calls.

Exercise

The assessment service team at Going Green must decide whether the microkernel's physical architecture should be **monolithic** (core and plugins in the same deployment unit) or **distributed** (plugins deployed separately from the core). They need your help with the trade-off analysis. Can you list some pros and cons for each option? We'll get you started. *Hint: Consider how each option would affect things like architectural characteristics.*

Monoliths generally provide better performance because they make fewer network calls.

Most monoliths only load plugins on startup, which can complicate deployment.

Monolithic

Pros

Performance

_____

_____

Cons

Single deployment

_____

_____

```
        Plugin  ◄─►
        Plugin  ◄─►   Core      ◄─►  Plugin
        Plugin  ◄─►   system    ◄─►  Plugin
                                ◄─►  Plugin
```

Distributed

Pros

_____

_____

_____

Cons

_____

_____

_____

```
   Plugin  ⇠─►
   Plugin  ──►   Core      ⇠─  Plugin
               system      ──► Plugin
                           ⇠─► Plugin
```

Solution on page 274

Plugin communication

To be useful, plugins must communicate with the core system. For example, the core will call a method (based on an interface) and utilize the results. This communication can be implemented in a couple of different ways, based on factors like physical architecture.

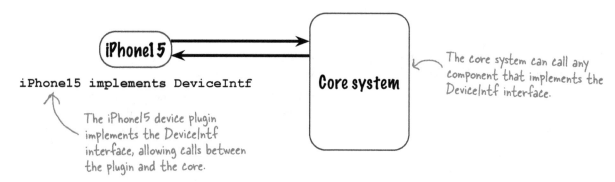

iPhone15 implements DeviceIntf

The iPhone15 device plugin implements the DeviceIntf interface, allowing calls between the plugin and the core.

The core system can call any component that implements the DeviceIntf interface.

How the actual call happens between the core and a plugin depends on the physical architecture you use to implement the plugins. In monolithic architectures, we implement plugins in the same technology stack as the core and deploy them as native components for the platform (like JAR files for Java, DLLs for .NET, or GEMs for Ruby).

As for distributed plugins, the core can call them with synchronous or asynchronous calls. Developers aren't restricted to the core's implementation platform, either—they can write plugins in a variety of languages.

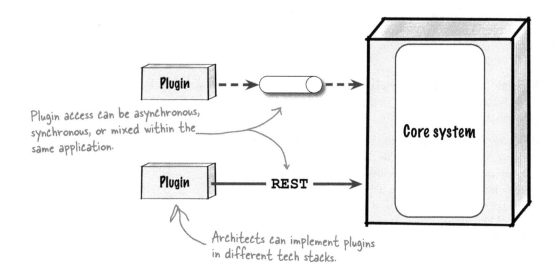

Plugin access can be asynchronous, synchronous, or mixed within the same application.

Architects can implement plugins in different tech stacks.

Today's Interview

Plugging into the star attraction of the
microkernel: the Plugin

Head First: Let's see... let me get my microphone
plugged in. Testing, testing... OK, welcome, Plugin!

Plugin: How appropriate! All *sorts* of things use me to
function. I'm happy to be here—and excited to clear up
some controversies.

Head First: Everyone says you're the star of the
microkernel architecture, yet the core gets more press
time and attention. Is that fair?

Plugin: Well, that may be true, but what good is the core
without me? It may be bigger, but without me, the core is
boring.

Head First: You certainly show up in lots of places.
What about your controversial role in non-microkernel
architectures? Lots of systems support plugins that aren't
microkernels...

Plugin: I'm happy wherever I appear. To be truthful,
though, I prefer microkernels. For other architectures,
plugins are just condiments—we're not necessary, but we
add some nice flavors. In a microkernel, though, I'm the
main course! The whole architecture is based on me. I
appreciate that level of importance.

Head First: Let's dig into something that seems to
appear in trade-off analyses all the time. Your distributed
version has some performance issues, no?

Plugin: Hey, you can't say bad things about all
plugins just because we have some trade-offs! Yes, it's
true that when we use network calls to communicate,
performance does take a hit. But you know what else?
Those distributed plugins can scale better, *and* you can
write them in a variety of languages. Different strokes
for different folks, right? And different plugin physical
architectures for different trade-offs.

Head First: OK, fair enough. But let's talk about
working with overly volatile cores.

Plugin: Alas, that's one of the downsides to starring in
a microkernel architecture—when the core decides to
change all the time. Change is *my* job! The more the core
changes, the more it's likely to interfere with what I'm
doing. I strive for professionalism, so I prefer to work with
nice, stable cores with no drama.

Head First: You get a lot of press because of your ability
to handle customization, but do you have other roles?
What else you can handle?

Plugin: Thanks for asking, Head First. It's always
annoying to be pigeonholed into my best-known role. I
can handle customizations without ugly, long `switch`
statements, using an elegant architectural style, without
even batting an eye. We plugins can be used for all kinds
of things—really, anything that needs good isolation.
For example, I show up all the time in A/B testing. The
architects keep the old behavior in PluginA, add the new
behavior in PluginB, and decide which to call. I also have
starring roles in integration hubs, developer tools, and lots
of other places.

Head First: Before we finish up, is there anything you'd
like to plug?

Plugin: You bet! Look for me in an architecture near you,
either as an integral part of a monolith or as an endpoint
for a distributed microkernel.

Cubicle conversation

Alex

Sam

Mara

Mara: Hi, all. Just stopping by to take a look at your trade-off analysis for the Going Green assessment service. Have you decided yet between a monolithic and a distributed physical architecture?

Sam: We're working on it. I did the trade-off analysis for the distributed version, and personally, I'm a big fan. Here's our summary:

Pros

Availability

Deployability

Scalability

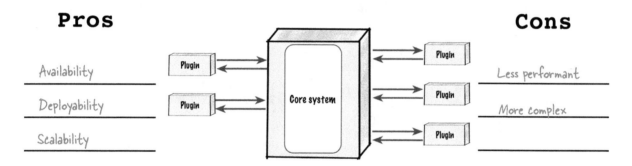

Cons

Less performant

More complex

Mara: Can you explain how you arrived at these conclusions?

Alex: Sure. For the distributed version, we don't have to restart the core system to add new devices. That gives us better *availability* than the monolithic version, since that requires a restart to load new device plugins. Also, it's simpler to deploy a single plugin than to redeploy the whole assessment service. Since the plugins don't run in the same process as the core, we can make the whole system more *scalable*. But that would take a toll on its *performance*—after all, network calls take a lot longer than in-process ones.

Mara: That sounds like a good trade-off. The business agrees that scalability is very important for the new system.

---

there are no
Dumb Questions

Q: Where is the user interface in a microkernel architecture?

A: It depends! If the system is monolithic, architects commonly include the UI as part of the core system. However, when you design a service in a distributed architecture as a microkernel, other parts of the system typically handle the UI.

Q: Can the UI utilize a microkernel?

A: You bet it can. In fact, lots of UI patterns (like the BFF pattern we mentioned earlier) use the microkernel structure to handle customized UI endpoints such as iOS, Android, and web browsers.

Q: Isn't a microkernel really just the Decorator design pattern?

A: Good catch! While their purposes are mostly the same, the microkernel architecture is one way to *implement* the Decorator design pattern. Compared to design patterns, architecture requires more thought about physical limitations and possibilities. For example, design patterns don't account for capabilities like scalability.

Q: Is the microkernel style the only way to handle customization?

A: Not at all. It's one of many ways. A microkernel architecture is useful when the structure of your system—its core capabilities that rarely change—requires discrete customization via plugins. For systems without that kind of structure, other architectural styles may be more appropriate.

Q: What's the internal structure of the core system? Is it just one big logical component?

A: In the microkernel style, we design the core system based on how we want to organize the logical components in the system. For example, if we want to separate capabilities within the core, we might choose to implement the core via layers, as we would in the layered architectural style. On the other hand, we might follow DDD and design the core around a bounded context, as in the modular monolith style. The microkernel style is often used in hybrid architectures where customizability is a driving characteristic.

I'm thinking it would be a bad idea to allow plugins to talk to one another. Am I right?

Plugins can talk to one another in a microkernel through the core system. But should they?

Plugins typically communicate with the core system by implementing an interface that the core supports. That makes it possible for plugins to communicate *with each other* "through" the core system. For example, the Eclipse IDE, which supports multiple languages, allows language-based tools (like compilers and debuggers) to interact with each other in this way.

Be cautious about allowing inter-plugin communication, though! It has some serious negative trade-offs. First, it requires consistent **contracts** between the core and the plugins, which eventually involves versioning. (More about contracts on the next page.) For example, one thing that makes Eclipse complex is the transitive dependencies between its components, which can cause versioning headaches. Second, dependencies between plugins create availability issues, because you must guarantee that all necessary plugins are present at runtime.

To understand the problems with letting plugins chat amongst themselves, we have to look at the two ways the core communicates with plugins.

Plugin contracts

When architects implement microkernel architectures, we usually ensure that the core calls plugins using a **contract** (another word for *interface*). That communication is *solely between the plugin and the core*, not between plugins. If you allow communication between plugins, the core has to act as their intermediary.

In the example system below, PluginA doesn't know or care about other plugins; it communicates only with the core. However, PluginX needs to communicate with PluginY, and that communication must be mediated by the core system.

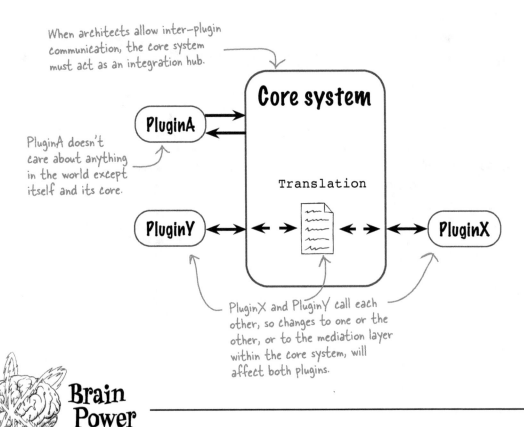

When architects allow inter-plugin communication, the core system must act as an integration hub.

PluginA doesn't care about anything in the world except itself and its core.

PluginX and PluginY call each other, so changes to one or the other, or to the mediation layer within the core system, will affect both plugins.

Brain Power

You know you have to worry about intermediary communication through the core system, but consider this: what happens when you update PluginY in a way that changes the contract between PluginX and PluginY? If you don't want to change PluginX when you change PluginY, how could you manage that communication?

Going Green goes green

After considering how best to implement the plugin interaction with the core, the team decides to define an interface (called *DeviceInterface*) for each plugin to implement. Now Going Green can add new devices just by implementing the interface and customizing the valuation process for that specific device.

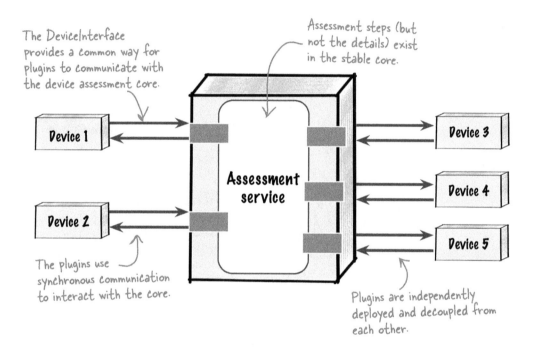

The DeviceInterface provides a common way for plugins to communicate with the device assessment core.

Assessment steps (but not the details) exist in the stable core.

The plugins use synchronous communication to interact with the core.

Plugins are independently deployed and decoupled from each other.

Your device assessment engine is a success. Well done!

To wrap up, let's quickly summarize the strong and weak points of this style of architecture.

Microkernel superpowers

The microkernel is a common architectural style. It's also one of the most common styles you'll find within hybrid architectures that require customization.

Custom behavior

Who you gonna call to customize part of your application? Microkernel to the rescue!

The microkernel is "shaped" in the best way to handle customizations.

Evolvability

Evolvability, as an architectural characteristic, means that architects can make fundamental underlying changes that gradually evolve the system away from its old behaviors. Unlike adaptable architectures, evolvable architectures only support the old behaviors for a short time. Plugins offer an excellent way to implement this capability.

Adaptability

Adaptability, as an architectural characteristic, implies the ability to keep existing functionalities and continue adding more. A microkernel supports this well; you can keep old plugins as you implement new ones.

Simplicity for the win!

Simple structure

A microkernel has two basic moving parts (the core and plugins), making it easy for developers to understand and implement.

Partitioning

In a microkernel, you can handle customization with design or with architecture. However, if you use design, the developers must be very diligent about following the design correctly. If the system is structured around plugins, the distinction is clearer.

The microkernel is a great example of an architectural approach to customization.

Microkernel kryptonite

The microkernel architecture's weaknesses mostly appear when architects use it improperly: for example, when the core changes too much or when plugins must communicate heavily with one another.

Misaligned volatility

In a microkernel, the core system should change very little once it is implemented. If it changes a lot, that is likely a sign that this is not the ideal architectural solution or you have made the wrong things plugins.

One of the most common mistakes in a microkernel is a too-volatile core, due to frequent domain changes.

Sharing between plugins

While it's often tempting, sharing dependencies (such as shared libraries) between plugins is generally a bad idea because it creates headaches around coupling and deployment.

To keep a microkernel from devolving into a big ball of mud, keep an close eye on coupling via sharing.

Chatty plugins

Allowing plugins to interact may be tempting, but it comes with a host of difficult trade-offs. Successful systems that use this approach (for example, Eclipse) do so at the cost of high complexity.

Performance

When using distributed plugins for a physical architecture, you might notice an impact on performance, depending on the communication protocols and how much information passes between the core and the plugins.

Microkernel star ratings

We've created a chart of star ratings, like the ones we showed you for layered and modular monolith architectures, to indicate how well microkernel architectures do with each of the architectural characteristics listed. One star means that the architectural characteristic is not well supported; five stars means it's very well supported.

Just like movie reviews.

Testing is straightforward in a microkernel; teams can test the core and plugins separately.

Architectural Characteristic	Star Rating
Maintainability	★ ★ ★
Testability	★ ★ ★
Deployability	★ ★ ★
Simplicity	★ ★ ★ ★
Evolvability	★ ★ ★
Performance	★ ★ ★
Scalability	★
Elasticity	★
Fault Tolerance	★
Overall Cost	$

A microkernel has a easy-to-understand structure.

Scalability is better when using distributed plugins.

Performance is better with embedded plugins.

Simplicity, in this case, leads to affordability.

Exercise

Which of the following systems might be well suited for the microkernel architectural style, and why? *Hint: Take into account its superpowers, its kryptonite, and the nature of each system.*

An online auction system where users can bid on items

Why? _____

_____

_____

☐ Well suited for microkernel

☐ Might be a fit for microkernel

☐ Not well suited for microkernel

A large backend financial system for processing and settling international wire transfers overnight

Why? _____

_____

_____

☐ Well suited for microkernel

☐ Might be a fit for microkernel

☐ Not well suited for microkernel

A company entering a new line of business that expects constant changes to its system

Why? _____

_____

_____

☐ Well suited for microkernel

☐ Might be a fit for microkernel

☐ Not well suited for microkernel

A small bakery that wants to start taking online orders

Why? _____

_____

_____

☐ Well suited for microkernel

☐ Might be a fit for microkernel

☐ Not well suited for microkernel

A trouble ticket system for electronics purchased with a support plan, in which field technicians come to customers to fix problems

Why? _____

_____

_____

☐ Well suited for microkernel

☐ Might be a fit for microkernel

☐ Not well suited for microkernel

→ Solution on page 275

Wrapping it up

Thanks to your efforts, Going Green is assessing devices quickly and accurately, and profitability has never been better. This case shows just how useful microkernel architectures can be. For problems that need a customizable, stable system, a microkernel is hard to beat.

Bullet Points

- The *microkernel* architectural style provides a structured way to handle customizations via plugins.

- Microkernel architectures consist of two main parts: the *core* and one or more *plugins*.

- The core system in a microkernel contains minimal functionality and has low volatility.

- Architects design plugins to customize and/or add behaviors to a system.

- Generally, plugins only communicate with the core system, not with each other.

- If plugins do need to communicate with each other, the core must mediate the communication and handle issues like versions and dependencies. It essentially serves as an integration layer.

- Microkernel architectures can be monolithic architectures or can be implemented as services in a distributed architecture.

- When built as a monolithic architecture, the core and plugins must be written in the same language.

- Plugin calls may be synchronous (for example, using REST in a distributed architecture) or asynchronous (using threads in a monolithic architecture or messaging in a distributed one). Whether remote calls are synchronous or asynchronous, architects can implement the plugins in a variety of technology stacks.

- Monolithic plugins generally offer better *performance* because calls take place in the same process.

- Monolithic microkernels suffer from the typical limitations of all monoliths, including limited operational capabilities such as scalability and elasticity.

- Microkernels that use distributed plugins may offer better scalability, because they use multiple processes and offer scalable communications (events).

- Microkernel architectures are best suited for problems with distinct categories of volatility.

- If a microkernel's core system changes often, its architects may have chosen the wrong architectural style or may have partitioned the work incorrectly.

- The microkernel style shows up in lots of places: IDEs, text processing tools, build and deployment tools, integrations, translation layers, insurance applications, and electronics recycling applications, just to name a few.

Microkernel Crossword

Ready to see how much you've learned about microkernel architecture? Plug into this crossword puzzle!

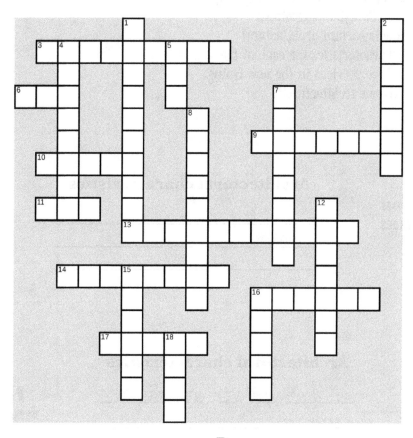

Across

3. Design pattern often used to implement microkernel architectures
6. With inter-plugin communication, the core serves as an integration _____
9. You can add new capabilities to a system by using these
10. Microkernel architectures can _____ to include new functionalities
11. Abbr. for a tool used to write code
13. Monolithic architectures _____ both plugins and core
14. Plugins are usually _____ independently from each other
16. A microkernel is great for creating systems with _____ rules and behaviors
17. You can use plugins written in more than one tech _____

Down

1. When plugins can talk to each other, their dependencies are _____
2. Example of an IDE that uses interacting plugins
4. _____ plugins provide better performance
5. Number of primary component types in a microkernel architecture
7. Constantly changing
8. Microkernel architectures often support several programming _____
12. When most monoliths load plugins
15. A tool that applies style and syntax rules to code
16. Plugins make _____ to talk to the core
18. What plugins are plugged into

→ Solution on page 276

BE the architect Solution

From page 249

Architects just can't stop analyzing stuff. Can you determine a few important architectural characteristics for each of the three services in the new Going Green architecture?

Public user interfaces

Architectural characteristics

Scalability

Availability

_____

Architectural characteristics

Agility (deployability, testability, etc.)

Maintainability

_____

Device assessment

Going Green needs to test and deploy new device assessments quickly, without breaking existing ones.

Recycling/ accounting

Architectural characteristics

Security

Data integrity

Auditability

Exercise Solution

From page 254

The microkernel architectural style shows up in lots of places. See if you can place the specific tools and categories below in the correct place on the spectrum, by determining how much of a microkernel each one is. *Hint: Each system's degree of "microkern-ality" depends on how useful it is* without *plugins.*

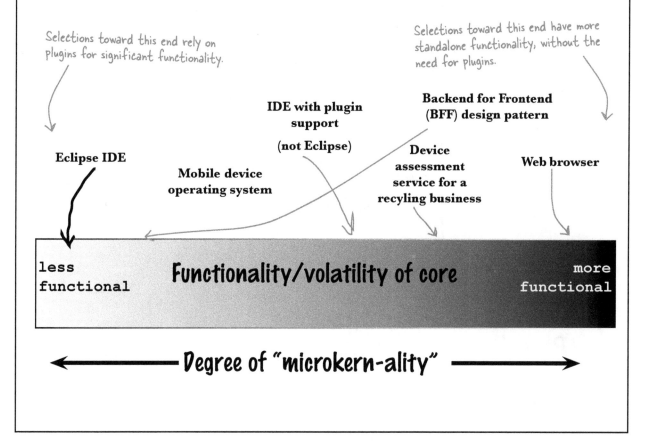

Selections toward this end rely on plugins for significant functionality.

Selections toward this end have more standalone functionality, without the need for plugins.

IDE with plugin support (not Eclipse)

Backend for Frontend (BFF) design pattern

Eclipse IDE

Mobile device operating system

Device assessment service for a recyling business

Web browser

less functional

Functionality/volatility of core

more functional

← ── Degree of "microkern-ality" ── →

Exercise Solution

From page 258

The assessment service team at Going Green must decide whether the microkernel's physical architecture should be ***monolithic*** (core and plugins in the same deployment unit) or ***distributed*** (plugins deployed separately from the core). They need your help with the trade-off analysis. Can you list some pros and cons for each option? *Hint: Consider how each option would affect things like architectural characteristics.*

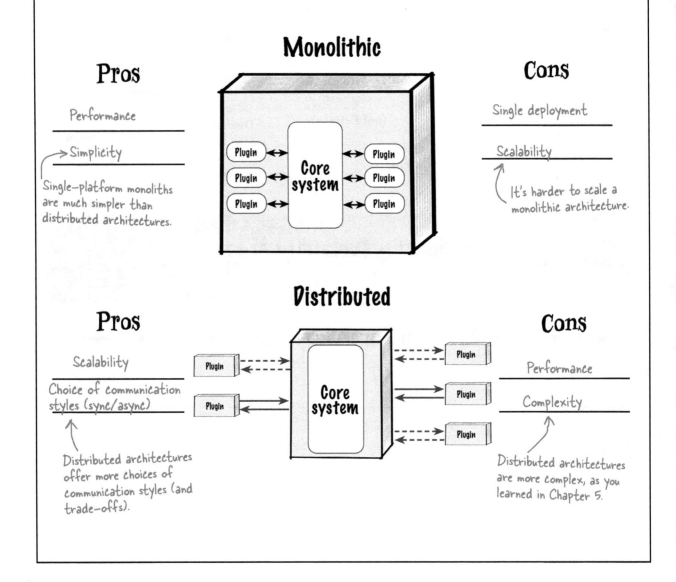

Monolithic

Pros

Performance

→ Simplicity

Single-platform monoliths are much simpler than distributed architectures.

Cons

Single deployment

Scalability

It's harder to scale a monolithic architecture.

Distributed

Pros

Scalability

Choice of communication styles (sync/async)

Distributed architectures offer more choices of communication styles (and trade-offs).

Cons

Performance

Complexity

Distributed architectures are more complex, as you learned in Chapter 5.

Exercise Solution

From page 269

Which of the following systems might be well suited for the microkernel architectural style, and why? *Hint: Take into account its superpowers, its kryptonite, and the nature of each system.*

An online auction system where users can bid on items

Why? This system requires high scalability but not a lot of customization, making it less suitable for a microkernel architecture.

☐ Well suited for microkernel
☐ Might be a fit for microkernel
☒ Not well suited for microkernel

A large backend financial system for processing and settling international wire transfers overnight

Why? Rules for wire transfers are likely to differ by country of origin. A microkernel is one way to address this problem. (However, scalability may be a concern for a monolithic microkernel.)

☒ Well suited for microkernel
☐ Might be a fit for microkernel
☐ Not well suited for microkernel

A company entering a new line of business that expects constant changes to its system

Why? If the company can partition changes to plugins and avoid having a volatile core, a microkernel will allow it to bring out new features in isolation.

☒ Well suited for microkernel
☐ Might be a fit for microkernel
☐ Not well suited for microkernel

A small bakery that wants to start taking online orders

Why? With no compelling reason for customization and a simple problem, a microkernel isn't a terrific fit here.

☐ Well suited for microkernel
☐ Might be a fit for microkernel
☒ Not well suited for microkernel

A trouble ticket system for electronics purchased with a support plan, in which field technicians come to customers to fix problems

Why? If customers, devices, or other parts of the system require customizations, a microkernel is one way to implement them.

☐ Well suited for microkernel
☒ Might be a fit for microkernel
☐ Not well suited for microkernel

Microkernel Crossword Solution

From page 271

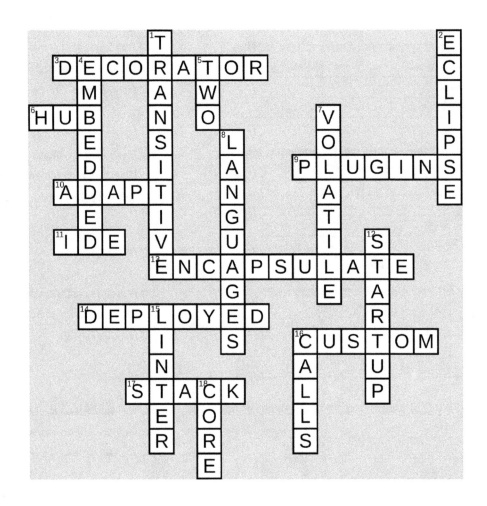

9 do it yourself

The TripEZ Travel App

Ready to extend your journey into software architecture? In this chapter, you're the software architect. You'll be determining architectural characteristics, building a logical architecture, making architectural decisions, and deciding whether to use a layered, modular, or microkernel architecture. The exercises in this chapter will give you an end-to-end view of what a software architect does and show you how much you've learned. Get ready to create an architecture for a startup company building a travel integration convenience site. *Bon voyage*—we hope you have a good trip building your architecture.

Making travel easier

You've just been hired as a software architect by an exciting new startup called TripEZ (pronounced like "trapeze") that wants to make travel easier, especially for "road warriors" who travel frequently. The TripEZ app will be an online trip management dashboard that allows travelers to see all of their existing reservations organized by trip, through either a web browser or their mobile devices.

TripEZ requirements document

☐ The system should continually poll the user's email account for travel-related emails.

☐ The system must interface with the systems of travel partners (like travel agencies, booking apps, airlines, hotels, and car rental companies) to update travel details. These include delays, cancellations, updates, and gate changes. To beat the competition, updates must appear in the app within five minutes.

☐ Users should be able to add, update, or delete existing reservations manually.

☐ Users should be able to group items in the dashboard by trip. Once the trip is complete, the items should automatically be removed from the dashboard.

☐ Users should be able to share their trip information by interfacing with standard social media sites and by sharing it with specific people.

☐ The system should have the richest user interface possible, across all deployment platforms.

☐ The system should provide end-of-year summary reports with a wide range of metrics about users' travel that year.

☐ TripEZ should gather analytical data—such as travel trends, locations, airline and hotel vendor preferences, and cancellation and update frequency—from users' trips for various purposes.

☐ The company would like to ship TripEZ in six months, to coincide with an important trade show.

Meet Travis, former pilot and consultant to TripEZ. He has a few more important requirements for the system.

Pay attention, because these things are important.

"TripEZ must integrate seamlessly with the existing standard interface systems used across the travel industry, including internationally.

It must integrate with the user's preferred travel agency (if any) to resolve problems quickly.

Finally, users must be able to access the system at all times. Unplanned downtime should be limited to a maximum of five minutes per month."

TripEZ's user workflow

Now that we have the requirements, let's get a better understanding of them by
looking at the primary workflow for travelers using TripEZ.

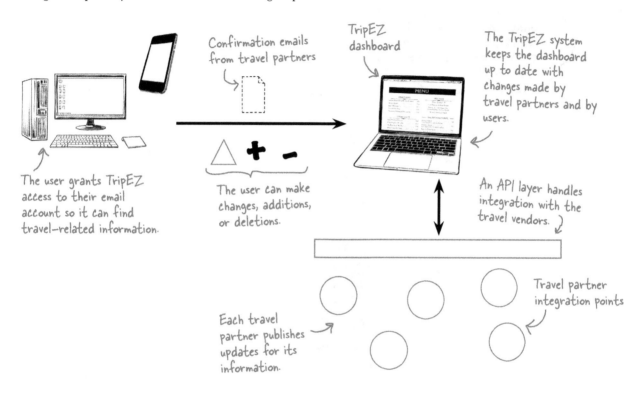

Confirmation emails
from travel partners

TripEZ
dashboard

The TripEZ system
keeps the dashboard
up to date with
changes made by
travel partners and by
users.

The user grants TripEZ
access to their email
account so it can find
travel-related information.

The user can make
changes, additions,
or deletions.

An API layer handles
integration with the
travel vendors.

Each travel
partner publishes
updates for its
information.

Travel partner
integration points

Sharpen your pencil

Given the requirements for TripEZ, list some challenges that you will need to address when
creating an architectural solution.

⟶ Solution on page 294

Planning the architecture

I've given you the requirements, so what's the big delay? Why aren't you developing the system? We only have six months!

← Even though Travis is impatient to see some progress, don't let that stop you from creating a solid, well–thought–out architecture.

We have to create an architecture first. ↙

As you've learned, architecture is a critical and necessary part of any software system. Without it, the system will likely fail to achieve any of its goals.

Before we start developing code, we have to create an architecture. This means going back to Chapter 1, where you learned about the four dimensions of software architecture.

Don't worry—we'll get the system done. But first, it's important to know what we're building.

The architects' roadmap

Let's get the TripEZ architecture started. You'll use the steps you've learned in previous chapters to translate the requirements into an architecture.

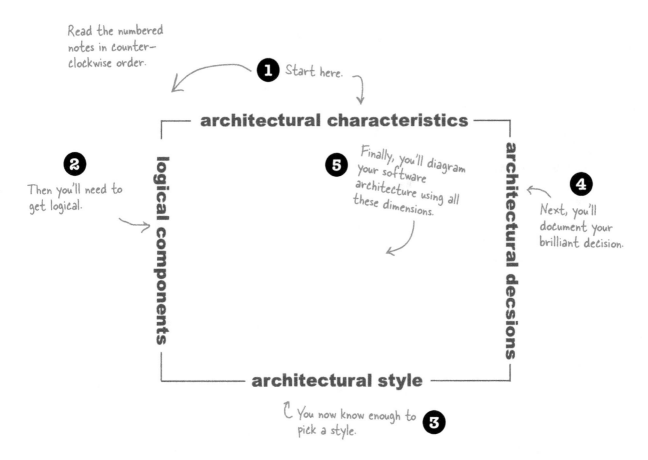

Read the numbered notes in counter-clockwise order.

1 Start here.

architectural characteristics

2

Then you'll need to get logical.

logical components

5 Finally, you'll diagram your software architecture using all these dimensions.

architectural decisions

4

Next, you'll document your brilliant decision.

architectural style

You now know enough to pick a style. **3**

This diagram will serve as your roadmap as you make your way through each of the exercises, so get used to seeing it. The next few pages will walk you through each of these steps.

Good luck on your journey—TripEZ is counting on you.

Step 1:
Identify architectural characteristics

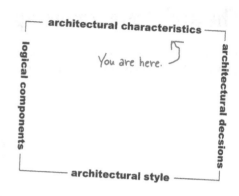

"TripEZ must integrate seamlessly with the existing standard interface systems used across the travel industry, including internationally.

It must integrate with the user's preferred travel agency (if any) to resolve problems quickly.

Finally, users must be able to access the system at all times. Unplanned downtime should be limited to a maximum of five minutes per month."

We copied the requirements here to make it easier for you to use them to identify the driving architectural characteristics.

TripEZ requirements document

☐ The system should continually poll the user's email account for travel-related emails.

☐ The system must interface with the interface systems of travel partners (like travel agencies, booking apps, airlines, hotels, and car rental companies) to update travel details. These include delays, cancellations, updates, and gate changes. To beat the competition, updates must appear in the app within five minutes.

☐ Users should be able to add, update, or delete existing reservations manually.

☐ Users should be able to group items in the dashboard by trip. Once the trip is complete, the items should automatically be removed from the dashboard.

☐ Users should be able to share their trip information by interfacing with standard social media sites and by sharing it with specific people.

☐ The system should have the richest user interface possible, across all deployment platforms.

☐ The system should provide end-of-year summary reports with a wide range of metrics about users' travel that year.

☐ TripEZ should gather analytical data—such as travel trends, locations, airline and hotel vendor preferences, and cancellation and update frequency—from users' trips for various purposes.

☐ The company would like to ship TripEZ in six months, to coincide with an important trade show.

Exercise

In Chapter 2, we showed you how to use this template to limit the number of architectural characteristics. Flip back to page 70 if you need a refresher on how to use it.

Top 3	Driving Characteristics	Implicit Characteristics
☐	_____	*feasibility (cost/time)*
☐	_____	*security*
☐	_____	*maintainability*
☐	_____	*observability*
☐	_____	
☐	_____	
☐	_____	

↖ These are implied characteristics. Move them to the Driving Characteristics column if you think they are <u>critical</u> to the success of the system.

↖ Pick the top three most important ones (in any order).

Go back to Chapter 2 if you need a refresher on the definitions of these common architectural characteristics.

Common Candidate Architectural Characteristics

performance	data integrity	deployability
responsiveness	data consistency	testability
availability	adaptability	configurability
fault tolerance	extensibility	customizability
scalability	interoperability	recoverability
elasticity	concurrency	auditability

→ Solution on page 293

Step 2:
Identify logical components

Good job! Now that you've identified the critical architectural characteristics for TripEZ, it's time to apply what you've learned to create logical components.

Referring to the requirements and primary workflow on the previous pages, use the actor/action approach described in Chapter 4 to identify actors and their actions. Then identify as many logical components as you can on the next page.

Here's some additional information you might find useful for this exercise:

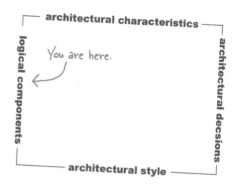

architectural characteristics

logical components

architectural decisions

architectural style

You are here.

- When users sign up for TripEZ, they provide credentials to allow the different travel services to provide up-to-date status reports on delays, cancellations, and so on.
- If a travel partner's integration point won't supply updates within the required five-minute window, the system should query the vendor.
- Updates, especially to the mobile application, should use as little data as possible to accommodate potentially spotty cell signals in remote places.
- TripEZ can't be held responsible for integration point availability; if the call fails, the system must return an error rather than failing silently (which would mislead the user into thinking no update was sent).

This allows the system to work with travel partners that can't meet its agreed—upon thresholds.

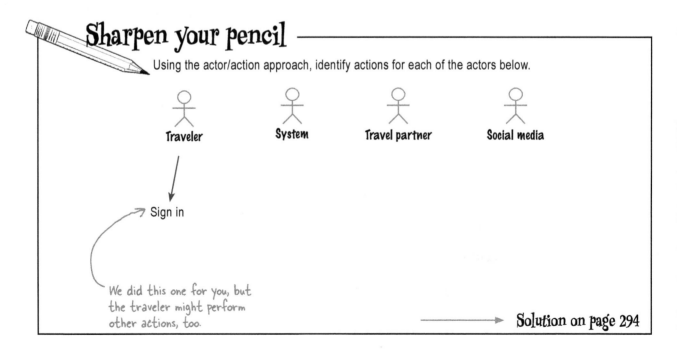

Sharpen your pencil

Using the actor/action approach, identify actions for each of the actors below.

Traveler   System   Travel partner   Social media

Sign in

We did this one for you, but the traveler might perform other actions, too.

Solution on page 294

Exercise

Using the space below, draw your logical components and their interactions.

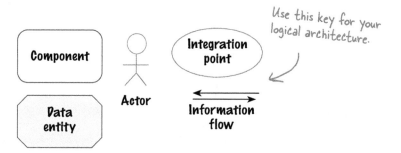

Use this key for your logical architecture.

Component

Actor

Integration point

Data entity

Information flow

⟶ Solution on page 295

Step 3:
Choose an architectural style

Leveraging what you've learned about the layered, modular monolith, and microkernel architectural styles, use the next page to analyze their pros and cons with respect to the TripEZ system. You'll also need to refer to the requirements, your logical architecture, and the star rating charts for each architectural style (we've added those below for you). Choose an architectural style based on your analysis.

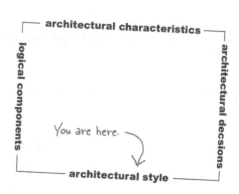

Layered

Architectural Characteristic	Star Rating
Maintainability	★
Testability	★ ★
Deployability	★
Simplicity	★ ★ ★ ★ ★
Evolvability	★
Performance	★ ★ ★
Scalability	★
Elasticity	★
Fault Tolerance	★
Overall Cost	$

Modular Monolith

Architectural Characteristic	Star Rating
Maintainability	★ ★ ★
Testability	★ ★ ★
Deployability	★ ★ ★
Simplicity	★ ★ ★ ★
Evolvability	★ ★ ★
Performance	★ ★ ★
Scalability	★
Elasticity	★
Fault Tolerance	★
Overall Cost	$ $

Microkernel

Architectural Characteristic	Star Rating
Maintainability	★ ★ ★
Testability	★ ★ ★
Deployability	★ ★ ★
Simplicity	★ ★ ★ ★
Evolvability	★ ★ ★
Performance	★ ★ ★
Scalability	★
Elasticity	★
Fault Tolerance	★
Overall Cost	$

The more stars, the better that characteristic is supported.

Apologies for the tiny font, but remember—you can always flip back to individual chapters to see the star ratings for a particular style.

Here are some considerations that might help you decide which architectural style would be better suited for TripEZ:

- Go back to your logical architecture diagram and see if you can identify distinct technical or business concerns. If so, a layered or modular monolith architecture might be a good choice.

- Think about different points of integration. If there are many, each with specific logic, then a microkernel architecture might be a good fit.

Exercise

Outline the pros and cons of each architectural style to help you make a choice about which one might be most appropriate for TripEZ.

Layered Monolith Architecture Analysis

Pros | Cons

Modular Monolith Architecture Analysis

Pros | Cons

Microkernel Architecture Analysis

Pros | Cons

List your winning choice here: _____

Solution on page 296

Step 4:
Document your decision

Congratulations on choosing which architectural style to use for TripEZ. Now's your chance to explain *why* you made the choice you did and document your architectural decision.

As you learned in Chapter 3, an **architectural decision record**, or ADR, is an effective way to document your architectural decisions. Use the ADR on the next page to document your architectural style decision. Assume this is your 11th architectural decision.

Revisit Chapter 3 if you need a refresher on architectural decision records.

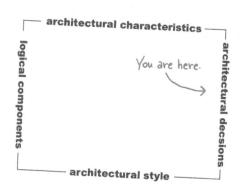

You are here.

What should I put in the Consequences section of my ADR if my architectural decision doesn't have any consequences?

Every architectural decision has consequences.

Maybe it's about cost, or maybe it's sacrificing a little bit of performance to have better security. Regardless, *every* architectural decision has consequences.

Think about the trade-off analysis you just did. Each one of those trade-offs implies a consequence—something you were willing to give up (or accept) to get something better. The Consequences section of an ADR is a great place to document your trade-off analysis and the corresponding consequences of your decision.

If you can't find any consequences in your architectural decision, keep looking, because they're there.

Exercise

Architectural Decision Record

Title:

Status: Proposed ⟵ We did this one for you.

Context:

Decision:

Consequences: ⟵ What is the impact of your decision? What trade-offs are you willing to accept?

⟶ Solutions on pages 297–299

Step 5:
Diagram your architecture

Now it's time to combine all four dimensions of software architecture and show us your vision of the TripEZ architecture. In this last exercise, you'll diagram your architecture on the following page using the key on this page.

We didn't give you a lot of room to diagram your architecture, and that's on purpose. While many architecture diagrams are very detailed, what we're asking you to do here is to sketch out a *high-level physical view* of the user interfaces, databases, and components that make up your architecture and how they all connect to each other.

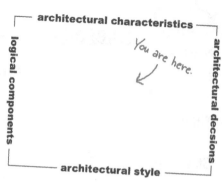

Physical Architecture Key

User Interface

Draw a computer screen to represent the ***user interface*** and indicate which types of ***users*** are interacting with it. For example, if you have separate user interfaces for desktops and mobile devices, show two computer screens.

Feel free to annotate your diagram to clarify points or describe things.

(Component)

Use a rounded box to represent a ***component***. These should match the logical components you identified in the previous exercise. Be sure to give your components a meaningful and descriptive names.

Layer

Use a box to a represent a ***layer*** (if your architecture needs layers). Again, be sure to give each layer a meaningful name.

Database

Draw a cylinder to represent each ***physical database*** in your solution.

Arrows represent communication to and from the user interface and database.

Exercise

Use this space and refer to the key on the previous page to sketch your physical architecture for TripEZ.

Solutions on pages 300–302

There are no right (or wrong) answers

Congratulations—you've just created an architecture!

What we're about to show you are the exercise "solutions." We've used quotes there because the solutions we present here are just some of *many* possible solutions. You see, there are no right or wrong answers in software architecture: it's all about analyzing trade-offs and being able to justify your decisions.

Compare your answers with the ones we're about to show you to see how your solutions differ. You can think about what you might have done differently, or confirm that you made what seems to you to be the most appropriate choice. We'll show you our TripEZ architectures for layered, modular monolith, *and* microkernel architectures, since all of these styles are viable options.

Software architecture is *always* a learning process. Each new problem brings a whole new set of conditions, constraints, and business and technical concerns. There is no one-size-fits-all architecture—it's up to you, the architect, to come up with the most appropriate architecture for your situation.

Bullet Points

- When analyzing requirements for a business problem, always gather additional information from the business stakeholders or project sponsor.

- While there's no "checklist" for creating an architecture, the four dimensions of software architecture (introduced in Chapter 1) provide a good roadmap.

- Identifying driving architectural characteristics requires you to analyze the business requirements and technical constraints.

- Implicit architectural characteristics become *driving characteristics* if they are critical or important to the success of the system.

- Make sure you can tie each driving characteristic back to some sort of requirement or business need.

- When identifying logical components and creating a corresponding logical architecture, try to avoid adding physical details such as services, databases, queues, and user interfaces—those artifacts go into the *physical architecture*.

- When choosing an architectural style, make sure you consider the characteristics of the architectural style, the problem domain, and the driving architectural characteristics you identified.

- *Hybrid architectures* (those combining two or more different architectural styles) are very common. If you use one, be sure to verify that it addresses your critical architectural characteristics.

- *Architectural decision records* (ADRs) are a great way to document your choices. They communicate the reasons for your architectural decisions as well as your trade-off analyses.

- When diagramming your physical architecture, be sure to include all the components you identified in your logical architecture.

- Remember, there are no right or wrong answers in software architecture. As long as you can provide a reasonable justification for your architectural decisions, you're on the right track.

Exercise Solution

From page 283

In Chapter 2, we showed you how to use this template to limit the number of architectural characteristics. Flip back to page 70 if you need a refresher on how to use it.

Top 3	Driving Characteristics	Implicit Characteristics
☐	**feasibility** *We only have six months.*	(*feasibility* *(cost/time)*)
☒	**performance**	*security*
☒	**scalability**	*maintainability*
☐	**elasticity**	*observability*
☒	**extensible/evolvable** ← *TripEZ is going to need lots of integrations with email providers and social media sites.*	
☐	**availability**	
☐		

Common Candidate Architectural Characteristics

performance	data integrity	deployability
responsiveness	data consistency	testability
availability	adaptability	configurability
fault tolerance	extensibility	customizability
scalability	interoperability	recoverability
elasticity	concurrency	auditability

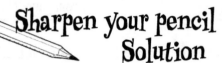

From page 279

Sharpen your pencil
Solution

Given the requirements for TripEZ, list some challenges that you will need to address when creating an architectural solution.

- Making sure that we can deliver alerts in time
- Supporting a sufficient number of users
- Finding a way to manage all the different integration points
- Integrating with social media accounts

From page 284

Sharpen your pencil
Solution

Using the actor/action approach, identify actions for each of the actors below.

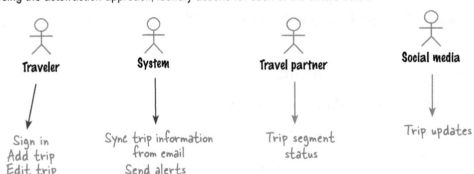

Traveler

Sign in
Add trip
Edit trip
Delete trip
Receive alerts

System

Sync trip information
from email
Send alerts

Travel partner

Trip segment
status

Social media

Trip updates

Exercise
Solution

From page 285

Using the space below, draw your logical components and their interactions.

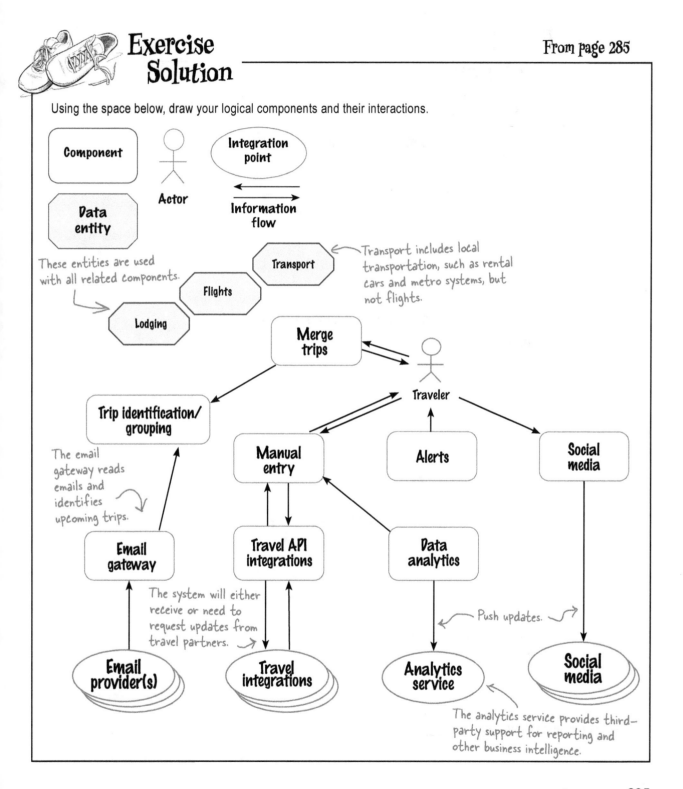

Component

Actor

Integration point

Data entity

Information flow

These entities are used with all related components.

Transport

Flights

Lodging

Transport includes local transportation, such as rental cars and metro systems, but not flights.

Merge trips

Traveler

Trip identification/ grouping

The email gateway reads emails and identifies upcoming trips.

Manual entry

Alerts

Social media

Email gateway

Travel API integrations

Data analytics

The system will either receive or need to request updates from travel partners.

Email provider(s)

Travel integrations

Analytics service

Social media

Push updates.

The analytics service provides third-party support for reporting and other business intelligence.

Exercise Solution

From page 287

Outline the pros and cons of each architectural style to help you make a choice about which one might be most appropriate for TripEZ.

Layered Monolith Architecture Analysis

Pros

A layered architecture, being a monolith, is fairly simple, so it provides a high degree of feasibility.

Partitioning by technical concerns makes adding third-party integrations easier.

Monolithic architectures lend themselves to better performance, which is one of TripEZ's priorities.

Cons

Making changes to the domain in a layered architecture can be cumbersome because the domain is smeared across multiple layers.

As TripEZ grows, the system will need to be monitored continuously to ensure that it can scale.

Modular Monolith Architecture Analysis

Pros

A modular monolith architecture, being a monolith, is fairly simple, so it provides a high degree of feasibility.

Partitioning by domains fits better here, because it eliminates the need to split domain parts out by their technical capabilities.

Monolithic architectures lend themselves to better performance, which is one of TripEZ's priorities.

Cons

Adding more integration partners may require changes to a large number of domains.

As TripEZ grows, the system will need to be monitored continuously to ensure that it can scale.

Microkernel Architecture Analysis

Pros

A monolithic microkernel architecture is fairly simple, so it provides a high degree of feasibility.

A microkernel is well suited to the job, given TripEZ's need for integration flexibility.

Monolithic microkernel architectures lend themselves to better performance, which is one of TripEZ's priorities.

Cons

Any changes that affect the core must be considered carefully.

As TripEZ grows, the system will need to be monitored continuously to ensure that it can scale.

List your winning choice here: _Turns out any of these would work; they'd just have different trade-offs._

We're going to show you ADRs and architecture diagrams for all three!

Exercise Solution

From page 289

Architectural Decision Record

Title: O11: Use of the layered monolith architectural style for the TripEZ system

Status: Proposed

Context:

TripEZ is a fast-growing startup that requires a simple architecture to ensure feasibility. Additionally, the company needs to ensure extensibility to accommodate multiple third-party integrations.

Decision:

We will use the layered monolith architectural style. Since TripEZ doesn't need separate architectural characteristics for different parts of its system, a layered monolith will suffice for the required architectural characteristics. The main constraint is scalability.

Additionally, separating the system by technical capabilities makes extensibility easier.

Consequences:

Because we chose a monolithic architecture, scalability may eventually grow to be a concern.

Building a layered architecture makes some domain-centric changes harder because the effort will affect multiple layers.

Architects will be able to change technical capabilities (such as adding support for new user interfaces) easily thanks to this architectural style's technical partitioning.

Exercise Solution

From page 289

Architectural Decision Record

Title: 011: Use of the modular monolith architectural style for the TripEZ system

Status: Proposed

Context:

TripEZ is a fast-growing startup that wants to make sure to model its architecture in a way that allows for the easiest possible migration to a distributed architecture, while still being simple enough to build on a tight schedule.

Decision:

We will use the modular monolith architectural style. We've chosen a development process that aligns well with the domain partitioning exhibited by this architecture.

Keeping each bounded context within a component boundary helps developers understand the system's organization. Additionally, the system can grow in a similar way to the problem domain.

Our organization has adopted domain-driven design, and this architectural style aligns nicely with that approach.

Consequences:

Because we've chosen a monolithic architecture, scalability may eventually grow to be a concern.

Holistic changes to technical capabilities (such as user interfaces) are more difficult in this architecture, since the UI is handled by a part of each bounded context.

Exercise Solution

From page 289

Architectural Decision Record

Title: O11: Use of the microkernel architectural style for the TripEZ system.

Status: Proposed

Context:

> You may have noticed that the context is slightly different, even though it's the same system. This reflects differing team priorities.

TripEZ is essentially an integration architecture, managing similar information from a variety of integration partners. This architecture will easily facilitate both isolation and customization for each integration point via plugins.

Decision:

We will use the microkernel architectural style.

Time to market and extensibility are important to the company, so modeling the architecture around a simple core with plugins for future additional integration partners will make it easy for developers to understand and implement.

We decided that the simplicity of a monolithic system outweighed the benefits (but added complexity) of distributed plugins.

Consequences:

In a monolithic architecture, scalability may eventually grow to be a concern. The team may consider distributing the plugins in the future, but we decided that it would be overengineering for now.

The core can be split so that the UI is handled by another microkernel, with different plugins for different UI types.

We should avoid adding fast-changing requirements to the core. It should be as stable as possible.

Exercise Solution

From page 291

Use this space and refer to the key on page 290 to sketch your physical architecture for TripEZ.

Layered monolithic architecture diagram

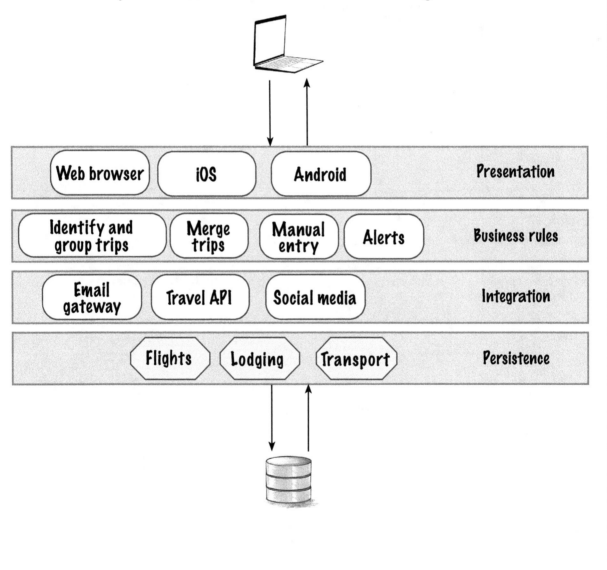

Exercise Solution

From page 291

Use this space and refer to the key on the page 290 to sketch your physical architecture for TripEZ.

Modular monolithic architecture diagram

All of these domains might have layers just like those in the Identify and Group Trips domain. We just aren't showing them.

Remember, this is a monolith with one backing database.

Identify and group trips

Add/edit/delete trips
- Presentation
- Business rules
- Persistence

Merge trips

Merge trips

Manual entry

Handle manual entry

Alerts

Alert user

Email gateway

Emails from partners

Travel API

Receive/poll travel APIs

Social media

Update social media

The persistence layer in the Manual Entry domain will manage all the data entities, like Flights, Lodging, etc.

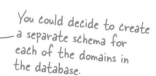

You could decide to create a separate schema for each of the domains in the database.

Exercise Solution

From page 291

Use this space and refer to the key on the prior page to sketch your physical architecture for TripEZ.

Microkernel architecture diagram

The entities that appear in the persistence layer in a layered architecture become part of the larger domain's components, including persistence logic.

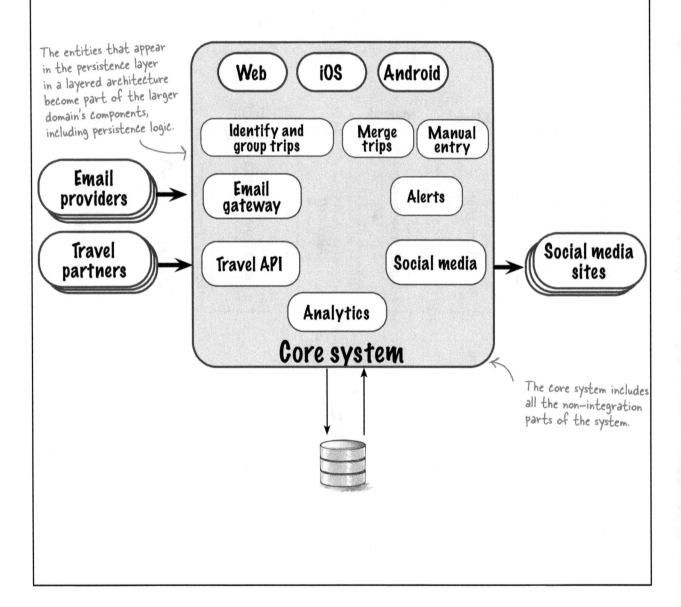

The core system includes all the non-integration parts of the system.

10 microservices architecture
Bit by Bit

How do you make an architecture easier to change? Business is changing faster than ever, and software architectures need to keep up. In this chapter you'll learn how to create a flexible architecture that can change as your business changes, scale as your business grows, and remain operational even when system failures occur. Intrigued? We hope so, because in this chapter we're going to show you *microservices*—an architectural style that solves all of these problems and more. Let's get started on our journey through microservices, bit by bit.

Are you feeling okay?

StayHealthy, Inc., is a company that specializes in medical monitoring systems for patients in hospitals. Using its systems, doctors and nurses can monitor a patient's heart rate, oxygen levels, body temperature, blood sugar levels, and more, and even determine whether the patient is sleeping or awake. If something goes wrong, a doctor or nurse is notified right away.

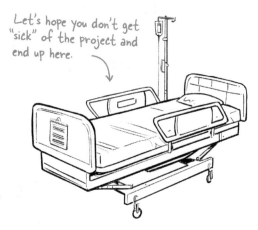

Let's hope you don't get "sick" of the project and end up here.

Recent advances in medicine have given rise to a new set of needs for medical monitoring. As a result, StayHealthy plans to leverage newer technology to replace its current patient medical monitoring software with a new system called MonitorMe. Guess what? You're the architect they chose for the new project.

Below are the requirements for the new system. You'll need to figure out what kind of architecture would be best suited for the job.

StayHealthy MonitorMe requirements document

☐ The system reads inputs from StayHealthy's patient monitoring equipment and sends the results to a single monitoring screen.

☐ MonitorMe must analyze each patient's vital signs and alert a medical professional if it detects a change that reaches a preset threshold.

☐ For each vital sign, the system must record all readings and measurements for the past five minutes. A medical professional should be able to review this five-minute history.

☐ Medical professionals select how they'd like to be notified if something goes wrong. Notifications can be sent to an assigned nurse or doctor's cell phone or to a central nurses' station.

☐ MonitorMe reads inputs from eight different input sources. It is vital that if any of these fails, the other inputs will still be monitored and recorded.

☐ The vital signs monitored by the MonitorMe system include heart rate, blood pressure, oxygen level, blood sugar, respiration rate, electrocardiogram (ECG), body temperature, and sleep status (sleep or awake).

☐ The system can measure the vital signs of multiple patients (up to 500) within a single hospital, meaning each physical hospital location has its own copy of the complete system (including the data).

Sharpen your pencil

Based on the problem domain and requirements document on the previous page, check off the **top five** architectural characteristics you think are **critical** to the MonitorMe architecture and indicate why you think they are critical.

☐ **Testability (the ease and completeness of testing)**
Reason: _____

☐ **Responsiveness (the time it takes to get a response to the medical professional)**
Reason: _____

☐ **Deployability (the difficulty and ceremony involved in releasing changes)**
Reason: _____

☐ **Abstraction (the level of isolation and knowledge between parts of the system)**
Reason: _____

☐ **Scalability (the system's ability to grow to accommodate more users or patients)**
Reason: _____

☐ **Fault tolerance (the system's ability to continue operating when parts of the system fail)**
Reason: _____

☐ **Data integrity (the data is consistent and correct across the system and there is no data loss)**
Reason: _____

☐ **Workflow (the system's ability to handle complex business workflows)**
Reason: _____

☐ **Concurrency (the system's ability to process concurrent requests or operations)**
Reason: _____

⟶ Solution on page 338

Cubicle conversation

Sam: I think we can all agree that microservices is a perfect fit for the new MonitorMe system.

Mara: Hold on—what brought you to that conclusion so quickly?

Sam: It's obvious, isn't it? From a domain perspective, we have independent monitoring functions, and we need high fault tolerance and comprehensive testability. Microservices does all this and more.

Assumptions like this are a common trap. We'll show you how to avoid it by better understanding the microservices architectural style and its trade-offs.

Alex: Slow down a second. I'm not familiar with microservices, and I have no idea how it supports all the things you say it does.

Mara: I agree with Alex. I know that we need a distributed architecture, so microservices might be a fit here. But let's back up and take a closer look before we jump to any conclusions.

Sam: Okay, I see your point—what might seem obvious to me might not be obvious to you. It's important that you both understand what microservices is all about, and then *together* we can decide if it's the right fit for MonitorMe. So let's get started.

What's a microservice?

What's in a name? When it comes to microservices, plenty. We'll show you what a microservice is and how it differs from other types of services.

Monitor All Vital Signs

Generally, a ***service*** is a separately deployed unit of software that performs some business or infrastructure process. For example, a single Monitor All Vital Signs service in MonitorMe might perform a lot of functions, including monitoring the patient's heart rate, blood pressure, temperature, and so on. This service does quite a bit, but we still call it a *service*.

← This large service monitors all of a patient's vital signs.

This is quite a small service because it only performs a single function—let's call it a "micro"—service.

The prefix ***micro-*** in microservice refers not to physical size, but to *what the service does*. For example, a Monitor Heart Rate service is single-purpose and does one thing really well—it monitors a heart rate. That's the idea behind microservices. By contrast, the larger Monitor All Vital Signs service performs many vital sign monitoring functions.

Monitor Heart Rate

A microservice is a single-purpose, separately deployed unit of software that does one thing really well.

Exercise

We're having trouble determining what *single-purpose* means. Can you help us by checking off all the functions below that you would consider single-purpose and therefore possible microservices?

- ☐ **Add a movie to your personal "to watch" list**
- ☐ **Pay for an order using your credit card**
- ☐ **Generate sales-forecasting and financial-performance reports**
- ☐ **Submit and process a loan application to get that new car you've always wanted**
- ☐ **Determining the shipping cost for an online order**

⟶ Solution on page 339

It's my data, not yours

Another feature that makes microservices special is that they own their own data. In other words, each microservice is the only one that can directly access its data.

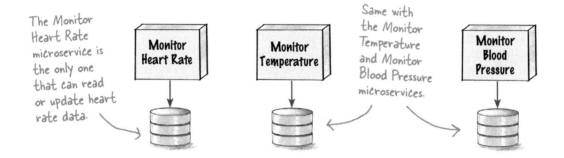

The Monitor Heart Rate microservice is the only one that can read or update heart rate data.

Same with the Monitor Temperature and Monitor Blood Pressure microservices.

Why? The primary reason is to *manage change control*. Say you have 50 microservices, all sharing the same data. If one microservice changes the structure of its data, which the other 49 microservices are *also* accessing, *all* of those other services will need to change *at the same time*. (Is your head exploding yet?)

A physical bounded context includes the microservice and all of its data.

Physically associating a microservice with its data is known as creating a ***physical bounded context***. Physical bounded contexts help manage change and coupling. If other microservices need access to data they don't own, they must ask the owning service for it.

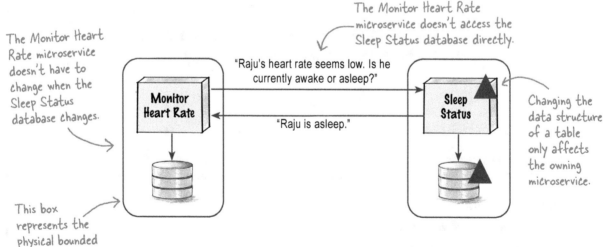

The Monitor Heart Rate microservice doesn't have to change when the Sleep Status database changes.

The Monitor Heart Rate microservice doesn't access the Sleep Status database directly.

"Raju's heart rate seems low. Is he currently awake or asleep?"

"Raju is asleep."

Changing the data structure of a table only affects the owning microservice.

This box represents the physical bounded context.

In the example above, the Monitor Heart Rate microservice is *asking for* the data rather than *directly accessing* the data. This way, even if the Sleep Status data structures change, the Monitor Heart Rate microservice doesn't have to. This is the whole idea behind physical bounded contexts.

Sharpen your pencil

We created the following services for an ecommerce site, but we need your help in figuring out the data ownership and bounded contexts. Can you associate the database tables below with the corresponding microservices that should own the data?

This is a microservice.

Customer Wishlist	Customer Profile	Product Catalog	Inventory Control	Order Shipping

This is a database table.

Contains customer bill-to and ship-to addresses
Customer Address

We did this one for you.

Contains all product details
Item Detail

Used to calculate shipping costs
Shipping Pricing

Contains items a customer may want to buy later
Wishlist Items

Holds credit card and payment information
Customer Wallet

Contains the number of items currently in stock
Inventory

Contains the warehouse in which each product is located
Item Location

Contains customer ID, name, email, and phone number
Customer Name

Contains all shipping details for an order
Shipment Manifest

Solution on page 340

How micro is "micro"?

Figuring out how big or small a microservice should be is hard. By now you know that *a microservice is a single-purpose service that's separately deployed*. But how do you determine the scope of that single purpose?

As an example, let's take a look at the MonitorMe functionality for blood pressure. Monitoring a vital sign involves capturing the input from the medical device attached to the patient, recording the input, analyzing the measurements, and alerting a nurse or doctor if something is wrong. We can model this functionality in one of three ways:

- **Option 1:** Create a single monitoring microservice that performs all monitoring and alerting functions.

- **Option 2:** Create two separate microservices—one that captures and records vital signs data, and one that analyzes the data and alerts staff if necessary.

- **Option 3:** Create four separate microservices, each one performing a specific blood pressure monitoring function.

"Single-purpose" here means <u>analyzing</u> the blood pressure data and <u>alerting</u> staff if something is wrong.

"Single-purpose" here means <u>monitoring</u> blood pressure, which includes all four of these functions.

The white boxes are the logical components.

"Single-purpose" here only means <u>recording</u> the blood pressure.

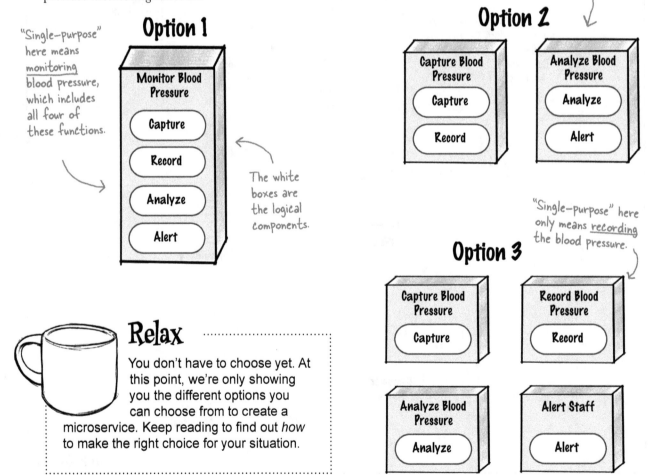

Relax

You don't have to choose yet. At this point, we're only showing you the different options you can choose from to create a microservice. Keep reading to find out *how* to make the right choice for your situation.

> Okay, so how am I supposed to know which of those options to use for monitoring blood pressure? Is this another one of those "guessing games," like with logical components?

No, granularity is not a guessing game.

Granularity—the scope of what a microservice does—is an important factor when identifying microservices. Microservices that are too fine-grained tend to communicate more with each other to complete business functions, leading to high levels of coupling, poor performance, and overall reliability issues. This is commonly referred to as the *Grains of Sand* antipattern, in which services are *so* small that they start to resemble sand on a beach. However, microservices that are too *coarse*-grained are harder and more expensive to maintain, test, and scale (which defeats the whole purpose of using microservices).

So how do you determine the most appropriate level of granularity for a microservice? By applying forces called granularity disintegrators and granularity integrators. **Granularity disintegrators** are forces that tell you to make your service smaller (meaning it's doing less work), whereas **granularity integrators** are forces that tell you to make the service bigger (meaning it's doing more work). Let's see how these forces work.

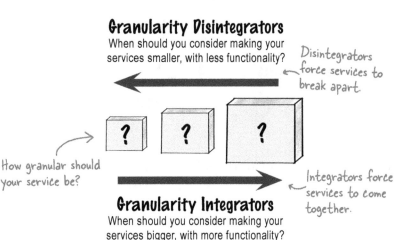

Granularity Disintegrators
When should you consider making your services smaller, with less functionality?

Disintegrators force services to break apart.

How granular should your service be?

Granularity Integrators
When should you consider making your services bigger, with more functionality?

Integrators force services to come together.

Granularity disintegrators

Granularity disintegrators are forces that help you decide whether you should break a service apart into several smaller ones. To show you how these forces can influence your decision to break a service apart, we'll take a look at MonitorMe's Monitor Basic Vital Signs functionality.

The three *basic* vital signs are blood pressure, temperature, and heart rate. Since they're all related, we could put them all in the same microservice *or* create separate microservices, one for each basic vital sign.

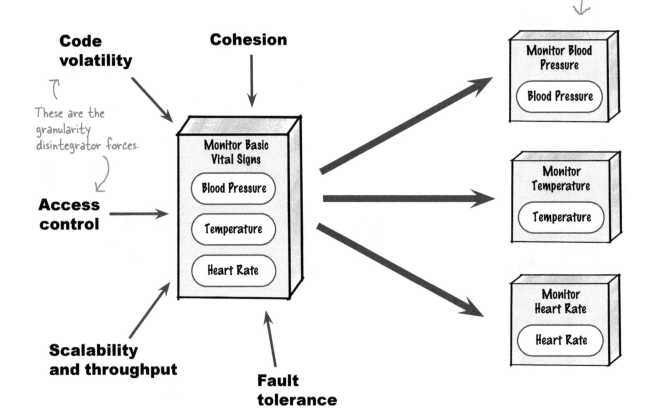

Let's analyze each of these forces to see how it might help you decide whether to break the monitoring functionality into separate microservices.

Why should you make microservices smaller?

Cohesion

A single-purpose microservice has functionality that is highly ***cohesive***—meaning all the things it does are closely related to each other. If the functionalities of a microservice lack cohesion, then it might be a good idea to break that microservice apart.

Fault tolerance and availability

Do certain functions in a microservice frequently produce fatal errors? In larger microservices, *all* functionalities become unavailable when a *part* of the microservice fails. However, if the faulty functionality is in its own separate microservice, it won't affect other functions.

Access control

The larger the service, the more difficult it is to control access to sensitive information. For example, a Patient Profile microservice containing functionality to access medical history might inadvertently allow unauthorized staff to access this sensitive (and protected) information.

Moving sensitive functionalities (like access to medical history) into their own microservices ***isolates*** them, making it easier to control access to that information.

This is also referred to as "volatility-based decomposition."

Code volatility

Does one part of the microservice change faster than others? Constant changes to one part of a large microservice mean you have to test the *entire* microservice, including functionalities you didn't change. That's a lot of extra work.

Moving a frequently changing function into its own separate microservice isolates those changes from other functions, making it much easier to maintain and test functionality.

Scalability and throughput

Do some parts of the microservice need more scalability than others? If so, breaking the service apart allows better control over which portions need to scale and which do not.

For example, suppose the heart rate monitoring function accepts sensor readings every second, but the temperature monitoring function accepts sensor readings once every 5 minutes. Separating these monitoring functions into distinct services allows each one to accommodate a different throughput rate.

Smaller microservices start up much faster than larger ones, making much-needed functionality available to the user sooner.

Granularity integrators

Granularity integrators work in the opposite direction from disintegrators—
they help you decide when to make services *bigger* and combine their
functionalities. We'll use the same Monitor Basic Vital Signs microservice we
broke apart earlier to illustrate why you might want to consider combining
separate microservices into one larger microservice.

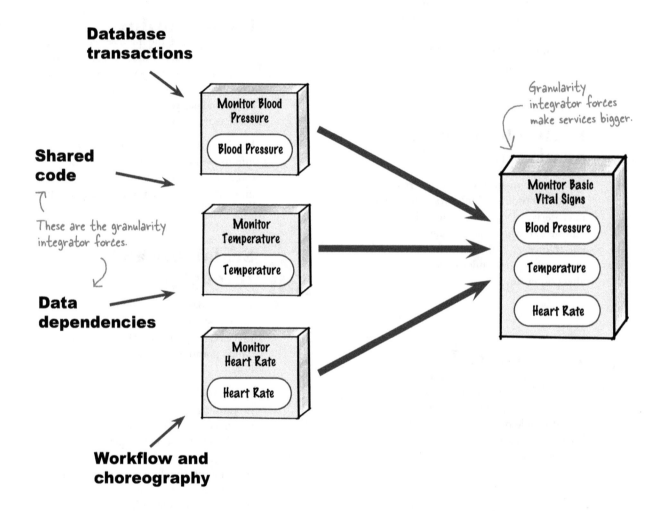

Let's analyze each of these forces to see how they might help you determine whether
you should put all this monitoring functionality into a single larger microservice.

Why should you make microservices bigger?

Database transactions

When requests involve multiple microservices, you can't perform a single database commit or rollback for all updates. Since each microservice update is in its own separate transaction, it must instead be committed or rolled back separately.

If *data consistency and integrity* are more important than any of the disintegrator forces, then it makes sense to combine the functionality into a single microservice so that operations take place in a single database transaction.

Data dependencies are one of the most common integration drivers.

Data dependencies

When you break a microservice apart, you also have to break its *data* apart. However, if the data is **highly coupled**, it will be very difficult to break it apart and form new physical bounded contexts.

An example of data coupling is when one database table refers to the key of another database table (known as a *foreign key constraint*). Another example of data coupling is when an entity (like *customer information*) is spread across multiple tables.

If your data is highly coupled and functions in the microservice need to share that data, it makes sense to keep the microservice large and combine the functions.

Workflow and choreography

If a single business request requires separate microservices to communicate with each other, that's **coupling**. Too much coupling between microservices can have many negative effects on the system.

For example, **performance** is affected by network, security, and data latency. **Scalability** is affected because each microservice in the call chain must scale as the other microservices scale (something that is hard to coordinate). **Fault tolerance** is affected because if one of the microservices in the chain becomes unresponsive or unavailable, the request cannot be processed.

If your workflow involves a lot of coordination between your microservices and these characteristics are important to you, consider combining them.

Too much communication between microservices can make an architecture look like spaghetti.

It's all about balance

Determining the appropriate level of granularity for a microservice isn't easy. You have to balance the trade-offs associated with each granularity disintegrator and integrator, and determine which trade-offs are more important. This usually involves collaborating with your product owner or business stakeholder, particularly if the trade-offs are significant.

Make it Stick

How small should a microservice be?
Use this tip and you will see.
Keep them coarse-grained when you begin,
Then move to fine-grained for the win!

You guessed it—there are trade-offs between these two forces, which is why you have to find the right balance between them.

Granularity disintegrators
When should you consider making your services smaller and separating functionalities?

Granularity integrators
When should you consider making your services bigger and combining functionalities?

Making our microservices smaller would give us better **scalability,** which is important to us.

Making our microservices bigger would give us better **data integrity,** which is important to us.

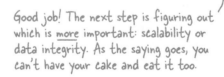

Good job! The next step is figuring out which is <u>more</u> important: scalability or data integrity. As the saying goes, you can't have your cake and eat it too.

Exercise

Now it's your turn to apply granularity disintegrators and granularity integrators to decide whether to implement the Monitor Basic Vital Signs functionality (which covers blood pressure, temperature, and heart rate) as a single microservice or three separate services. Here is some additional information:

* A patient's heart rate and blood pressure are the two most critical basic vital signs to monitor. If something should go wrong with temperature monitoring, heart rate and blood pressure monitoring must continue to work.

* All three basic vital signs share an alert functionality to notify medical professionals if something goes wrong.

* The heart rate monitoring functionality accepts sensor readings once a second, whereas the temperature and blood pressure monitoring functions only accept sensor readings once every 5 minutes.

* Each basic vital sign's data is recorded and stored separately, as simple JSON name/value pairs in a single document database. For example, the heart rate readings are stored as follows:

BPM stands for "beats per minute."

```
{"patient_id": "123",
 "timestamp": "10452955668",
 "bpm": "64"}
```

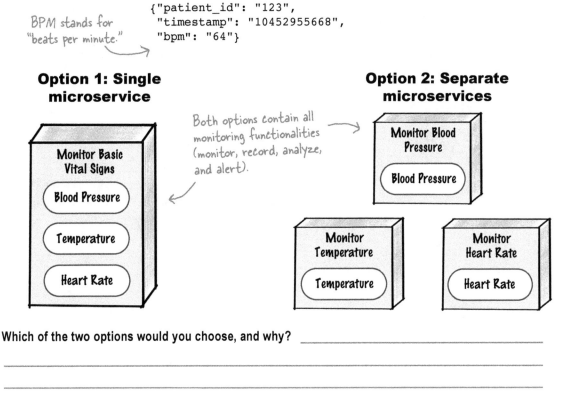

Option 1: Single microservice

Monitor Basic Vital Signs
- Blood Pressure
- Temperature
- Heart Rate

Both options contain all monitoring functionalities (monitor, record, analyze, and alert).

Option 2: Separate microservices

Monitor Blood Pressure
- Blood Pressure

Monitor Temperature
- Temperature

Monitor Heart Rate
- Heart Rate

Which of the two options would you choose, and why? _____

_____

_____

_____

_____

Solution on page 341

> If microservices is all about breaking business functionalities into separate services, what do you do with shared functionalities like logging, authorization, and date utilities?

You can still share code in microservices.

Code reuse is a necessary part of software development. Without it, you would have duplicate functionality almost everywhere in your system. Functions like logging, metrics streaming, user authorization, and basic utilities like transforming date formats are common in most (if not all) systems.

In monolithic systems, this is easy—you write the common functionality once and use it everywhere in the system, because it's all compiled together as one unit. But in *distributed* architectures like microservices, it's not that easy. That's because each microservice is a separately deployed unit of software.

So where does all that common functionality go in microservices? Usually into either a *shared library* or a *shared service*. In the following pages, we'll show you the trade-offs between these choices.

Sharing functionality

All of MonitorMe's vital-sign monitoring microservices have shared functionality
to alert a medical professional if something is wrong with the patient. Let's look
at the code:

```java
package monitorme.common;

public class AlertNurse {
    public static void sendAlert(AlertType type, String data) {
        ...
    }
}
```

Temperature

This is Java code.

"41 degrees Celsius"

Let's say we create three separate microservices for monitoring blood pressure,
temperature, and heart rate. Each one needs this common alert functionality.

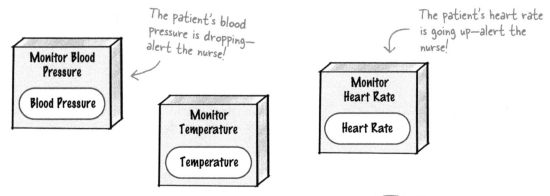

The patient's blood pressure is dropping—alert the nurse!

The patient's heart rate is going up—alert the nurse!

Where should the source code for the common alert functionality go? We *could*
replicate the code in each microservice, but that would lead to issues if anyone
changed it to fix a bug or add new functionality. That leaves us with two choices
for where to put the code: in a shared service or in a shared library. Let's look at
both options.

"Replication" means that each microservice has its own copy of the source code. This is only useful for truly static source code.

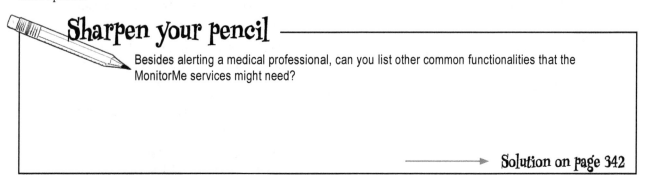

Sharpen your pencil

Besides alerting a medical professional, can you list other common functionalities that the
MonitorMe services might need?

Solution on page 342

Code reuse with a shared service

A ***shared service*** is a separate microservice that contains a shared functionality that other microservices can call remotely.

If we put the MonitorMe alert functionality in its own separate shared service, each monitoring microservice will need to call that shared service if it detects something wrong with the patient.

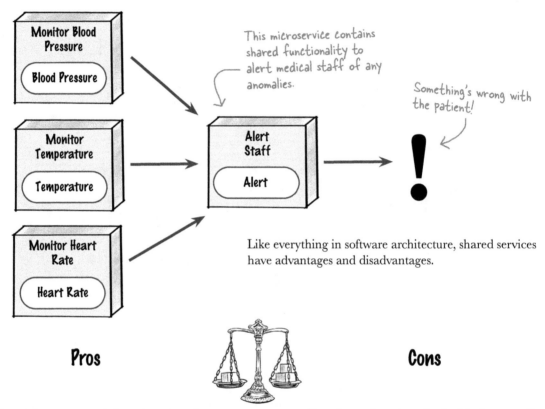

Like everything in software architecture, shared services have advantages and disadvantages.

Pros

Changing common code in a shared service doesn't require changing other microservices.

The shared service can be written in any language and on any platform, which is handy when you have microservices implemented in multiple languages.

Cons

Changing a shared service is risky because it can immediately affect other microservices that call it.

Because the shared functionality is remote, network latency can slow its performance.

If the shared service is unavailable, microservices that need the shared functions cannot operate.

The shared service must scale whenever other microservices that call it scale.

Code reuse with a shared library

A more common approach to shared functionality is to put it in a custom shared library. A **shared library** is an independent artifact (like a JAR file in Java or a DLL in C#) that is included with each microservice at compile time. This means that once the microservice is deployed, *each* microservice has *all* of the shared functionality available to it.

Most platforms and programming languages have their own shared-library file formats.

Let's see how the shared MonitorMe alerting functionality might look if we were to use a shared library rather than a shared service.

This is the Alert shared library that contains the shared alerting functionality.

This service no longer has to call a remote microservice to alert the nurse. Cool!

Do you see how the shared alert functionality is included as part of each microservice's deployment unit? This means each microservice can simply use the shared code to alert a medical professional, without having to make a remote call to a separate service.

Pros

Performance, availability, and scalability are better because the shared functionality is not remote. Instead, it's bound at compile time to each microservice.

Changing code in a shared library is less risky, because shared libraries can be versioned to provide agility and backward compatibility.

Because shared libraries can be versioned, you don't have to do this all at once.

Cons

You'll need multiple shared libraries if your microservices are written in different programming languages or use different platforms.

Managing dependencies between microservices and shared libraries can become difficult if you have a lot of microservices (which is typical in this architectural style).

If you change a shared functionality, you must retest and redeploy the microservices that use it.

Fireside Chats

Tonight's talk: **A shared service and a shared library answer the question: "Who's cooler?"**

Shared Service

Hey there, "old school." You still around?

Not a chance, bud. Don't you get it? In the distributed architecture world, I'm king. *Everything* is services—including me, the shared functionality. Need to reauthorize a user? Need to alert a nurse that the patient is having issues? Just call me. What could be easier?

Fine, you got me there. But when I have to change, I just do it. No one else has to be involved. When you change, every service you're attached to has to retest and redeploy. How disruptive you are!

At least *I'm* not a conformist. Face it—for every programming language in your environment, you have to replicate yourself. I, on the other hand, am independent. I can be implemented in *any* language or platform because I don't have the same attachment problem you have.

Whatever. Later, conformist—I'm gonna go find someone to hang out with who appreciates me.

Shared Library

"Old school?" Let me tell you something—not only am I still around, I'll outlive you by a long shot.

Right. And when you aren't around, what then? You see, unlike you, I'm *always* around, right by each microservice's side.

Oh please! I can clone myself into multiple versions. That makes me a lot safer to change. You, on the other hand, are full of risk—you can break the entire system when you redeploy! You really like to live dangerously, don't you?

Attachment problem? Really? Listen—my attachment to services means I'm faster, more available, more scalable, and more reliable than you.

And... now you're not available. See what I mean?

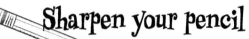

Sharpen your pencil

Now that you've seen the two main options for sharing functionality in the microservices architectural style, it's your turn to decide—should the alert functionality in MonitorMe be a shared library or a shared service? Make sure you consider external forces (like the problem domain) in addition to the pros and cons of each option, and justify your choice.

Option 1: Shared service   Option 2: Shared library

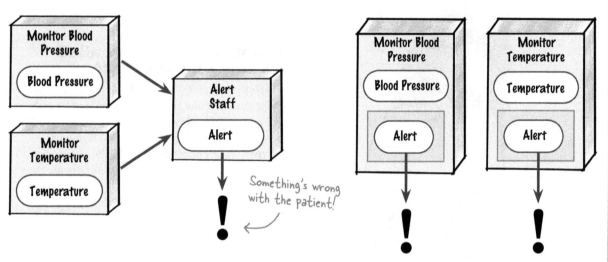

Put your decision and reasoning here.

☐ **Option 1: Shared service**
☐ **Option 2: Shared library**
Reason: _____
_____
_____
_____
_____
_____
_____

⟶ Solution on page 343

Suppose I need information from multiple services. Can I do that in a microservices architecture?

Yes, you can! This is called *workflow management.*

A *workflow* is when fulfilling a single business request—a task request that comes from a user interface—needs more than one microservice. You can manage a workflow in microservices by using either of two techniques: *orchestration* or *choreography*. In the next couple of pages, we'll show you how these work and discuss their pros and cons.

there are no
Dumb Questions

Q: If I make a request involving a workflow that needs multiple microservices to give me an answer, why break those microservices apart? Wouldn't it be better to make a single service and avoid workflows in the first place?

A: Great question. Remember the granularity disintegrators from several pages ago? Some of those factors—like scalability, fault tolerance, code volatility, and better, more secure access control—might be important enough to warrant keeping the microservices separate, even if it means you'll have to add a bit of complexity later to tie those services together with a workflow.

Managing workflows

A *workflow* is required when two or more microservices are needed to complete a single business request. The request might be a nurse (say, Juan) asking "How is the patient doing today?" To answer, the system must gather information about the patient's temperature, heart rate, and blood pressure. This means calling multiple microservices, one for each vital sign.

However, Juan doesn't want to make three separate requests to the MonitorMe system. He would like to make *a single request* to get all the vital signs information. This means the three monitoring microservices need to be coordinated in a workflow.

Let's look at how to make this happen in microservices by using either **orchestration** (centralized workflow management) or **choreography** (decentralized workflow management).

> Juan is in charge of the patient today.

> **Let's see how the patient is doing today...**

> Juan wants to get this data with a <u>single request</u>.

Monitor Heart Rate	Monitor Temperature	Monitor Blood Pressure
Heart Rate	Temperature	Blood Pressure

> Juan needs information from all three microservices, which means they need to be in a <u>workflow</u>.

Exercise

Can you think of any workflows involving multiple microservices that might exist for the MonitorMe patient vital signs monitoring system? List them in the space below.

> We did this one for you.

Get the status of a patient's basic vital signs (temperature, blood pressure, and heart rate).

Solution on page 344

Orchestration: Conducting microservices

When you go to a symphony concert, who do you see in the front, leading all the musicians? The conductor, of course. This is a great way to think about orchestration in microservices.

Orchestration is about coordinating all the microservices needed for a workflow. A centralized microservice—the ***orchestrator***—does this, very much like a conductor coordinates all the musicians performing in a symphony orchestra.

An ***orchestration service*** is a separate microservice that is responsible for calling all the microservices involved in the workflow. It also handles errors and passes consolidated data back to the caller (usually the user interface).

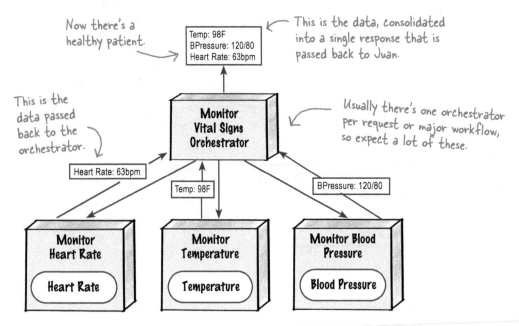

Now there's a healthy patient.

This is the data, consolidated into a single response that is passed back to Juan.

Temp: 98F
BPressure: 120/80
Heart Rate: 63bpm

This is the data passed back to the orchestrator.

Monitor Vital Signs Orchestrator

Usually there's one orchestrator per request or major workflow, so expect a lot of these.

Heart Rate: 63bpm

Temp: 98F

BPressure: 120/80

Monitor Heart Rate

Heart Rate

Monitor Temperature

Temperature

Monitor Blood Pressure

Blood Pressure

That's a lot to manage. I hope the job pays well.

Job Posting: Microservices Orchestrator

Looking for a microservices orchestrator to manage monitoring a patient's basic vital signs. Duties and responsibilities include:

- Call the right microservices in the right order.
- Always know the current state of the workflow and what happens next.
- Consolidate all the data from each microservice.
- Handle errors if any of the microservices fails.

Like everything, orchestration has trade-offs. Let's be positive and start with the good.

The good...

Sort of like a GPS—it always knows where you are.

Centralized workflow

Request workflows are centralized and well understood. You only need to go to the orchestrator to understand the complete workflow.

Workflow state

Since the orchestrator always knows where the request is in the workflow, if there's a failure, restarting the request where the workflow left off is much easier.

Error handling

Error handling is consolidated into the orchestrator, so each microservice doesn't need to worry about what to do if an error occurs—the orchestrator handles it.

Workflow changes

It's easy to change the workflow because all changes occur in one central place.

Performance

Orchestration tends to be slowed by communication between the orchestrator and the microservices, and because the orchestrator typically saves the workflow state to a database each time something changes.

Scalability

The central orchestrator can become a bottleneck as requests increase, because every request must go through it before reaching any microservices.

Tight coupling

Because the orchestrator and microservices need to communicate constantly, orchestration tends to be highly coupled.

Availability

If the conductor leaves the orchestra, the concert is over. Similarly, if the orchestration microservice is unavailable, the request cannot be processed. This single point of failure is usually addressed by creating multiple instances of the orchestrator.

The bad...

Sort of like having an understudy conductor backstage in case the conductor gets sick.

Choreography: Let's dance

Whereas orchestras are conducted, dances are ***choreographed***. Rarely do you see a conductor leading a group of classical or modern dancers—instead, the dancers learn their parts and then communicate with each other. This is a great way to think about choreography in microservices.

Let's say the MonitorMe system's blood pressure monitoring functionality is separated into four separate microservices, which communicate to complete the workflow of the monitoring operation.

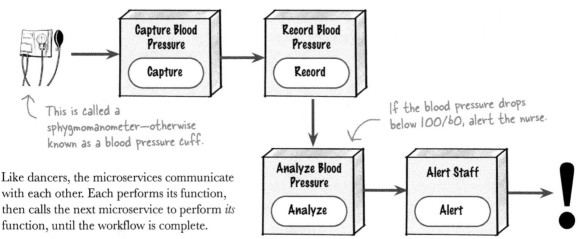

↰ This is called a sphygmomanometer—otherwise known as a blood pressure cuff.

If the blood pressure drops below 100/60, alert the nurse.

Like dancers, the microservices communicate with each other. Each performs its function, then calls the next microservice to perform *its* function, until the workflow is complete.

Don't lead the dancers!

When using choreography, make sure you don't fall into the trap of turning one of the microservices into an orchestrator. This is known as the Front Controller *pattern. This pattern is useful for orchestration, but not for choreography.*

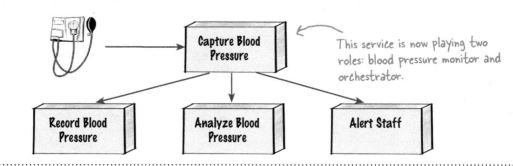

This service is now playing two roles: blood pressure monitor and orchestrator.

Guess what? Choreography has trade-offs as well.

The good...

Responsiveness
Since there's no central orchestrator to communicate with continually, responsiveness and performance tend to be better.

Loose coupling
Since microservices don't depend on a central orchestration service to direct them, the system tends to be less coupled.

Scalability
Each microservice can scale to meet its throughput demands, independent of other microservices in the workflow.

Fast, scalable systems usually use choreography. However, watch out for the trade-offs.

Error handling
Each microservice is responsible for managing the error workflow if an error occurs. This can lead to too much communication between services.

Recoverability
When a user retries a request that has failed or is still in progress, it's really hard for the system to know where to restart. That's because no single service is responsible for directing the request to a specific microservice in the workflow—each one only sends it to the next microservice in the call chain.

State management
It's hard to know what state the workflow is in when using choreography, because there's no central conductor controlling the workflow. Usually, one of the microservices (typically the first one in the call chain) is designated the **state owner,** and other microservices send it their state.

The bad...

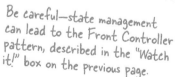

Be careful—state management can lead to the Front Controller pattern, described in the "Watch it!" box on the previous page.

Exercise

StayHealthy, Inc., stands behind MonitorMe and its monitoring devices and display screens. If a problem occurs with any software or physical hardware, someone from the medical facility can go online and create a trouble ticket. A field technician will receive the trouble ticket on their mobile phone, come to the medical facility, fix the problem, and mark the ticket as fixed.

It's up to you: Would you manage the microservices for the trouble ticket system workflow using orchestration or choreography? Be sure to include the reasons for your choice.

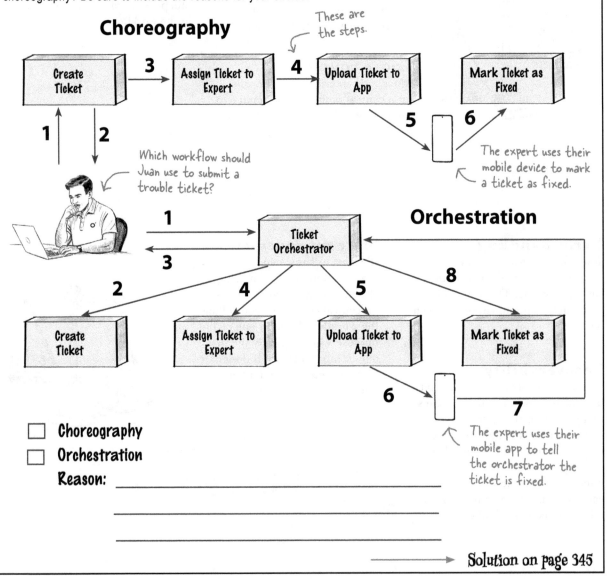

☐ **Choreography**
☐ **Orchestration**
Reason: _____

_____

_____

Solution on page 345

The microservices architectural style seems overly complex to me. There are so many hard decisions to make. Why would I ever bother to use microservices?

You're right—the microservices architectural style *is* complex. But it's also powerful.

Using microservices helps us address complex business problems. Not only does this architectural style excel at supporting operational characteristics such as scalability, reliability, availability, and fault tolerance, but it also allows the system to respond quickly to changes in both business and technology (known as *agility*).

That said, the microservices architectural style may not be a fit for every system. In the next few pages we'll show you some of the superpowers of microservices as well as its weaknesses.

Microservices architecture superpowers

Every architectural style has its superpowers. Here are some reasons to use the microservices architectural style.

Maintainability

Because microservices are single-purpose and separately deployed, you can more easily locate code that needs to change for a particular function.

Testability

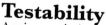

A microservice's testing scope is much smaller than that of a larger monolithic application or a system with large services. This limited scope makes it easier to fully test a microservice's functionality.

Evolvability

It's relatively easy to add functionality to a microservices architecture: you create a new service, test it, and deploy it alongside other existing microservices in your system.

Deployability

Because microservices are deployed as separate units of software, there are fewer risks involved with releasing a microservice than with large monolithic systems. You can also deploy microservices more frequently—sometimes daily.

Scalability

Microservices scale at a *function* level rather than a *system* level. This means that you scale only the functionalities you need to meet increased user load and demand, saving resources and lowering costs.

Fault tolerance

If a particular microservice fails, it doesn't bring down the entire system—only that function. Users can continue to use other functions.

Microservices architecture kryptonite

Are there reasons *not* to use the microservices architectural style? You bet there are. Just like kryptonite diminishes a superhero's powers, certain business and architectural characteristics diminish the case for using microservices. Watch out for them!

Complexity

Microservices is one of the most complex architectural styles. It involves so many hard decisions—about granularity, transactions, workflow, contracts, shared code, communication protocols, team topologies, and deployment strategies, just to name a few.

Performance

The more microservices communicate with each other, the worse their performance will be. They may have to wait for the network, undergo additional security checks, and make extra database calls.

Complex workflows

Workflows occur when you need to call multiple microservices for a single business request. If the functionality of your system is too tightly coupled, breaking it into separately deployed services will only result in a big ball of distributed mud. Yuck!

Remember—a physical bounded context includes the microservice as well as all of its data.

Monolithic databases

Each microservice must own its own data and form a physical bounded context. If your *data* can't be broken apart for whatever reason, stay away from this architectural style.

Technically partitioned teams

Does your organization consist of siloed teams of user interface developers, backend developers, and database people? If so, microservices won't work for you (a reflection of Conway's Law). Microservices architecture requires cross-functional teams. Each team owns its own group of microservices, all the way from the user interface to the database.

Microservices star ratings

Below is a useful chart for understanding what microservices architecture is good at and what it's not so good at. One star means that the architectural characteristic is not well supported; five stars means the characteristic is very well supported.

Just like movie reviews.

Architectural Characteristic	Star Rating
Maintainability	★ ★ ★ ★ ★
Testability	★ ★ ★ ★ ★
Deployability	★ ★ ★ ★ ★
Simplicity	★
Evolvability	★ ★ ★ ★ ★
Performance	★ ★
Scalability	★ ★ ★ ★ ★
Elasticity	★ ★ ★ ★
Fault Tolerance	★ ★ ★ ★ ★
Overall Cost	$ $ $ $ $

These characteristics contribute to agility—the ability to respond quickly to change.

Microservices are HARD.

We can scale microservices at a function level.

Too much communication between microservices slows down requests.

Overall cost is high due to licensing fees, breaking apart data, optimizing deployment pipelines, and reorganizing teams.

As you can see, the microservices architectural style is pretty good in terms of agility (maintainability, testability, and deployability) and operational characteristics. However, it's *not* so great when it comes to performance, simplicity, and cost.

You might be wondering about the low performance rating. This is because of latency as services communicate with each other. This latency takes on three forms: *network latency* (the time it takes the request to get to the service), *security latency* (the time it takes to reauthorize a user, for example), and *data latency* (since each microservice makes its own database calls).

Exercise

Which of the following systems might be well suited for the microservices architectural style, and why? *Hint: Take into account microservices' superpowers, its kryptonite, and the problem domain.*

An online auction system where users can bid on items

Why? _____

_____

☐ Well suited for microservices

☐ Might be a fit for microservices

☐ Not well suited for microservices

A large backend financial system for processing and settling international wire transfers overnight

Why? _____

_____

☐ Well suited for microservices

☐ Might be a fit for microservices

☐ Not well suited for microservices

A company entering a new line of business that expects constant changes to its system

Why? _____

_____

☐ Well suited for microservices

☐ Might be a fit for microservices

☐ Not well suited for microservices

A small bakery that wants to start taking online orders

Why? _____

_____

☐ Well suited for microservices

☐ Might be a fit for microservices

☐ Not well suited for microservices

A trouble ticket system for electronics purchased with a support plan, in which field technicians come to customers to fix problems

Why? _____

_____

☐ Well suited for microservices

☐ Might be a fit for microservices

☐ Not well suited for microservices

⟶ Solution on page 346

Wrapping it up

Congratulations! The MonitorMe system is up and running, and it's a success. It's all thanks to your understanding of microservices and what types of systems this approach is good for.

You've learned that while microservices can be a complicated architectural style, it also has superpowers that can help solve complex business problems (like the MonitorMe system we've been working on). Let's close this chapter by reviewing some key points about microservices.

Bullet Points

- A *microservice* is a single-purpose, separately deployed unit of software that does one thing really well.

- A *physical bounded context* means that a microservice owns its own data and is the only microservice that can access that data. If a microservice needs data that is owned by another microservice, it must ask for it.

- The *granularity* of a microservice is a measure of its size—not physically, but the scope of what it does.

- Forces that guide you to make your microservices smaller are called *granularity disintegrators*.

- Forces that guide you to make your microservices bigger are called *granularity integrators*.

- Balance granularity disintegrators and integrators to find the most appropriate level of granularity for a microservice.

- You can make microservices coarse-grained to start with, then finer-grained as you learn more about them.

- Two techniques for sharing functionality in microservices are *shared services* and *shared libraries*.

- A *shared service* is a microservice that contains a functionality shared by multiple microservices. It's deployed separately and each microservice calls it remotely. Shared services are more agile overall and are good for heterogeneous environments. However, they are not good for scalability, fault tolerance, or performance.

- A *shared library* is an independent artifact (like a JAR or DLL file) that is bound to a microservice at compile time. Shared libraries offer better operational characteristics, like scalability, performance, and fault tolerance, but make it harder to manage dependencies and control changes.

- A *workflow* is when multiple microservices are needed for a single business request or business process.

- Workflows that use *orchestration* require a central orchestrator microservice, which works like a conductor in a symphony orchestra.

- In workflows that use *choreography,* the services talk to each other, like dancers performing together.

- Scalability, fault tolerance, evolvability, and overall agility (maintainability, testability, and deployability) are the superpowers of the microservices architectural style.

- Performance, complexity, cost, monolithic databases that can't be broken apart, and high semantic coupling are kryptonite to microservices.

- Microservices should be as independent as possible; too much communication between them will degrade the benefits of this architectural style.

Microservices Crossword

Ready to have some fun and test your knowledge about what you've learned?

Across

1. Microservices make it easier for a system to do this
5. When you make a service smaller, you make it more _____
7. Each microservice _____ its own data
11. Workflow where microservices communicate with each other
14. A _____service does one thing really well
15. Microservices is this type of architecture
17. _____ tolerance keeps a problem from bringing down the whole system
18. Microservices are _____-purpose
19. When you need more than one microservice to do the job, it's a _____

Down

1. _____ handling is part of an orchestrator's job
2. Kind of component found within a microservice
3. Kind of force that pushes you to make a microservice bigger
4. Watch out for the _____ Controller pattern
6. Each microservice is a separately deployed _____ of software
8. Code resource that's often shared
9. A context that restricts data access
10. Workflow where one microservice rules all the others
12. Type of bounded context or architecture diagram
13. Good security includes restricting _____ to data
16. A bad design pattern is an _____pattern

→ Solution on page 347

Sharpen your pencil
Solution

From page 305

Based on the problem domain and requirements document on page 304, check off the **top five** architectural characteristics you think are **critical** to the MonitorMe architecture and indicate why you think they are critical.

☒ **Testability (the ease of and completeness of testing)**

Reason: Because this is a critical medical system, we can't let bugs get into the system (completeness)

☒ **Responsiveness (the time it takes to get a response to the medical professional)**

Reason: A patient's life could depend on how fast the medical professional is notified of a problem

☐ **Deployability (the frequency and ceremony involved with releasing changes)**

Reason: Not critical—there are no requirements stating there will be many changes in the system

☐ **Abstraction (the level of isolation and knowledge between parts of the system)**

Reason: Not critical—there are no requirements regarding abstraction

☐ **Scalability (the system's ability to grow to accommodate more users or patients)**

Reason: Not critical—the system is scoped to a single hospital only (hospital beds are the limiting factor)

☒ **Fault tolerance (the system's ability to continue operating when parts of the system fail)**

Reason: One vital sign monitoring failure can't stop the other vital signs functions from monitoring the patient

☒ **Data integrity (the data is consistent and correct across the system and there is no data loss)**

Reason: The data about a patient's health must be as accurate as possible

☐ **Workflow (the system's ability to handle complex business workflows)**

Reason: Not critical—each vital sign is monitored separately and no complex workflows are required

☒ **Concurrency (the system's ability to process concurrent requests or operations)**

Reason: The system must be able to monitor many different vital signs at the exact same time

Exercise
Solution

From page 307

We're having trouble determining what *single-purpose* means. Can you help us by checking off all the functions below that you would consider single-purpose and therefore possible microservices?

☒ **Add a movie to your personal "to watch" list**

☒ **Pay for an order using your credit card**

☐ **Generate sales forecasting and financial performance reports** ✓ ⟶ These are complex processes with lots of different functions.

☐ **Submit and process a loan application to get that new car you've always wanted** ⟵

☒ **Determining the shipping cost for an online order**

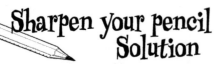

Sharpen your pencil
Solution

We created the following services for an ecommerce site, but we need your help in figuring out the data ownership and bounded contexts. Can you associate the database tables below with the corresponding microservices that should own the data?

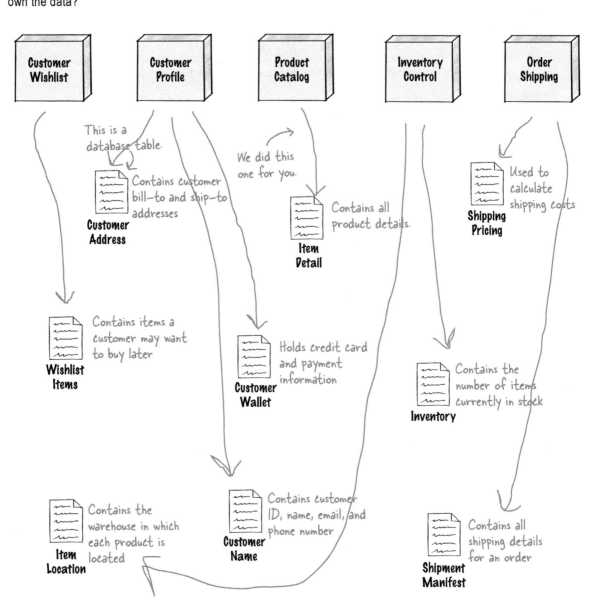

Exercise Solution

From page 317

Now it's your turn to apply granularity disintegrators and granularity integrators to decide whether to implement the Monitor Basic Vital Signs functionality (which covers blood pressure, temperature, and heart rate) as a single microservice or three separate services. Here is some additional information:

* A patient's heart rate and blood pressure are the two most critical basic vital signs to monitor. If something should go wrong with temperature monitoring, heart rate and blood pressure monitoring must continue to work.

* All three basic vital signs share an alert functionality to notify medical professionals if something goes wrong.

* The heart rate monitoring functionality accepts sensor readings once a second, whereas the temperature and blood pressure monitoring functions only accept sensor readings once every 5 minutes.

Each basic vital sign's data is recorded and stored separately, as simple JSON name/value pairs in a single document database. For example, the heart rate readings are stored as follows:

```
{"patient_id": "123",
 "timestamp": "10452955668",
 "bpm": "64"}
```

BPM stands for beats per minute.

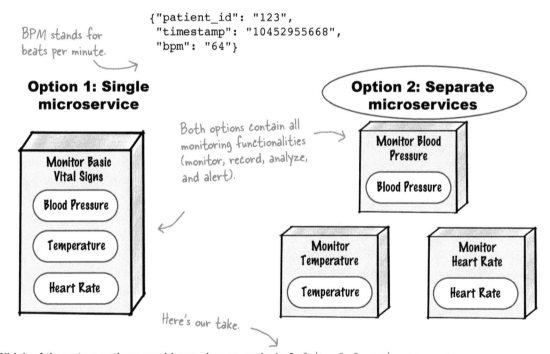

Option 1: Single microservice

Monitor Basic Vital Signs
Blood Pressure
Temperature
Heart Rate

Both options contain all monitoring functionalities (monitor, record, analyze, and alert).

Option 2: Separate microservices

Monitor Blood Pressure
Blood Pressure

Monitor Temperature
Temperature

Monitor Heart Rate
Heart Rate

Here's our take.

Which of these two options would you choose, and why? _Option 2: Separate microservices._
Having separate services provides better fault tolerance in case one of the monitoring functions causes the
service to go down. Also, data is recorded and stored separately, which works well with physical bounded
contexts in separate databases to provide better fault tolerance. Finally, each separate service can scale
as needed based on the varying input rates (once a second for heart rate, every 5 minutes for others).

Sharpen your pencil
Solution

From page 319

Besides alerting a medical professional, can you list other common functionalities that the MonitorMe services might need?

Observability—streaming service response times, errors, uptime, and other metrics and measurements

Logging—reporting on errors and other service functionality alerts

Auditing—recording when an alert was sent and which medical professional received it

Security—restricting access to a monitoring service to authorized medical professionals only

Sharpen your pencil
Solution

Now that you've seen the two main options for sharing functionality in the microservices architectural style, it's your turn to decide—should the alert functionality in MonitorMe be a shared library or a shared service? Make sure you consider external forces (like the problem domain) in addition to the pros and cons of each option, and justify your choice.

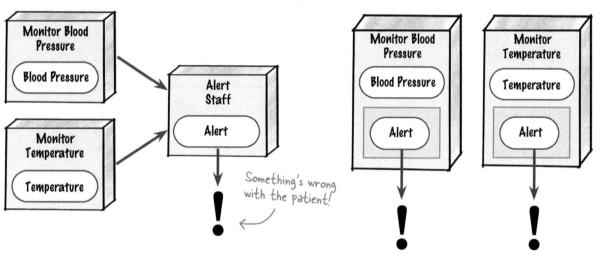

Option 1: Shared service

Option 2: Shared library

Something's wrong with the patient!

This is our decision and reasoning.

☐ **Option 1: Shared service**

☒ **Option 2: Shared library**

Reason: We chose option 2 (shared library) because it provides:

—better performance (the medical professional will be alerted faster)

—better reliability and fault tolerance (if the Alert Staff shared service went down, the

system couldn't alert the medical professional)

—better concurrency (if multiple problems occur at the same time)

Exercise Solution

From page 325

Can you think of any workflows involving multiple microservices that might exist for the MonitorMe patient vital signs monitoring system? Here are our ideas.

Get the status of a patient's basic vital signs (temperature, blood pressure, and heart rate)

Find out which vital signs are being monitored for a given patient (requires queries to multiple monitoring services)

Register a new patient to be monitored—lots of different information is gathered, like name, identity, demographics, medical history, and so on, all of which could be separate microservices

Exercise Solution

From page 330

StayHealthy, Inc., stands behind MonitorMe and its monitoring devices and display screens. If a problem occurs with any software or physical hardware, someone from the medical facility can go online and create a trouble ticket. A field technician will receive the trouble ticket on their mobile phone, come to the medical facility, fix the problem, and mark the ticket as fixed.

It's up to you: would you manage the microservices for the trouble ticket system workflow using orchestration or choreography? Be sure to include the reasons for your choice.

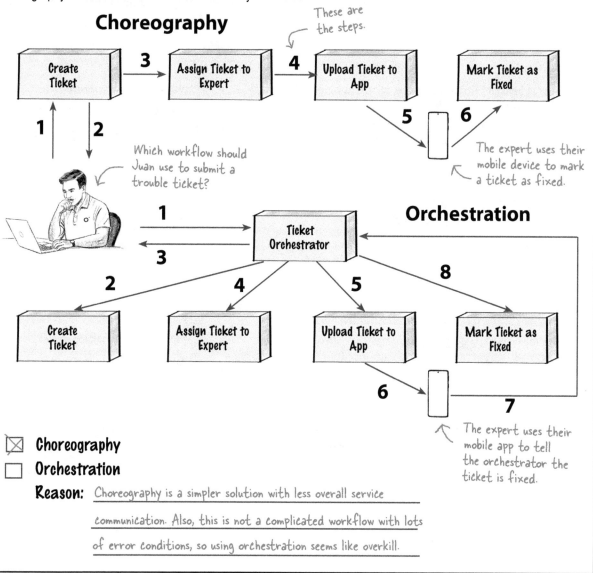

☒ **Choreography**

☐ **Orchestration**

Reason: Choreography is a simpler solution with less overall service communication. Also, this is not a complicated workflow with lots of error conditions, so using orchestration seems like overkill.

Exercise Solution

From page 335

Which of the following systems might be well suited for the microservices architectural style, and why? *Hint: Take into account microservices' superpowers, its kryptonite, and the problem domain.* Here are our answers.

An online auction system where users can bid on items

Why? High scalability and elasticity needs; high concurrency; independent functions

- ☒ Well suited for microservices
- ☐ Might be a fit for microservices
- ☐ Not well suited for microservices

A large backend financial system for processing and settling international wire transfers overnight

Why? Microservices' superpowers aren't needed in this kind of complex system

- ☐ Well suited for microservices
- ☐ Might be a fit for microservices
- ☒ Not well suited for microservices

A company entering a new line of business that expects constant changes to its system

Why? High agility and evolvability mean microservices could fit, but we need more info

- ☐ Well suited for microservices
- ☒ Might be a fit for microservices
- ☐ Not well suited for microservices

A small bakery that wants to start taking online orders

Why? The high cost and complexity of microservices would be too much for a small bakery

- ☐ Well suited for microservices
- ☐ Might be a fit for microservices
- ☒ Not well suited for microservices

A trouble ticket system for electronics purchased with a support plan, in which field technicians come to customers to fix problems

Why? Independent functions; good scalability and elasticity; simple workflows

- ☒ Well suited for microservices
- ☐ Might be a fit for microservices
- ☐ Not well suited for microservices

Microservices Crossword Solution

From page 337

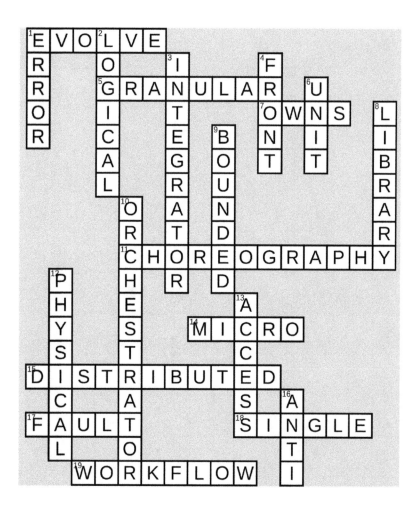

11 event-driven architecture
Asynchronous Adventures

What if your architecture could do lots of things at the same time? As businesses grow and become more successful, they need to be able to handle more and more users, without slowing down or crashing systems. In this chapter, you'll learn how to design high-performance systems that can scale as a business grows. Get ready for *event-driven architecture*, a highly popular distributed architectural style. It's very fast, highly scalable, and easy to extend—but it's also quite complex. You'll be learning about lots of new concepts in this chapter, including things like events, messages, and asynchronous communication, so you can create an architecture that can do many things at once. Fasten your seatbelt, and let's go on an asynchronous adventure through event-driven architecture.

Too slow

Imagine going to your favorite diner to order their famous grilled cheese sandwich, crispy fries, and a chocolate milkshake. Sounds easy, right? But what if the person taking your order had to make all of those things one at a time, without any help? Not only would everything take longer, but the diner wouldn't be able to serve as many customers. Let's visualize that workflow:

1. Take the next customer's lunch order (1 minute)

2. Accept payment from the customer (1 minute)

3. Cook the grilled cheese sandwich (4 minutes)

4. Cook the french fries (5 minutes)

5. Make the chocolate milkshake (4 minutes)

6. Plate the food and serve the customer

Each order takes 15 minutes, meaning the diner can only serve four customers during the lunch-hour rush.

This customer isn't happy with her cold lunch.

This is no way to run a diner! Let's see if we can make things go a little faster so they can serve more customers.

Brain Power

Pretend you are a customer of this diner. How would you suggest they speed things up?

Write your ideas here.

Speeding things up

If the diner hires three more workers (one to make the sandwiches, one to cook the french fries, and one to make milkshakes) and they prepare all parts of the meal at once, completing orders will take half as long. That effectively doubles the number of customers the diner can serve during the lunch hour.

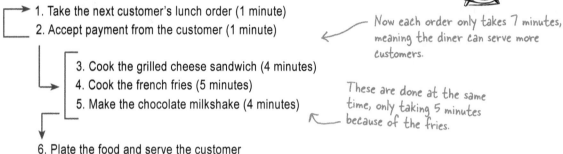

1. Take the next customer's lunch order (1 minute)
2. Accept payment from the customer (1 minute)

3. Cook the grilled cheese sandwich (4 minutes)
4. Cook the french fries (5 minutes)
5. Make the chocolate milkshake (4 minutes)

6. Plate the food and serve the customer

Now each order only takes 7 minutes, meaning the diner can serve more customers.

These are done at the same time, only taking 5 minutes because of the fries.

Doing all three activities *at the same time* significantly reduces customers' wait time (we'll call that *responsiveness*). Because meals can be made faster, the server taking orders can now handle more customers (we'll call that *scalability*).

This is the fundamental concept behind **event-driven architecture (EDA)**—breaking up processing into separate *services*, with each of those services performing its function at the same time by responding to an **event** (something that just happened). In EDA, services communicate *asynchronously* through an **event channel**, meaning they don't wait for responses from other services to complete their work.

Note: we'll be referring to event-driven architecture as EDA going forward, because we're cool like that (and, thankfully, we don't get paid by the word).

Don't worry— we'll cover all of these terms.

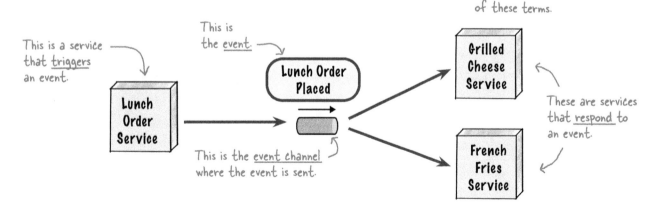

This is a service that triggers an event.

This is the event.

Lunch Order Service

Lunch Order Placed

This is the event channel where the event is sent.

Grilled Cheese Service

French Fries Service

These are services that respond to an event.

We know this is a lot to take in at once, so we'll take it step by step. But before we jump in, let us introduce you to Der Nile, a large German online-ordering company that is having growing pains and needs your help.

Der Nile flows faster than ever

Der Nile is Germany's largest online retailer, selling everything from diapers to hair-growth supplements.

Business is booming—so much, as a matter of fact, that the company's online ordering system is stressed to the breaking point. Der Nile's customers demand fast systems and quick order fulfillment, and the current system simply can't handle the volume of orders coming in. Processing orders takes too long, and fulfillment times are increasing.

Der Nile would like to create a new ordering system from scratch to handle this growth—and needs your help in designing it.

Here is the basic flow of the legacy online-ordering system currently in place:

Der Nile wants to make online shopping fun.

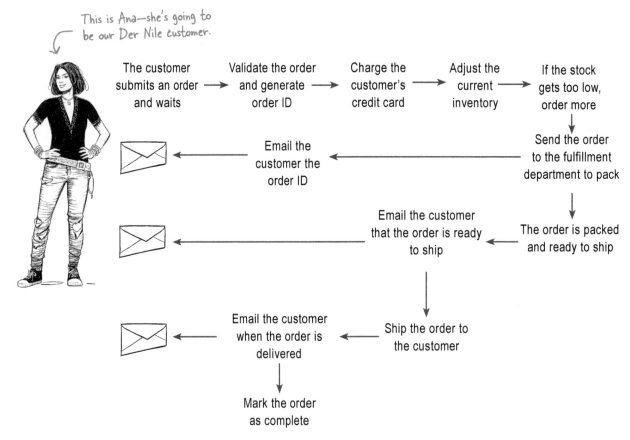

This is Ana—she's going to be our Der Nile customer.

The customer submits an order and waits → Validate the order and generate order ID → Charge the customer's credit card → Adjust the current inventory → If the stock gets too low, order more

Email the customer the order ID ← Send the order to the fulfillment department to pack

Email the customer that the order is ready to ship ← The order is packed and ready to ship

Email the customer when the order is delivered ← Ship the order to the customer

Mark the order as complete

Exercise

As the architect, how can you modify the current workflow (shown on the previous page) to speed things up a bit? Draw your ideas for a new workflow in the space below. *Hint: What can you do at the same time?*

— Start here.

The customer
submits an order ⟶
and waits

Solution on page 391

What is an event?

Back in the late 1950s, a journalist asked Prime Minister Harold Macmillan of the United Kingdom what troubled him the most. "Events, my dear boy, events," was his famous reply. Events may have troubled Harold Macmillan, but they can be a lot of help to us in solving complex business problems.

An *event* is something that happens, especially something of importance. Things like the World Cup, musical concerts, big promotions at work, weddings, and birthday celebrations are all important events.

Publishing this book was an important event for the authors.

In software systems, certain user actions trigger events—things that happen, like placing a bid for an item up for auction, filing an insurance claim, or making a purchase.

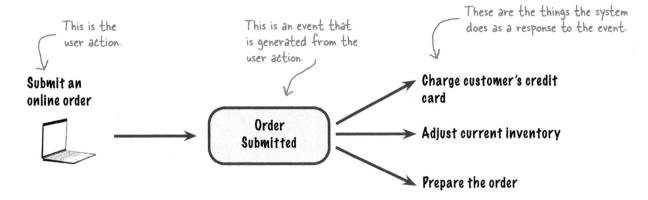

This is the user action.

This is an event that is generated from the user action.

These are the things the system does as a response to the event.

Submit an online order

Order Submitted

Charge customer's credit card

Adjust current inventory

Prepare the order

Events are a way for a service to let the rest of the system know that something important has just happened. In EDA, events are the means of passing information to other services.

Friendly reminder: EDA is event-driven architecture.

An event usually contains data, like *all* the details of an online order. On occasion, it might only have *key* information (like the order ID). In the latter case, services that must do something when they receive the event will have go to a data store to get additional information about it.

The data inside an event is referred to as its <u>payload</u>.

Order Submitted

Order ID: 123

This event only passes along the order ID.

Order Submitted

Order ID: 123
Customer ID: 99876
Date Placed: 22 May
Item List: [Items]
Street: 123 Main St
City: Anytown
...

This event passes along all the information about the order that was just submitted.

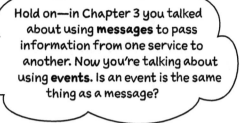

Hold on—in Chapter 3 you talked about using **messages** to pass information from one service to another. Now you're talking about using **events**. Is an event is the same thing as a message?

This is often referred to as "fire-and-forget."

More on this soon.

No, an event is not the same thing as a message.
Although they both deliver information to other parts of the system, there are some important differences between them.

An **event** is used to **broadcast** some action that a service just performed to other services in the system. For example, a service might tell the rest of the system: *A customer just placed an order.* A service sending an event **never waits** for a response. The service generally has no knowledge about what other services (if any) are listening for that event, or what they'll do with that information if they respond to it.

A **message**, on the other hand, is a **command**, such as *Apply the payment for this order*, or a **request**, like *Give me shipping options for this customer.* Because messages are only meant to reach one other service, the other services in the system are unaware of the message. Services sometimes stop and wait for a response (for instance, if they are sending a request for information). Other times, the service might just issue a command and trust that the receiving service will do its job.

Turn the page to see more differences between an event and a message.

Events versus messages

Here are two really important differences between events and messages:

1. Events are broadcast to other services using topics, whereas messages are sent to a single service using queues.

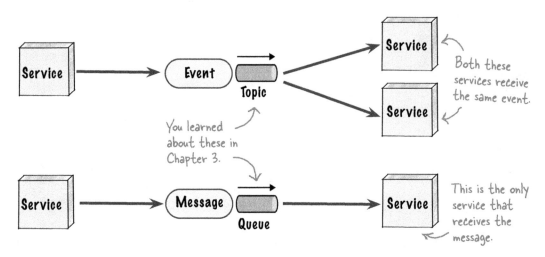

2. Events always broadcast something that has already happened, whereas messages request something that needs to be done.

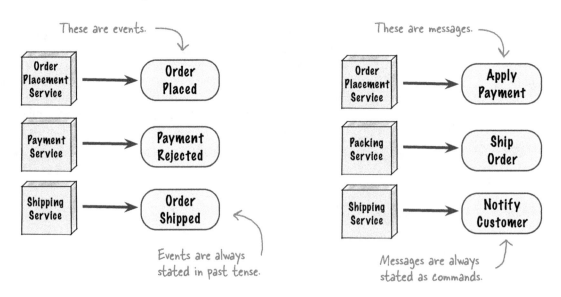

Sharpen your pencil

It's time to test your knowledge about events and messages. For each of the quotes below, mark whether it is more likely an event or a message, and indicate why.

"Adventurous Air flight 12, turn left, heading 230 degrees."

☐ Event ☐ Message

Reason: _____

_____

"In other news, a winter storm front has just moved into the area."

☐ Event ☐ Message

Reason: _____

_____

"Okay, class, turn to page 42 in your workbooks." ← *Be careful—this one's tricky!*

☐ Event ☐ Message

Reason: _____

_____

"Hello, everyone! Sorry I'm late."

☐ Event ☐ Message

Reason: _____

_____

"Oh no! I just missed my train!"

☐ Event ☐ Message

Reason: _____

_____

"Excuse me, sir—do you have the time?"

☐ Event ☐ Message

Reason: _____

_____

Solution on page 392

Initiating and derived events

Events that originate from a customer or end user are called ***initiating events***. These are a special type of event that kicks off a business process.

Once a service responds to an initiating event, it might in turn broadcast what it did to the rest of the system, within the scope of that initiating event. These events are called ***derived events*** because they are internal events generated in response to the initiating event.

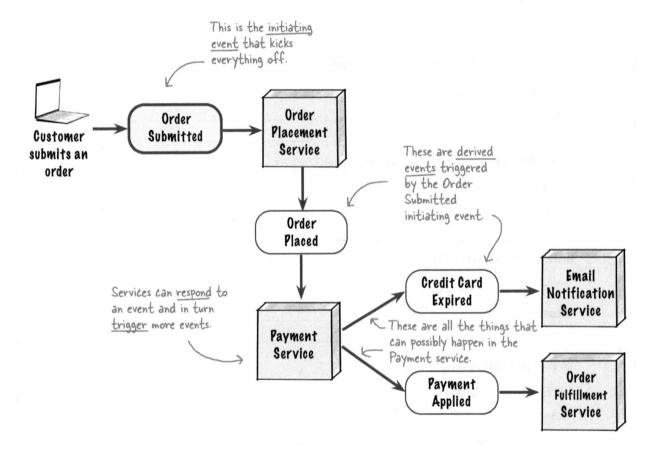

Did you notice that the Payment service generates two different derived events? This is typical in EDA. Anything a service generates or causes to happen can be a derived event.

Exercise

Based on the *Credit Card Charged* initiating event and the corresponding processing below, can you identify what the derived events should be for each service? Think of as many possible outcomes as you can.

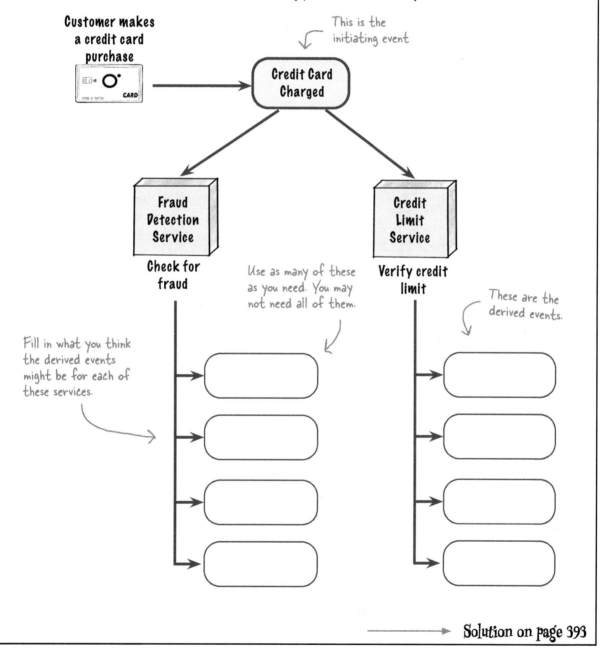

Customer makes a credit card purchase

This is the initiating event

Credit Card Charged

Fraud Detection Service

Check for fraud

Use as many of these as you need. You may not need all of them.

Credit Limit Service

Verify credit limit

These are the derived events.

Fill in what you think the derived events might be for each of these services.

Solution on page 393

Is anyone listening?

When you post something on social media, you often get a reaction—someone liking or commenting on your post. But how many times have you posted something only to get no reaction? Maybe you wondered: *Did anyone see my post? Did anyone care?*

In EDA, any action a service performs *should* trigger a derived event. However, there is a chance that no one cares about certain events. So why publish those events? Because this provides **architectural extensibility**—the ability to extend the system to add new functionality.

Extensibility is one of the architectural characteristics you learned about in Chapter 2.

Let's say customers in the Der Nile online ordering system get notified when an order is shipped and also when it has been delivered. The Email Notification service handles this by sending the customer an email. That event in turn triggers a *Customer Notified* derived event.

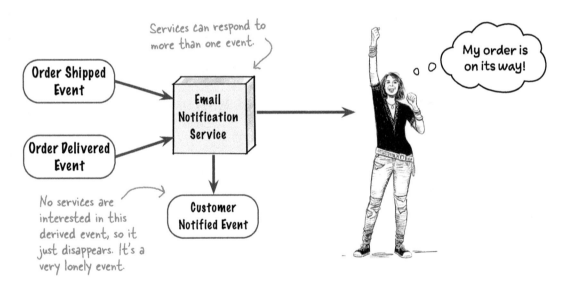

Services can respond to more than one event.

No services are interested in this derived event, so it just disappears. It's a very lonely event.

Now let's suppose Der Nile wants to do some analytics to learn what times of the day the system sends the most customer notification emails. Since the *Customer Notified* derived event is already being published, you can simply create a new Notification Analytics service and tell it to listen for that event. *You don't need to modify any other parts of the system.*

This new service can simply subscribe to the existing Customer Notified event.

This event is no longer lonely.

Asynchronous communication

I thought you said this architecture was really fast. How is this any faster than microservices?

Event-driven architecture is fast because it uses mostly asynchronous (or "async" for short) communication.

You're probably most familiar with communication styles such as REST or HTTP, particularly when you need to call an API or another service. These are forms of *synchronous communication*. With synchronous (or "sync") communication, when a service sends information, it must sit and wait for a response from the receiving service before doing anything else (even if it's just acknowledging receipt of the information). This slows systems down and makes them less scalable. It's like calling a friend—you have to wait for your phone to make a connection to your friend's phone, let it ring, and wait for your friend to answer before you can talk.

Asynchronous communication is a fancy way of saying that services don't wait for a response or acknowledgment from other services when sending them information. This creates systems that are highly decoupled and very fast. It's one of the unique features of event-driven architecture. It's like sending your friend a text—you can do other things while you wait for their response.

Having to wait for a response is really slow.

Not having to wait means you can go do other things.

Fireside Chats

Tonight's talk: **Asynchronous and synchronous communication debate: Who's more useful?**

Asynchronous Communication	Synchronous Communication

Asynchronous Communication

Well, it's about time you showed up.

Yeah, I've noticed. You're as slow as a herd of snails traveling through peanut butter.

Wait? You want me to *wait?* That's your whole problem—you're always waiting around for answers. No one has to wait when I'm around. And that makes me fast—*really* fast.

I trust others to get the job done, unlike you. You need verification for *everything*, all the time.

I don't. I can't be responsible for everyone, you know. I let others deal with their own issues.

Oh, I'm sorry—did you say something? I wasn't listening.

Sorry—I wasn't paying attention. What was that?

Synchronous Communication

Sorry I'm late. I can't seem to multitask, so everything I do takes *such* a long time.

Now, wait just one minute!

That may be so, but your problem is that you never know what's going on. You ask others to do things, but you never find out whether those things actually got done or not.

Yeah, right. Tell me: when an error occurs downstream, how do you deal with it?

And what if you need information from someone else before you can finish your work? What do you do then?

That's exactly my point! You never listen to anyone else. I may be slow, but at least I pay attention to what's going on and communicate with others.

Sigh...

Fire-and-forget

Asynchronous communication is one of the foundations of event-driven architecture. When a service broadcasts information to other services, it doesn't wait for a response, nor does it care whether the services are available or not. This is known as *fire-and-forget* communication—the event is sent (that's the *fire* part), and the service moves on to do other things (that's the *forget* part). Architects usually use a dotted line to represent async communication between services.

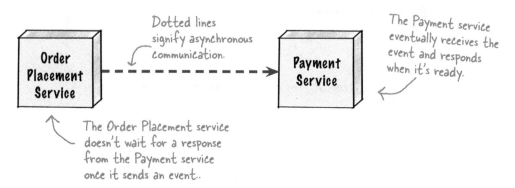

Dotted lines signify asynchronous communication.

The Payment service eventually receives the event and responds when it's ready.

The Order Placement service doesn't wait for a response from the Payment service once it sends an event..

Synchronous communication, on the other hand, means that the sending service must stop and wait for a response from the service it's calling before continuing its work. This means that the service being called *must* be available to respond, or an error occurs. Architects usually represent synchronous communication using a solid line.

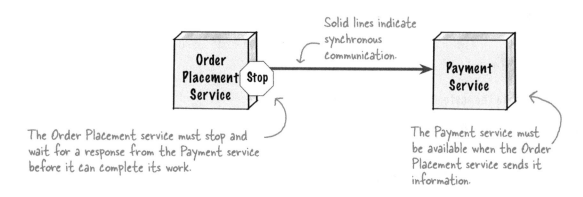

Solid lines indicate synchronous communication.

The Order Placement service must stop and wait for a response from the Payment service before it can complete its work.

The Payment service must be available when the Order Placement service sends it information.

Event-driven architecture relies on <u>asynchronous communication</u> when sending and receiving events.

Sharpen your pencil

For each of these tasks, would you use asynchronous or synchronous communication?

Give me the shipping options for this order.

☐ Asynchronous ☐ Synchronous ☐ Either one would work

Apply payment for this order and let me know if the payment goes through.

☐ Asynchronous ☐ Synchronous ☐ Either one would work

Fulfill this order for me by picking the items off the shelf and packing them in a box.

☐ Asynchronous ☐ Synchronous ☐ Either one would work

Give me the current status of this order.

☐ Asynchronous ☐ Synchronous ☐ Either one would work

Our inventory of this item is getting low—please order more stock.

☐ Asynchronous ☐ Synchronous ☐ Either one would work

Tell the customer that their order has been shipped and is on its way.

☐ Asynchronous ☐ Synchronous ☐ Either one would work

Update the customer's profile picture.

☐ Asynchronous ☐ Synchronous ☐ Either one would work

Post a customer's review on the product page.

☐ Asynchronous ☐ Synchronous ☐ Either one would work

Solution on page 394

Asynchronous for the win

Communicating between services asynchronously has a lot of advantages. The first is better ***responsiveness***—in async, it takes less time to complete a request.

Suppose a customer places an online order in Der Nile. It takes 600 milliseconds (ms), or just over half a second, for the Order Placement service to validate and place the order, and 1,200 ms for the Payment service to apply the payment. With async, the customer would wait 600 ms to get a response. With sync, however, they would have to wait 1,800 ms (just shy of 2 seconds). That's a big difference in response times.

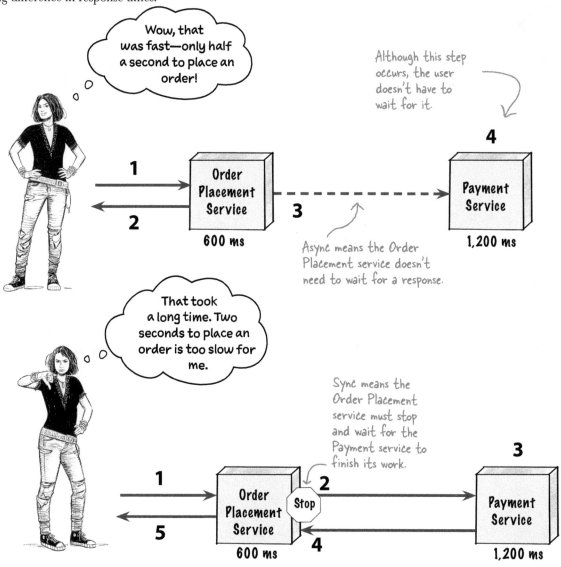

Asynchronous for the win (continued)

The other big advantage of async is **availability**. Let's see what happens with async and sync if the Payment service is unavailable or becomes unresponsive.

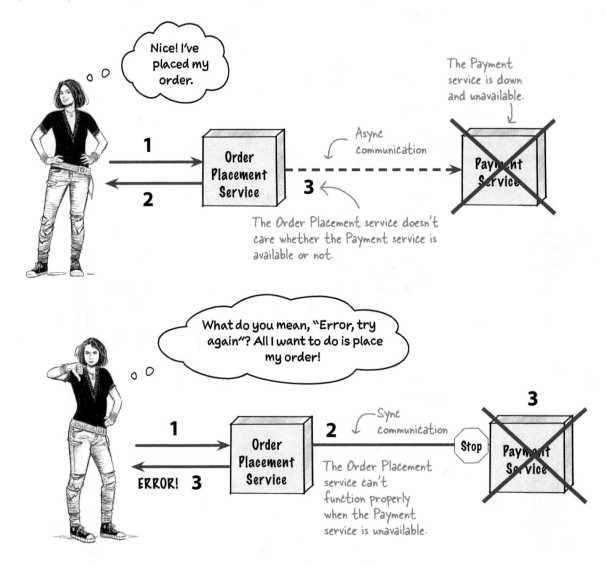

Have we convinced you that asynchronous communication is great? Let's take a look at its trade-offs next.

Remember the First Law—everything in software architecture is a trade-off.

Synchronous for the win

The main disadvantage of async communication is ***error handling***. With sync communication, if there's a problem with the payment method, the customer knows right away and has a chance to fix it and resubmit the order. However, with async, the customer thinks everything is fine because the system hasn't told them otherwise— but the Order Placement service can't process the order until the customer corrects the payment problem. This makes error handling much more complex.

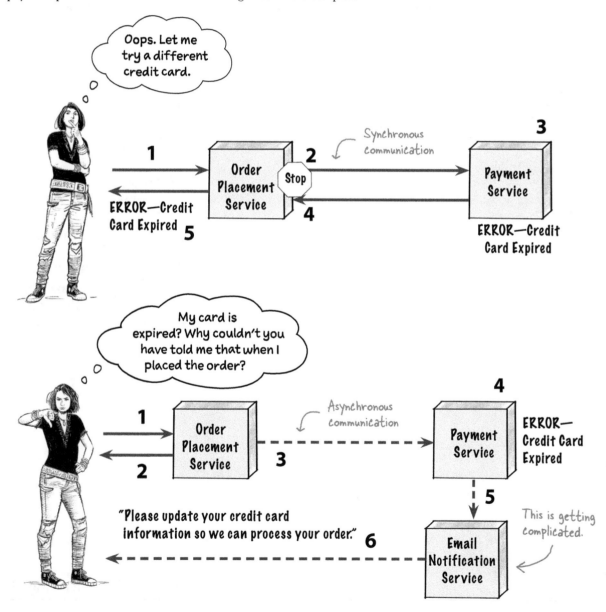

Sharpen your pencil

Now's your chance to test what you've learned so far about event-driven architecture, events, and asynchronous processing. Der Nile's inventory occasionally gets out of sync, as shown below. When this happens, the order cannot be fulfilled and goes into a back-order state. Der Nile never makes a customer pay for items that are back-ordered, and the customer can choose whether to wait or cancel the order.

As the architect for Der Nile, what additional events and services would you create to address this situation?

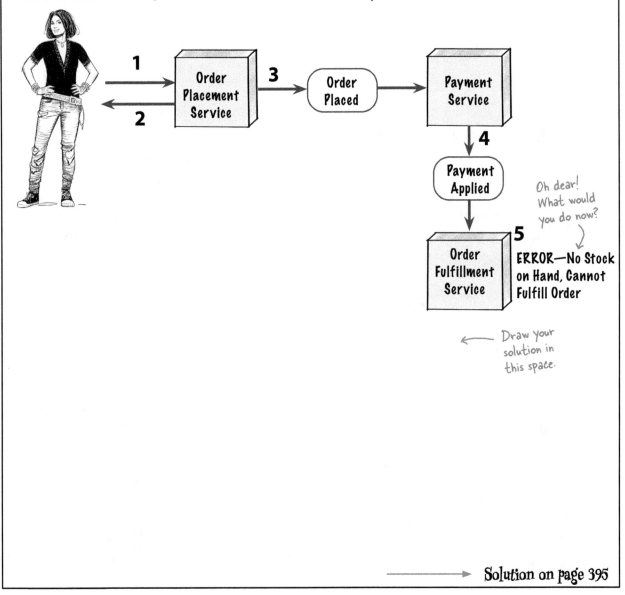

Oh dear! What would you do now?

← *Draw your solution in this space.*

Solution on page 395

Database topologies

> Hang on. All you've talked about so far are events and services. Data matters too, ya know. When are you going to start talking about databases in event-driven architecture?

We're glad you brought that up.

Data can be a complex topic in EDA. Because EDA is so asynchronous, services are highly *decoupled* from *one another*. However, if all the services share a single database, then they end up being highly *coupled* to the *database*. On the other hand, if each service owns its own data, like with microservices (discussed in the previous chapter), then services become highly coupled to each other because they need to synchronously ask each other for the data. In either case, data forms a coupling point—something we try to avoid in EDA.

In the next couple of pages we're going to show you various ways for dealing with databases in EDA: ***monolithic databases***, ***domain-partitioned databases***, and the ***database-per-service*** pattern. We'll talk about their trade-offs to help you decide which one is most appropriate for your situation.

Monolithic database

In the **monolithic database** topology, *all services share a single database.*
The main advantage is that when services need data they don't own,
they can go directly to the database. This means they don't have to make
synchronous calls to other services to get data. For example, if the Order
Placement service needs the current inventory and shipping options for a
customer's order, it can simply query that information from the database.

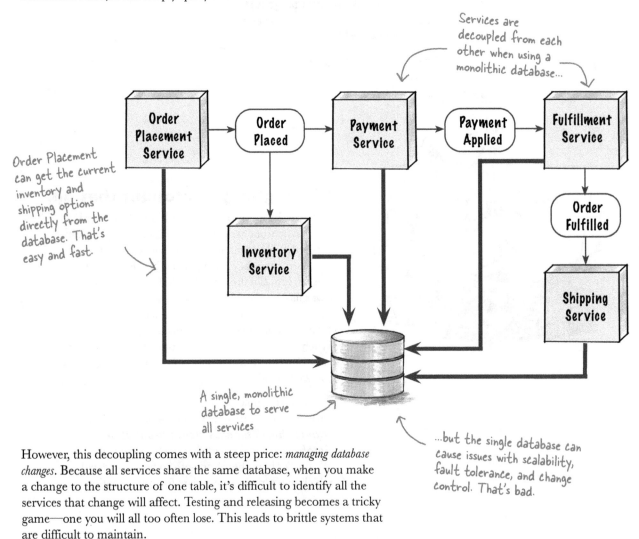

Services are decoupled from each other when using a monolithic database...

Order Placement can get the current inventory and shipping options directly from the database. That's easy and fast.

A single, monolithic database to serve all services

...but the single database can cause issues with scalability, fault tolerance, and change control. That's bad.

However, this decoupling comes with a steep price: *managing database
changes*. Because all services share the same database, when you make
a change to the structure of one table, it's difficult to identify all the
services that change will affect. Testing and releasing becomes a tricky
game—one you will all too often lose. This leads to brittle systems that
are difficult to maintain.

What's more, the shared database becomes a single point of failure, and
one that may not be able to scale as the system grows.

Monolithic database topology scorecard

Here's a scorecard for the monolithic database topology.

Monolithic databases are not necessarily good or bad—it all depends on what's important to you.

Monolithic Database Topology Scorecard

☑ **GOOD** — Service coupling:

Low		High

Services are highly decoupled because they don't need to synchronously communicate with each other to get data.

☑ **GOOD** — Performance:

Low		High

Data retrieval is fast because services are accessing the database directly, not through synchronous remote calls to other services.

☑ **GOOD** — Simplicity:

Low		High

The monolithic database is a simple topology. Complex joins and queries are done in the database rather than in the services.

☒ **BAD** — Ease of change:

Low		High

Changing the structure of a database table can affect lots of distributed services, making systems hard to test.

☒ **BAD** — Fault tolerance:

Low		High

If the single monolithic database goes down, the entire system goes down, impacting overall fault tolerance and availability.

☒ **BAD** — Scalability:

Low		High

It's harder to scale and provide elasticity because the database must scale along with the services, and because services could run out of connections to the database.

Domain-partitioned databases

With ***domain-partitioned*** databases, each ***domain*** in the system has its own database. This means any service that belongs to a particular domain will share the database for that domain. For example, the Order Placement, Payment, and Inventory services are all part of the *Order Placement* domain, so they all share the same physical database.

See Chapter 10 for a review of the physical bounded context.

However, since each domain forms its own broad physical bounded context, a service in one domain can't directly access a database to get data from another domain. This means it must make a synchronous call to another service to get the data—and now these services are coupled.

The Order Placement service must synchronously call the Shipping service to get the shipping options.

Dotted lines represent separate domains.

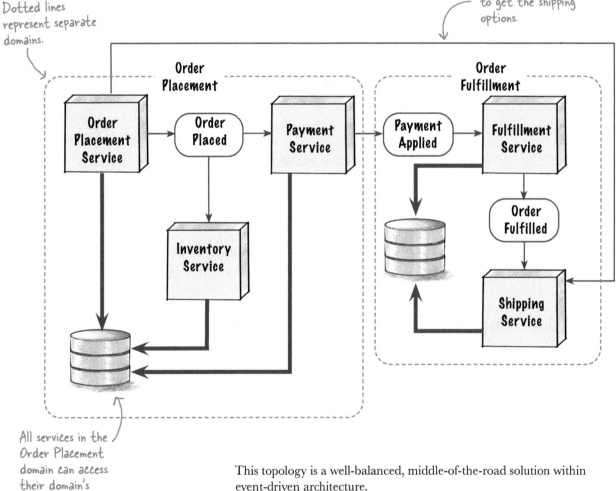

All services in the Order Placement domain can access their domain's database directly.

This topology is a well-balanced, middle-of-the-road solution within event-driven architecture.

Domain-partitioned databases topology scorecard

Here's a scorecard for the domain-partitioned databases topology.

The domain-partitioned databases topology provides a good balance.

Domain-Partitioned Databases Topology Scorecard

☒ **Service coupling:**
BAD

Low		High

While services *within* a domain are still highly decoupled because of shared data, services must make synchronous calls to other services to get data from *outside* their domain.

☑ **Performance:**
GOOD

Low		High

Data retrieval is fast for services *within* a domain because they are accessing the database directly. However, performance becomes slower when services access data synchronously *outside* their domain.

☑ **Simplicity:**
GOOD

Low		High

Since most data is naturally partitioned by domain, this topology is not overly complex (but it's still not as simple as a monolithic topology).

☒ **Ease of change:**
BAD

Low		High

Changing the structure of a database table only affects services within the domain, limiting the number of services impacted.

☒ **Fault tolerance:**
BAD

Low		High

Database failures only affect services within the domain, making this topology a little more fault tolerant than the monolithic topology.

☒ **Scalability:**
BAD

Low		High

While still a con, scalability is a little better here than in the monolithic topology. Databases only need to scale at the domain level, rather than across the entire system.

Database-per-service

Remember the *database-per-service* pattern from Chapter 10? It isn't just for microservices—you can use it for EDA as well.

The database-per-service pattern is just what it sounds like. Every service has its own database, forming an even tighter physical bounded context than with the domain-partitioned topology. Here, making database changes is a breeze, because the only service affected is the one that owns the data (that is, does writes to the database). You get better fault tolerance and better scalability, too. What's not to like?

We hope you have plenty of money! This can get expensive.

Unfortunately, plenty. You see, whenever services need additional data they don't have, they have to *ask* for that data from the service that owns it using synchronous calls. That results in a lot of coupling and communication between services, not to mention much slower performance.

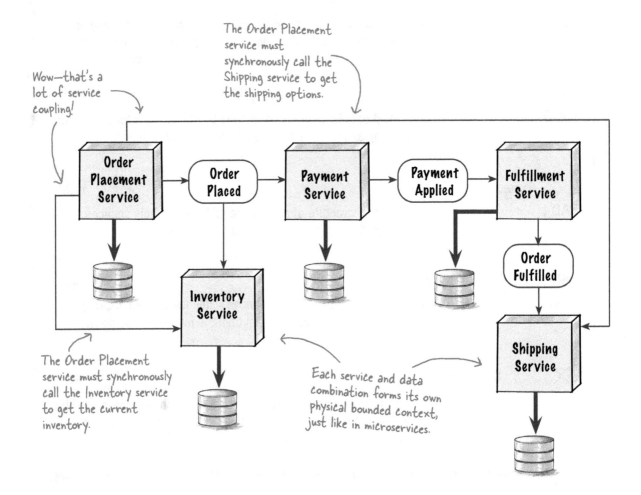

Wow—that's a lot of service coupling!

The Order Placement service must synchronously call the Shipping service to get the shipping options.

The Order Placement service must synchronously call the Inventory service to get the current inventory.

Each service and data combination forms its own physical bounded context, just like in microservices.

Database-per-service topology scorecard

Here's a scorecard for the database-per-service topology.

This topology is the exact opposite of the monolithic topology, from a pros-and-cons perspective.

Database-Per-Service Topology Scorecard

☒ **BAD** — Service coupling:

Low		High

Since services only have access to data they own, they must make synchronous calls to other services to get additional data. This highly couples services in a highly *decoupled* architecture. That's bad.

☒ **BAD** — Performance:

Low		High

Because services must make synchronous calls to retrieve other data, performance becomes much slower than in the other topologies.

☒ **BAD** — Simplicity:

Low		High

Breaking data apart into small physical bounded contexts is very hard, due to coupling between data tables and artifacts (such as foreign keys, triggers, views, and stored procedures).

☑ **GOOD** — Ease of change:

Low		High

Changing the structure of a database table only affects a single service within the physical bounded context, making database changes much easier than in other topologies.

☑ **GOOD** — Fault tolerance:

Low		High

Database failures only affect the owning service, making this the most fault tolerant of the three topologies.

☑ **GOOD** — Scalability:

Low		High

Databases scale at the service level, making this a great topology for high scalability and elasticity needs.

Exercise

For each of these business needs, select which topologies you would consider. You can select more than one topology.

We expect anywhere between 20 and 300,000 customers to be on the system at once.

☐ Monolithic Database ☐ Domain-Partitioned Databases ☐ Database-Per-Service

The system must be as fast as possible.

☐ Monolithic Database ☐ Domain-Partitioned Databases ☐ Database-Per-Service

This medical monitoring system can never completely fail—parts of it must always stay running.

☐ Monolithic Database ☐ Domain-Partitioned Databases ☐ Database-Per-Service

We're anticipating changing the database a lot in this new line of business.

☐ Monolithic Database ☐ Domain-Partitioned Databases ☐ Database-Per-Service

We have to get the new system up and running as soon as possible.

☐ Monolithic Database ☐ Domain-Partitioned Databases ☐ Database-Per-Service

Our data model is extremely large and complex, with lots of interrelated data.

☐ Monolithic Database ☐ Domain-Partitioned Databases ☐ Database-Per-Service

⟶ Solution on page 396

> Event-driven architecture using the database-per-service topology looks a lot like microservices to me. What's the difference?

Even though they may appear simliar, EDA and microservices are very different.

We're glad you noticed some similarities between the two architectural styles. Both are distributed architectures good for scalability, agility, elasticity, and fault tolerance.

Over the next few pages, we'll show you some important differences. But before we move on, how about trying the short exercise below to see if you can spot any yourself?

If you don't know, that's okay—keep reading!

Sharpen your pencil

List any differences you can think of between event-driven architecture and microservices.

Solution on page 397

EDA versus microservices

Welcome to the EDA versus microservices Top Six Differences countdown! Over the next few pages, we're going to count down six important differences between these architectural styles, starting with number 6. Ready? Let's go!

It's time for the Head First differences countdown!

Number 6: Performance

The first difference in our countdown, at number 6, is *performance*.

In their book *Fundamentals of Software Architecture* (O'Reilly), two of your authors created star ratings for each architectural style. We gave microservices only two stars out of five for performance, but we gave EDA five stars. Why?

Well, EDA combines asynchronous processing with the ability to do multiple things at once, creating very fast systems. Microservices, however, because of their bounded contexts and fine-grained nature, frequently need to communicate *synchronously*. This creates a lot of latency, which slows the system down considerably.

Architectural Characteristic	Star Rating
Performance	★ ★ ★ ★ ★

Event-Driven Architecture

Architectural Characteristic	Star Rating
Performance	★ ★

Microservices Architecture

Number 5: Physical bounded contexts

Coming in at number 5 in our countdown is *physical bounded contexts*. Microservices won't work without these.

In EDA, however, while a physical bounded context is nice to have, it's certainly not foundational (or even required). Because data sharing is pretty typical in EDA, this architecture doesn't restrict data ownership as strictly as microservices does.

These services and their data are each in a physical bounded context.

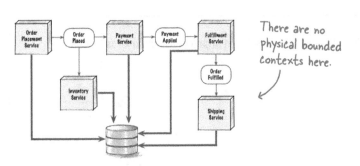

There are no physical bounded contexts here.

Event-Driven Architecture

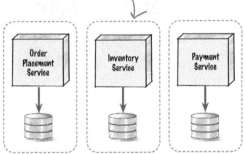

Microservices Architecture

Number 4: Data granularity

Another constraint with microservices that doesn't exist in EDA is ***data granularity***.

By definition, a microservices architecture requires each service to own its own data. This means you have to break apart your data into fine-grained databases or database ***schemas***—collections of tables that a service owns (writes to). But in EDA, you can choose a single monolithic database, domain-partitioned databases, *or* the database-per-service pattern.

You can refresh your memory of this restriction and why it exists by going back to Chapter 10.

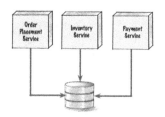

Event-Driven Architecture

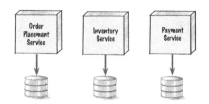

Microservices Architecture

Number 3: Service granularity

Number 3 in our differences countdown has to do with ***service granularity***. Recall from Chapter 10 that a microservice is a *single-purpose service that does one thing really well*. As a result, microservices tend to be fine-grained.

EDA has no such restrictions. Services in an event-driven architecture (formally called ***event processors***) can be whatever size they need to be—fine-grained, coarse-grained, it doesn't matter.

These services can be any size.

These services are all required to be single-purpose—hence the name "micro."

| Event Processor | Event Processor | Event Processor |

Event-Driven Architecture

| Microservice | Microservice | Microservice |

Microservices Architecture

Number 2: Event versus request processing

We're almost there. Coming in at number 2 is another fundamental difference: ***event processing versus request processing***. Event-driven architecture is built on *event processing*—responding to something that has happened, and in turn triggering more events. Microservices architecture, on the other hand, is built on *request processing*—responding to something that needs to happen, like a command or a request, and processing that request.

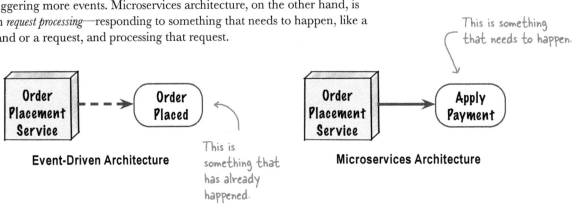

Number 1: Communication style

And finally, coming in at number 1 is the most fundamental difference between EDA and microservices: ***communication style***. EDA typically uses asynchronous communication between services, whereas microservices typically rely on synchronous communication using REST. EDA can occasionally use synchronous calls for things like retrieving data it doesn't have access to, and microservices can use asynchronous communication when commands don't require a response. But those are exceptions rather than the rule.

In microservices, communication is usually done using REST, which needs a response to continue processing.

| Order Placement Service | — Async → | Payment Service |

Event-Driven Architecture

| Order Placement Service | — Sync → | Payment Service |

Microservices Architecture

Who Does What?

Oh dear! We tried to organize these facts , but got them all mixed up. Can you help us figure out which statements are about EDA and which are about microservices? Careful—some facts apply to both.

I require a bounded context.

I can use the database-per-service pattern.

Event-Driven
Architecture

I create systems that can scale.

I mostly use synchronous communication.

I create high-performance systems.

I save you money because I don't cost a lot.

We did this
one for you.

I rely mainly on asynchronous communication.

Microservices
Architecture

I communicate to services using events.

I'm really good at fault tolerance.

I can use a monolithic database.

Solution on page 398

Hybrids: Event-driven microservices

Even with all the differences between EDA and microservices, there's no reason you can't combine them. Doing this creates a *hybrid* architecture called *event-driven microservices*.

You might have observed that the EDA database-per-service pattern for Der Nile looks a lot like microservices. However, just using the database-per-service pattern doesn't make it event-driven microservices. To see what we mean, take a look at this EDA.

A hybrid architecture combines multiple architectural styles.

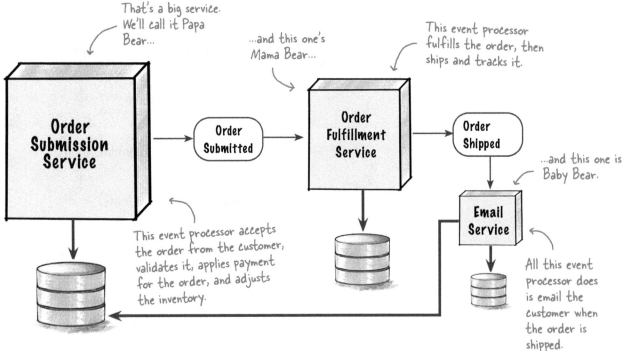

That's a big service. We'll call it Papa Bear...

...and this one's Mama Bear...

This event processor fulfills the order, then ships and tracks it.

...and this one is Baby Bear.

This event processor accepts the order from the customer, validates it, applies payment for the order, and adjusts the inventory.

All this event processor does is email the customer when the order is shipped.

Sharpen your pencil

The above architecture is an acceptable and well-formed EDA, but *not* a well-formed microservices architecture. Two fundamental principles are missing that would make it event-driven microservices. Can you list what those two missing things are?

1. _____   2. _____

Solution on page 399

To make this architecture an event-driven microservices hybrid, we have to apply two very important principles of microservices: single-purpose services and physical bounded contexts.

The Order Submission service has to accept an order, validate it, apply the payment, and adjust the inventory. It's certainly *not* a single-purpose service. That's perfectly acceptable in EDA, but not in microservices. The same is true of the Order Fulfillment service. To make this an event-driven *microservices* architecture, we'd have to split these services into separate *single-purpose* services, each triggering its own events.

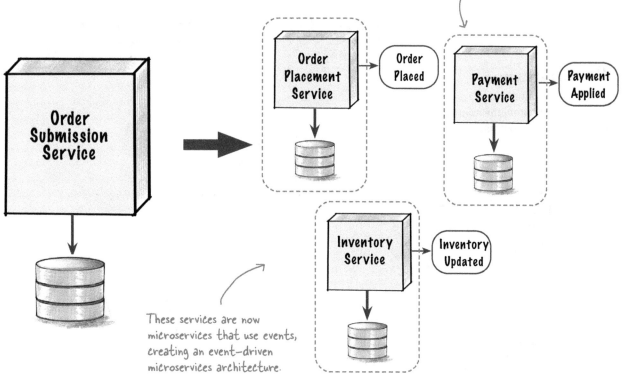

This is a physical bounded context, meaning no one else can access the payment data directly.

These services are now microservices that use events, creating an event-driven microservices architecture.

You might have noticed on the previous page that the Email service is accessing the Order Submission database directly. In microservices, this isn't allowed because of the physical bounded context. In the new hybrid architecture, to retrieve the order data, the Email service needs to call the Order Submission service (now the Order Placement service, since we broke that service up). The implementation of tight physical bounded contexts isolates data access to the owning service.

Event-driven architecture superpowers

It's time to check out the superpowers of the EDA style.

Maintainability
Services in EDA are highly decoupled, making them fairly independent and therefore easier to maintain.

Performance
Because EDA mostly uses asynchronous communication and can multitask, it's very fast.

Evolvability
EDA services always trigger derived events, onto which we can easily add functionality. This makes EDA highly evolvable.

Scalability
Event-driven architectures are highly scalable because of asynchronous processing and service decoupling. Each service can scale independently of others, with the event channels acting as pressure release valves if bottlenecks occur.

Fault tolerance
Because services are highly decoupled in EDA, if one service goes down, it doesn't bring down other services in the workflow.

Event-driven architecture kryptonite

Kryptonite diminishes a superhero's powers, just like these system features and characteristics diminish the power of EDA. Watch out for them!

Complexity

EDA is highly complex because it typically uses asynchronous communication and parallel event processing, and because of its varied database topologies and their trade-offs.

Testability

It's really hard to test asynchronous processing and parallel tasks, making testability a weakness in EDA.

Synchronous calls

If you have lots of synchronous calls between services and workflows that require synchronously dependent services, EDA is not for you.

We know you need a database—what we're saying here is that databases can couple an otherwise highly decoupled system.

Databases

Regardless of the database topology you choose, services are coupled: either to the database or to each other. There are not a lot of good trade-offs here.

Event-driven architecture star ratings

Below is a useful chart for better understanding what EDA is good at and what it's not so good at. One star means that the architectural characteristic is not well supported; five stars means it's very well supported.

Just like movie reviews.

Architectural Characteristic	Star Rating
Maintainability	★ ★ ★ ★
Testability	★ ★
Deployability	★ ★ ★
Simplicity	★
Evolvability	★ ★ ★ ★ ★
Performance	★ ★ ★ ★ ★
Scalability	★ ★ ★ ★ ★
Elasticity	★ ★ ★ ★
Fault Tolerance	★ ★ ★ ★ ★
Overall Cost	$ $ $

While it's easy to find where to change code, testing and deployment are risky and hard.

Things like error handling and asynchronous communication make EDA complex.

Less service coupling means better scalability and elasticity.

Finally, an architectural style that performs well!

Because most things are asynchronous and decoupled, fault tolerance is really high.

EDA is great for operational characteristics like performance, scalability, elasticity, evolvability, and fault tolerance, but struggles when it comes to simplicity and testing. Asynchronous communication is hard to test, and it's also hard to verify that a change in one service or event hasn't affected other services.

Exercise

Which of the following systems might be well suited for the event-driven architectural style, and why? *Hint: Think about EDA's superpowers, its kryptonite, and the problem domain.*

An online auction system where users can bid on items

Why? _____

_____

☐ Well suited for event-driven architecture

☐ Might be a fit for event-driven architecture

☐ Not well suited for event-driven architecture

A large backend financial system for processing and settling international wire transfers overnight

Why? _____

_____

☐ Well suited for event-driven architecture

☐ Might be a fit for event-driven architecture

☐ Not well suited for event-driven architecture

A company entering a new line of business that expects constant changes to its system

Why? _____

_____

☐ Well suited for event-driven architecture

☐ Might be a fit for event-driven architecture

☐ Not well suited for event-driven architecture

A small bakery that wants to start taking online orders

Why? _____

_____

☐ Well suited for event-driven architecture

☐ Might be a fit for event-driven architecture

☐ Not well suited for event-driven architecture

A social media site where users can post and respond to comments

Why? _____

_____

☐ Well suited for event-driven architecture

☐ Might be a fit for event-driven architecture

☐ Not well suited for event-driven architecture

Solution on page 400

Putting it all together

Now, the part you've been waiting for—the complete picture of the Der Nile online ordering system using event-driven architecture. Since there are lots of database topologies to choose from, we'll focus on the core parts of the system: event processors (services) and events.

Lots of errors can occur in this architecture, which would generate corresponding error events. We're not showing those events here—only the "happy path" events.

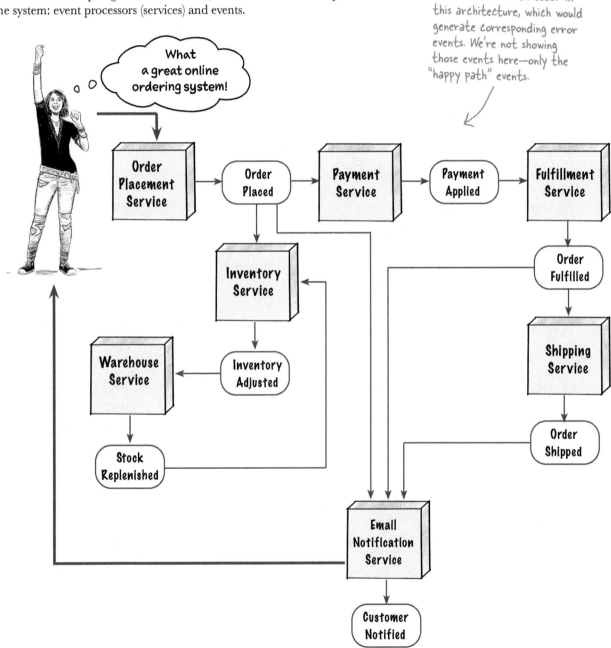

What a great online ordering system!

Wrapping up

Well done! Thanks to your diligent work and EDA knowledge, Der Nile is scaling up and performing to meet its high customer demand, with room to grow even more. Let's close this chapter by reviewing some key points about event-driven architecture.

Bullet Points

- An *event* is something that happens in the system. Events are the fundamental way services communicate with each other in EDA.

- Events are not the same thing as messages—*events* broadcast some action a service just performed to other services in the system, whereas *messages* are commands or requests directed to a single service.

- An *initiating event* originates from a customer or end user and kicks off a business process.

- A *derived event* is generated by a service in response to an initiating event.

- Any action a service performs should trigger a derived event to provide *architectural extensibility*—the ability to extend the system to add new functionality.

- EDA is fast because it generally uses *asynchronous (async) communication*—services don't wait for a response or acknowledgment from other services when sending them information.

- Asynchronous communication is sometimes called *fire-and-forget*.

- Architects usually use a dotted line to represent async communication between services and a solid line to represent sync communication.

- Unlike microservices, event-driven architecture can use a variety of database topologies:

    - With the *monolithic database* topology, all services share a single database.

    - With the *domain-partitioned databases* topology, each domain in the system has its own database, shared by all of the services within that domain.

    - In the *database-per-service pattern*, each service has its own database in a bounded context.

- Event-driven architecture and microservices are very different architectural styles:

    - EDA relies mostly on *asynchronous* communication between services, whereas microservices typically rely on *synchronous* communication using REST.

    - EDA is built on *event processing*—processing things that have already happened. A microservices architecture is built on *request processing*— processing a command or request about something that needs to happen.

    - Microservices are fine-grained and single-purpose, whereas services in EDA can be any size.

    - Microservices requires each service to own its own data, whereas in EDA services can (and usually do) share data.

- You can combine microservices and EDA to create a hybrid architecture called *event-driven microservices*.

- EDA is very complex because it uses asynchronous communication and parallel event processing, and has varied database topologies.

- It's really hard to test asynchronous processing and parallel tasks, making testability a weakness in EDA.

- Derived events provide *hooks* to add functionality, making EDA highly evolvable.

- EDA is highly scalable because of asynchronous processing and service decoupling.

Event-Driven Crossword

Ready to have some fun and test your knowledge about events, asynchronous communication, event processors, and multitasking? Try this crossword puzzle about the event-driven architectural style.

Across

2. How each part of a process is completed and in what order
3. _____-and-forget communication
5. When you combine a service with a database, you get a physical bounded _____
6. Reducing users' wait time is the goal of making a system more _____
8. Async communications don't _____ for a response
12. Type of communication that requires a response
13. Architectural characteristic that deals with speed
18. Some architectures are easier to _____ with new features
19. These communications are sent to a single service using queues
20. Certain conditions may _____ an event

Down

1. A way of organizing databases in an architecture
4. Something important that happens
7. Type of event that kicks off a business process
9. Type of event that flows from other events
10. Abbr. for an external communication hub that an app may call
11. An event is used to _____ news that something has happened
12. Part of an architecture that performs a function
14. _____-partitioned databases
15. Events are delivered via an event _____
16. A message can be a command or a _____
17. Services can _____ for event notifications

Solution on page 401

Exercise Solution

From page 353

As the architect, how can you modify the current workflow shown on page 352 to speed things up a bit? Draw your ideas for a new workflow in the space below. *Hint: What can you do at the same time?* Here's our solution.

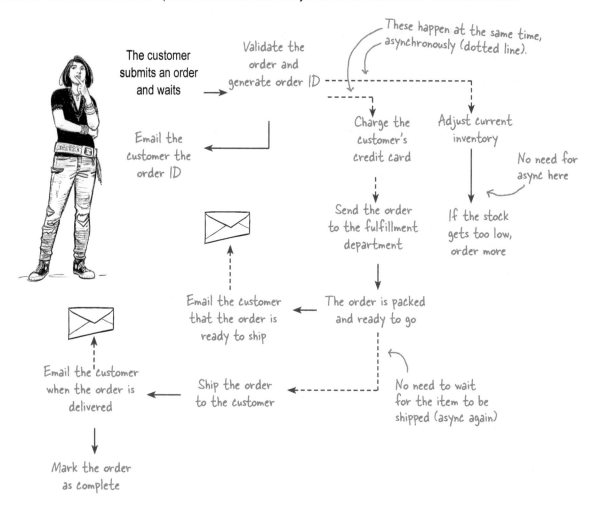

These happen at the same time, asynchronously (dotted line).

The customer submits an order and waits

Validate the order and generate order ID

Charge the customer's credit card

Adjust current inventory

No need for async here

Email the customer the order ID

Send the order to the fulfillment department

If the stock gets too low, order more

Email the customer that the order is ready to ship

The order is packed and ready to go

Email the customer when the order is delivered

Ship the order to the customer

No need to wait for the item to be shipped (async again)

Mark the order as complete

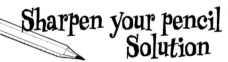

Sharpen your pencil
Solution

From page 357

It's time to test your knowledge about events and messages. For each of the quotes below, mark whether it is more likely an event or a message, and indicate why.

"Adventurous Air flight 12, turn left, heading 230 degrees."

☐ Event   ☒ Message

Reason: This is a command sent to only one airplane about something that needs to happen.

"In other news, a winter storm front has just moved into the area."

☒ Event   ☐ Message

Reason: This is being broadcast to lots of people about something that has just happened.

"Okay, class, turn to page 42 in your workbooks."   ← Be careful—this one's tricky!

☐ Event   ☒ Message

Reason: Even though this is being broadcast to lots of students, it's a command about something that needs to happen.

"Hello, everyone! Sorry I'm late."

☒ Event   ☐ Message

Reason: This is something that happened that is being broadcast to many people. No response is expected.

"Oh no! I just missed my train!"

☒ Event   ☐ Message

Reason: Even though no one might be listening, this is something that just happened. It isn't directed toward any one individual.

"Excuse me, sir—do you have the time?"

☐ Event   ☒ Message

Reason: This is a request made to a single individual about something that needs to happen.

Exercise Solution

From page 359

Based on the *Credit Card Charged* initiating event and the corresponding processing below, can you identify what the derived events should be for each service? Think of as many possible outcomes as you can. Here's our take.

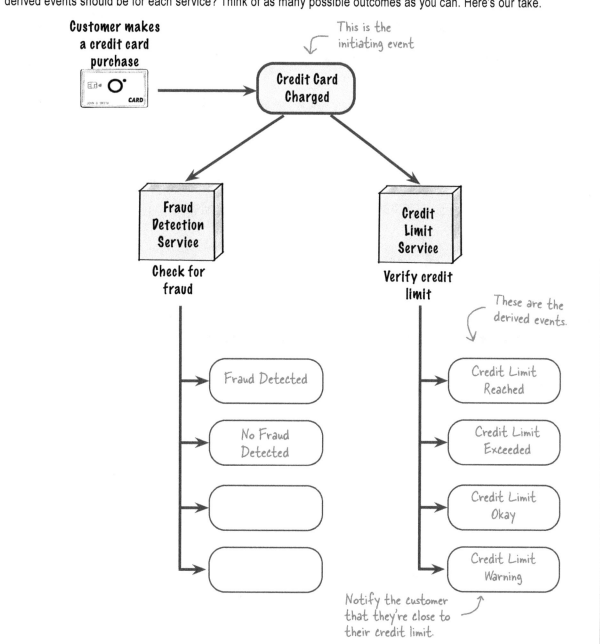

Customer makes
a credit card
purchase

This is the
initiating event

Credit Card
Charged

Fraud
Detection
Service

Check for
fraud

Credit
Limit
Service

Verify credit
limit

These are the
derived events.

Fraud Detected

No Fraud
Detected

Credit Limit
Reached

Credit Limit
Exceeded

Credit Limit
Okay

Credit Limit
Warning

Notify the customer
that they're close to
their credit limit.

Sharpen your pencil
Solution

From page 364

For each of these tasks, would you use asynchronous or synchronous communication?

Give me the shipping options for this order.

☐ Asynchronous ☒ Synchronous ☐ Either one would work

Apply payment for this order and let me know if the payment goes through.

☐ Asynchronous ☒ Synchronous ☐ Either one would work

Fulfill this order for me by picking the items off the shelf and packing them in a box.

☒ Asynchronous ☐ Synchronous ☐ Either one would work

Give me the current status of this order.

☐ Asynchronous ☒ Synchronous ☐ Either one would work

Our inventory of this item is getting low—please order more stock.

☒ Asynchronous ☐ Synchronous ☐ Either one would work

Tell the customer that their order has been shipped and is on its way.

☒ Asynchronous ☐ Synchronous ☐ Either one would work

Update the customer's profile picture.

☐ Asynchronous ☐ Synchronous ☒ Either one would work

Post a customer's review on the product page.

☐ Asynchronous ☐ Synchronous ☒ Either one would work

Sharpen your pencil
Solution

From page 368

Now's your chance to test what you've learned so far about event-driven architecture, events, and asynchronous processing. Der Nile's inventory occasionally gets out of sync, as shown below. When this happens, the order cannot be fulfilled and goes into a back-order state. Der Nile never makes a customer pay for items that are back-ordered, and the customer can choose whether to wait or cancel the order.

As the architect for Der Nile, what additional events and services would you create to address this situation?

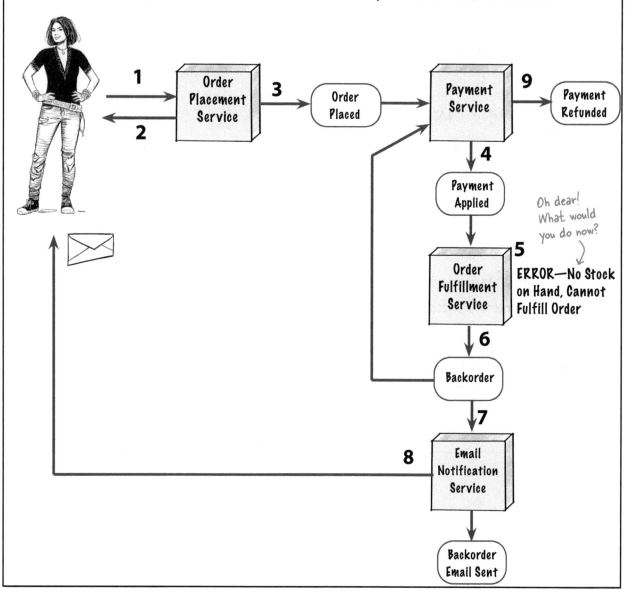

Exercise Solution

From page 376

For each of these business needs, select which topologies you would consider. You can select more than one topology.

We expect anywhere between 20 and 300,000 customers to be on the system at once.

☐ Monolithic Database   ☒ Domain-Partitioned Databases   ☒ Database-Per-Service

The system must be as fast as possible.

☒ Monolithic Database   ☒ Domain-Partitioned Databases   ☐ Database-Per-Service

This medical monitoring system can never completely fail—parts of it must always stay running.

☐ Monolithic Database   ☐ Domain-Partitioned Database   ☒ Database-Per-Service

We're anticipating changing the database a lot in this new line of business.

☐ Monolithic Database   ☒ Domain-Partitioned Databases   ☒ Database-Per-Service

We have to get the new system up and running as soon as possible.

☒ Monolithic Database   ☒ Domain-Partitioned Databases   ☐ Database-Per-Service

Our data model is extremely large and complex, with lots of interrelated data.

☒ Monolithic Database   ☐ Domain-Partitioned Databases   ☐ Database-Per-Service

From page 377

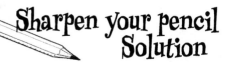

Sharpen your pencil
Solution

List any differences you can think of between event-driven architecture and microservices.

Performance

Physical bounded contexts

Data granularity

Service granularity

Event vs. request processing

Asynchronous versus synchronous processing

These are some of the ones we came up with.

From page 381

Who Does What? Solution

Oh dear! We tried to organize these facts, but got them all mixed up. Can you help us figure out which statements are about EDA and which are about microservices? Careful—some facts apply to both.

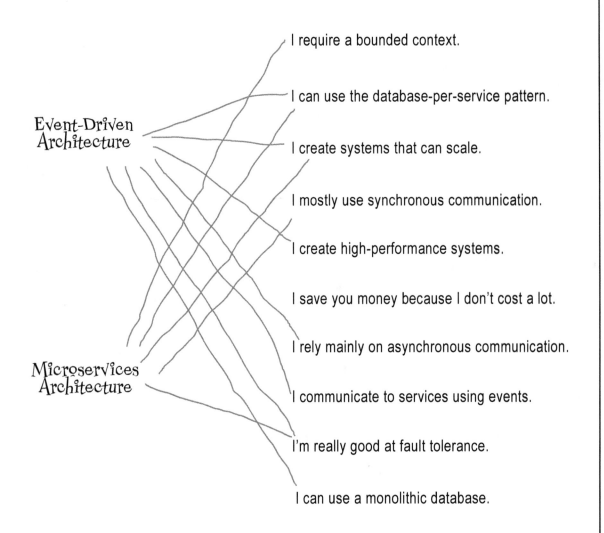

Event-Driven Architecture

Microservices Architecture

- I require a bounded context.
- I can use the database-per-service pattern.
- I create systems that can scale.
- I mostly use synchronous communication.
- I create high-performance systems.
- I save you money because I don't cost a lot.
- I rely mainly on asynchronous communication.
- I communicate to services using events.
- I'm really good at fault tolerance.
- I can use a monolithic database.

Sharpen your pencil
Solution

From page 382

The architecture on page 382 is an acceptable and well-formed EDA, but *not* a well-formed microservices architecture. Two fundamental principles are missing that would make it event-driven microservices. Can you list what those two missing things are?

1. Single-purpose services

2. Physical bounded context (data ownership)

Exercise Solution

From page 387

Which of the following systems might be well suited for the event-driven architectural style, and why? *Hint: Think about EDA's superpowers, its kryptonite, and the problem domain.*

An online auction system where users can bid on items

Why? The problem domain fits EDA, and this system needs high levels of scalability, elasticity, and responsiveness.

☒ **Well suited for event-driven architecture**
☐ **Might be a fit for event-driven architecture**
☐ **Not well suited for event-driven architecture**

A large backend financial system for processing and settling international wire transfers overnight

Why? None of EDA's superpowers are needed for this problem.

☐ **Well suited for event-driven architecture**
☐ **Might be a fit for event-driven architecture**
☒ **Not well suited for event-driven architecture**

A company entering a new line of business that expects constant changes to its system

Why? EDA might be a possibility, since it makes change easier.

☐ **Well suited for event-driven architecture**
☒ **Might be a fit for event-driven architecture**
☐ **Not well suited for event-driven architecture**

A small bakery that wants to start taking online orders

Why? EDA is too complex and expensive for a small bakery.

☐ **Well suited for event-driven architecture**
☐ **Might be a fit for event-driven architecture**
☒ **Not well suited for event-driven architecture**

A social media site where users can post and respond to comments

Why? The async and broadcast capabilities of EDA are a good fit here.

☒ **Well suited for event-driven architecture**
☐ **Might be a fit for event-driven architecture**
☐ **Not well suited for event-driven architecture**

Event-Driven Crossword Solution

From page 390

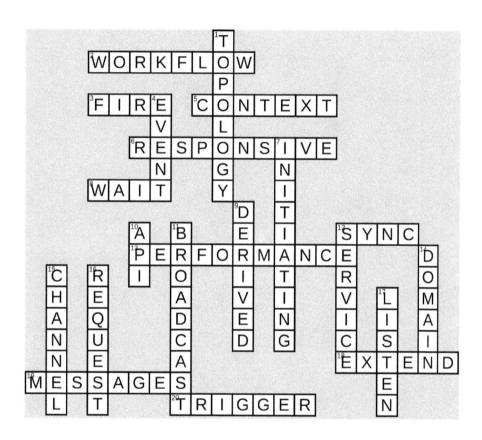

12 *do it yourself*
Testing Your Knowledge

Ready to test your skills in creating a distributed architecture? In this
chapter, you're the software architect. You'll be determining architectural characteristics, building a
logical architecture, making architectural decisions, and deciding whether to use microservices or
event-driven architecture. The exercises in this chapter will give you an end-to-end view of what a
software architect does and show you how much you've learned. Get ready to create an architecture
for a student standardized test–taking system called Make the Grade. Good luck—we hope you get an
A on your architecture!

Welcome to Make the Grade

Congratulations—you've just been hired by Dataville Public Schools to build a new system for standardized testing. All students in a specific grade level will take the same test to determine how well students, teachers, and the schools are doing.

Make the Grade requirements document

☐ Students will take a web-based test in their homeroom, proctored by their homeroom teacher. Because tests are timed (2 hours), the system must present questions as fast as possible.

☐ Each student is presented with a multiple-choice question on the screen. Once they answer it, the system captures the answer and delivers the next question. Students may skip questions, but may not go back to prior ones—only moving forward is allowed.

☐ Once captured, each answer is automatically graded (correct or incorrect) and the results are stored in a central relational database, which has only 300 database connections available.

☐ Anywhere from 20 to 200,000 students could be taking tests at the exact same time.

☐ The Dataville Public Schools testing administrator is responsible for scheduling tests and for maintaining tests, answer keys, and the list of students (used when students sign in to the system).

☐ Rita, the head of Dataville Public Schools, uses the system to generate student reports, teacher evaluations, and school reports after *all* testing is complete.

☐ The proctor (teacher) uses the system to find out when tests are scheduled.

Meet Rita, head of Dataville Public Schools.

Rita has some other important requirements for the system.

Pay attention, because these things are important.

"It's *imperative* that no student answers are lost, even if the system crashes."

"We need this system in place for the *start of the next term*, which is in six months."

"You absolutely have to make sure that students *cannot* hack into the system and steal the test answer keys."

"Testing doesn't occur every day. Some days there are only 20 students taking a test; other days there could be 200,000 at the exact same time. Sometimes tests might be staggered throughout the day."

Student testing workflow

Now that you have the requirements, let's take a look at the primary workflow of the Make the Grade system so you can better understand those requirements.

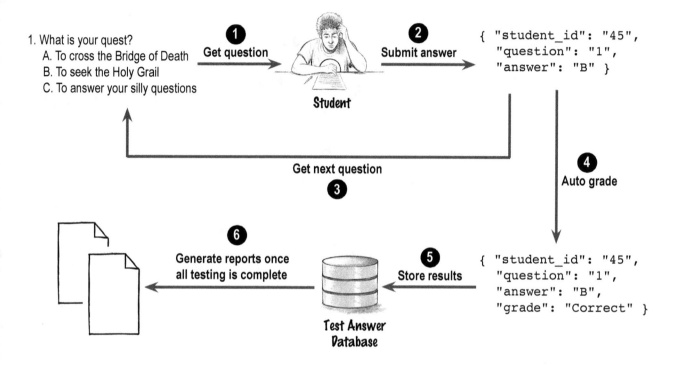

1. What is your quest?
   A. To cross the Bridge of Death
   B. To seek the Holy Grail
   C. To answer your silly questions

1 Get question

Student

2 Submit answer

```
{ "student_id": "45",
  "question": "1",
  "answer": "B" }
```

Get next question
3

4 Auto grade

6 Generate reports once all testing is complete

5 Store results

Test Answer Database

```
{ "student_id": "45",
  "question": "1",
  "answer": "B",
  "grade": "Correct" }
```

Sharpen your pencil

Given the requirements for Make the Grade, list some challenges that you will need to address when creating an architectural solution.

Solution on page 420

Planning the architecture

I've given you the requirements, so what's the big delay? Why aren't you developing the system? We only have six months.

Make The Grade requirements document

* Students will take a web-based test from their assigned classroom and teacher. Because tests are timed (2 hours), the system must present questions as fast as possible.

* Each student is presented a question on the screen. Once they answer it, the system captures the answer and delivers the next question to the student. Students may skip questions, but they may not go back to prior questions.

* Once captured, the student answer is automatically graded (correct or incorrect) and the results stored in a central student answer database, which is relational and only has 300 connections available.

* There can be anywhere from 20 to 200,000 students all taking the same test at the exact same time.

* The testing administrator schedules tests, maintains tests and corresponding answer keys, and also maintains the list of students (this is used when the student signs into the system).

* The administrator also generates student reports, teacher reports, school reports, and testing reports (common questions students always get wrong, and so on) for the education department after all testing is complete.

Even though Rita is impatient to see some progress, don't let that sway you from creating a solid and well-thought-out architecture.

We have to create an architecture first.

As you've learned, architecture is a critical part of any software system. Without it, the system will likely fail to achieve any of its goals.

Before you start developing code, you have to create an architecture. This means going back to what you learned in Chapter 1 about the four dimensions of software architecture.

Don't worry—we'll get the system done. But first, it's important to know what we're building.

The architects' roadmap

Let's get the Make the Grade architecture started. You'll use the steps you've learned to translate requirements into an architecture.

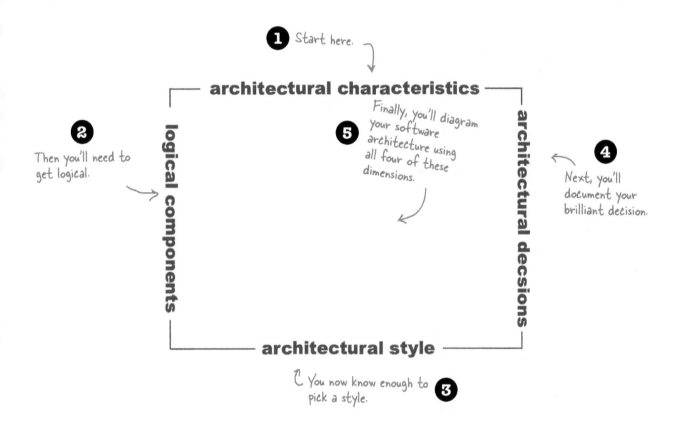

This diagram will serve as your roadmap as you make your way through each of the exercises, so get used to seeing it. The next few pages will walk you through these steps.

Good luck on your journey—Dataville Public Schools is counting on you.

Step 1:
Identify architectural characteristics

In this first step, you'll use the requirements below to identify the architectural characteristics that are critical for the success of the Make the Grade student test-taking system. On the next page, identify *up to seven* driving characteristics. Then select the three you think are the *most critical* for the system to be successful.

Remember, *implicit characteristics* are those that are implied in virtually every software architecture. (Would you ever *not* worry about security?) If you see one you feel is *critical* for the success of the system, move it over to the driving characteristics area.

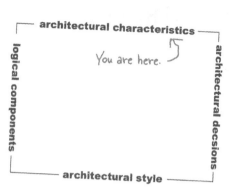

"It's **imperative** that no student answers are lost, even if the system crashes."

"We need this system in place for the **start of the next term**, which is in six months."

"You absolutely have to make sure that students **cannot** hack into the system and steal the test answer keys."

"Testing doesn't occur every day. Some days there are only 20 students taking a test; other days there could be 200,000 at the exact same time. Sometimes tests might be staggered throughout the day."

We copied the requirements here to make it easier for you to use them to identify the driving architectural characteristics.

Make the Grade requirements document

☐ Students will take a web-based test in their homeroom, proctored by their homeroom teacher. Because tests are timed (2 hours), the system must present questions as fast as possible.

☐ Each student is presented with a multiple-choice question on the screen. Once they answer it, the system captures the answer and delivers the next question. Students may skip questions, but may not go back to prior ones—only moving forward is allowed.

☐ Once captured, each answer is automatically graded (correct or incorrect) and the results are stored in a central relational database, which has only 300 database connections available.

☐ Anywhere from 20 to 200,000 students could be taking tests at the exact same time.

☐ The Dataville Public Schools testing administrator is responsible for scheduling tests and for maintaining tests, answer keys, and the list of students (used when students sign in to the system).

☐ Rita, the head of Dataville Public Schools, uses the system to generate student reports, teacher evaluations, and school reports after *all* testing is complete.

☐ The proctor (teacher) uses the system to find out when tests are scheduled.

Exercise

In Chapter 2, we showed you how to use this template to limit the number of architectural characteristics. Flip back to page 70 if you need a refresher on how to use it.

Top 3   Driving Characteristics   Implicit Characteristics

☐   _____   *feasibility (cost/time)*
                                             _____

☐   _____   *security*
                                               _____

☐   _____   *maintainability*
                                               _____

☐   _____   *observability*
                                               _____

☐   _____   These are implied characteristics. Move them to the Driving Characteristics column if you think they are <u>critical</u> to the success of the system.

☐   _____

☐   _____   Go back to Chapter 2 if you need a refresher on the definitions of these common architectural characteristics.

↖ Pick the top three most important ones (in any order).

Possible Candidate Architectural Characteristics

performance	data integrity	deployability
responsiveness	data consistency	testability
availability	adaptability	configurability
fault tolerance	extensibility	customizability
scalability	interoperability	recoverability
elasticity	concurrency	auditability

———————▶ Solution on page 421

Step 2:
Identify logical components

Good job! Now that you've identified the critical architectural characteristics for Make the Grade, it's time to apply what you learned in Chapter 4 to create logical components.

Using the requirements and primary workflow on the previous pages, use the actor/action approach to identify the *users and their actions*. Then identify as many **logical components** as you can on the next page.

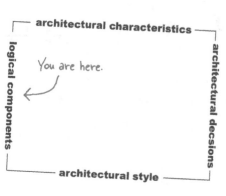

Here's some additional information you might find useful for this exercise:

- Students sign in to the system using their student ID. The system will verify the date, student ID, test, and teacher when a student signs in.

- Rita, the head of Dataville Public Schools, will wait at least one day after testing has finished before generating reports.

  This gives the system time to record all the answers in the database.

- The classroom teacher acts as the *proctor* for the test, watching the students to make sure they don't cheat and providing assistance. The teachers use the system to find out when a test is scheduled for their class.

- When a test is created, the questions and answers are sent to the test administrator, who enters them into the system. The same goes for any modifications to existing tests.

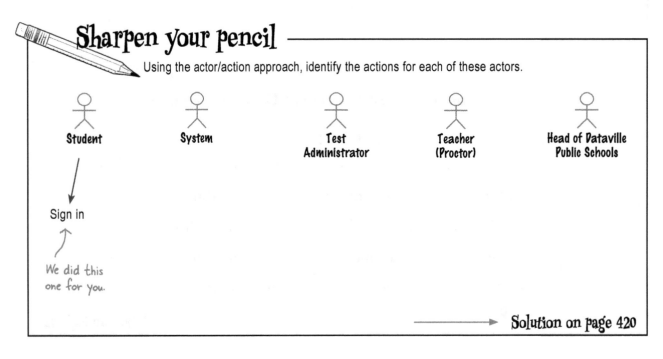

Sharpen your pencil

Using the actor/action approach, identify the actions for each of these actors.

Student   System   Test Administrator   Teacher (Proctor)   Head of Dataville Public Schools

Sign in

We did this one for you.

Solution on page 420

Exercise

Using the space below, draw your logical components and their interactions.

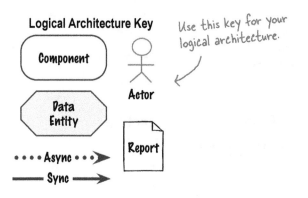

Logical Architecture Key

Use this key for your logical architecture.

Component

Data Entity

Actor

Report

• • • • Async • • • ▶

——— Sync ———▶

———————▶ Solution on page 422

Step 3:
Choose an architectural style

We know that this system will have separate parts that require different architectural characteristics, so it makes sense to use a ***distributed architecture***, such as microservices or event-driven architecture. Leveraging what you've learned about both styles, use the next page to analyze their pros and cons with respect to the Make the Grade test-taking system. You will also need to go back to the requirements, your logical architecture, and the star rating charts for each architectural style (we've added those for you below). Choose an architectural style based on your analysis.

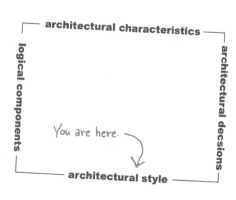

The more stars, the better that characteristic is supported.

Microservices

Architectural Characteristic	Star Rating
Maintainability	★ ★ ★ ★ ★
Testability	★ ★ ★ ★ ★
Deployability	★ ★ ★ ★ ★
Simplicity	★
Evolvability	★ ★ ★ ★ ★
Performance	★ ★
Scalability	★ ★ ★ ★ ★
Elasticity	★ ★ ★ ★
Fault Tolerance	★ ★ ★ ★ ★
Overall Cost	$ $ $ $ $

Both of these styles are complex. Welcome to distributed architecture.

Event-Driven Architecture

Architectural Characteristic	Star Rating
Maintainability	★ ★ ★ ★
Testability	★ ★
Deployability	★ ★ ★
Simplicity	★
Evolvability	★ ★ ★ ★ ★
Performance	★ ★ ★ ★ ★
Scalability	★ ★ ★ ★ ★
Elasticity	★ ★ ★ ★
Fault Tolerance	★ ★ ★ ★ ★
Overall Cost	$ $ $

These three characteristics are the same for both styles.

Here are some considerations that might help you decide which architectural style would be better suited for Make the Grade:

- Go back to your logical architecture diagram and count the actions you identified that you would consider *events*. If you find there aren't many events, event-driven architecture might not be the right choice.

- Think about the nature of the data in the system. If most of the data is shared, then microservices probably isn't the right choice.

- Think about how many actions you identified are *synchronous* and how many are *asynchronous*. If you have a lot of synchronous actions, event-driven architecture might not be a good fit.

Exercise

Outline the pros and cons of each architectural style to help you make a choice about which one might be most appropriate for Make the Grade.

Microservices Architecture Analysis

Pros   Cons

Event-Driven Architecture Analysis

Pros   Cons

List your winning choice here: _____

Solution on page 423

Step 4:
Document your decision

Good work: you've just chosen which architectural style you are going to use for Make the Grade. Now's your chance to explain *why* you made the choice you did and document your architectural decision.

As you learned in Chapter 3, an **architectural decision record**, or ADR, is an effective way to document your architectural decisions. Use the ADR on the next page to document your architectural style decision. Assume that this is your 11th architectural decision.

Revisit Chapter 3 if you need a refresher on architectural decision records.

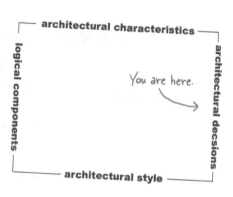

You are here.

architectural characteristics

logical components

architectural decisions

architectural style

What should I put in the Consequences section of my ADR if my architectural decision doesn't have any consequences?

Every architectural decision has consequences.

Maybe it's cost, or maybe it's sacrificing a little bit of performance to have better security. Regardless, *every* architectural decision has consequences.

Think about the trade-off analysis you just did. Each one of those trade-offs implies a consequence—something you were willing to give up (or accept) to get something better. The *Consequences* section of an ADR is a great place to document your trade-off analysis and the corresponding consequences of your decision.

If you can't find any consequences in your architectural decision, keep looking, because they're there.

Exercise

Architectural Decision Record

Title:

Status: Proposed   ← *We did this one for you.*

Context:

Decision:

Consequences: ← *What is the impact of your decision? What trade-offs are you willing to accept?*

→ Solution on page 424

Step 5:
Diagram your architecture

Now it's time to combine all four dimensions of software architecture and show us your vision of the Make the Grade architecture. In this last exercise, you'll diagram your architecture on the following page using the key on this page.

There's not a lot of room to diagram your architecture, but that's intentional. While a lot of detail can go into architecture diagrams, what we're asking you to do is sketch out a **high-level** physical view showing the user interfaces, services, databases, communication type (sync or async), and how all of these architectural artifacts connect to each other.

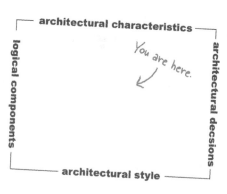

Physical Architecture Key

User Interface

Draw a computer screen to represent the **user interface**, and indicate which type(s) of **users** are interacting with it. For example, if you have separate user interfaces for the test administrator and the education department (for generating reports), show two computer screens. If they share a single user interface, show one computer screen with multiple actors interacting with it.

Feel free to annotate your diagram to clarify points or describe things.

Use a box to represent a service. Be sure to include the **components** that the services implement, which should match the logical components you identified in the prior exercise. Also, indicate which user interfaces access the service and which other services communicate with the service. Last, give your service a **meaningful and descriptive name**.

Database

Draw a cylinder to represent each **physical database** in your solution. Your label should indicate what type of data it stores (for example, **Student Answers**). Show which services write to the database and which services are read-only by **drawing arrows** to indicate the data flow to and from the services. (Writes assume reads.)

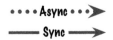

Draw dotted lines to represent **asynchronous** communication (such as using a queue, topic, or stream), and solid lines to represent **synchronous** (blocking) communication between services and user interfaces.

If your architecture uses messages or events, draw a box or an envelope to indicate the **data** being passed (for example, **Student Answer**) or the **event** being triggered (for example, **Answer Submitted**).

Event or Message

Exercise

Use this space and refer to the key on the previous page to sketch your physical architecture for Make the Grade.

Solutions on pages 425–426

There are no right (or wrong) answers!

Congratulations—you've just created an architecture!

What we're about to show you are the exercise "solutions." We've used quotes there because our answers are not the only ones possible. You see, there are no right or wrong answers in software architecture: it's all about analyzing trade-offs and being able to justify your decisions.

Compare your answers with the ones we're about to show you. See how your solutions differ and think about what you might have done differently, or confirm that you made what seems to you to be the most appropriate choice. We'll show you our Make the Grade architectures for microservices *and* event-driven architecture, since both these styles are viable options.

Software architecture is *always* a learning process. Each new problem brings a whole new set of conditions, constraints, and business and technical concerns. There is no one-size-fits-all architecture—it's up to you, the architect, to come up with the most appropriate architecture for your situation.

⌐ Bullet Points

- When analyzing requirements for a business problem, always gather additional information from the business stakeholders or project sponsor.

- While there's no "checklist" for creating an architecture, the four dimensions of software architecture (introduced in Chapter 1) provide a good roadmap.

- Identifying driving architectural characteristics requires you to analyze the business requirements and technical constraints.

- Implicit architectural characteristics become *driving characteristics* if they are critical or important to the success of the system.

- Make sure you can tie each driving characteristic back to some sort of requirement or business need.

- When identifying logical components and creating a corresponding logical architecture, try to avoid adding physical details such as services, databases, queues, and user interfaces—those artifacts go into the *physical architecture*.

- When choosing an architectural style, make sure you take into account the characteristics of the architectural style, the problem domain, and the driving architectural characteristics you identified.

- *Hybrid architectures* (those combining two or more different architectural styles) are very common. Just be sure to verify that the hybrid architecture still addresses your critical architectural characteristics.

- *Architectural decision records* (ADRs) are a great way to document your choices. They communicate the reasons for your architectural decisions as well as your trade-off analyses.

- When diagramming your physical architecture, be sure to include all the components you identified in your logical architecture.

- Remember that there are no right or wrong answers in software architecture. As long as you can provide a reasonable justification for your architectural decisions, you are on the right track for success.

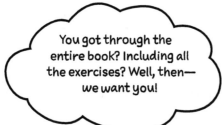

You are well on your way to thinking architecturally!

We are going to assume that you actually read this book all the way through and didn't just jump to the end. If so, we congratulate you for it! Job well done.

Congratulations!

You've made it to the end.

Though there is still the appendix.

And the index.

And there's a website...

You aren't getting away that easily!

(Go ahead, you can admit it—you just can't get enough of software architecture, can you?)

Sharpen your pencil Solution

From page 405

Given the requirements for Make the Grade, list some challenges that you will need to address when creating an architectural solution.

- Storing up to 200,000 simultaneous student answers in a relational database that has only 300 connections.

- Delivering the next question to each student as fast as possible while making sure student answers are not lost.

- Coming up with a viable solution that can be delivered within a six-month time frame.

- Making the system elastic to reduce cost and resource use when testing is not happening or there are only a few students taking a test.

Sharpen your pencil Solution

From page 410

Using the actor/action approach, identify the actions for each of these actors.

Student

System
→ Grade answer
→ Write to database

Test Administrator
→ Schedule tests
→ Maintain tests
→ Maintain list of students

Teacher (Proctor)
→ Get test schedule

Head of Dataville Public Schools
→ Generate reports

Get next question

Sign in
↑
We did this one for you.

Submit answer

Exercise Solution

From page 409

In Chapter 2, we showed you how to use this template to limit the number of architectural characteristics. Flip back to page 70 if you need a refresher on how to use it.

Top 3	Driving Characteristics	Implicit Characteristics
☐	Feasibility — We only have six months!	← *feasibility (cost/time)*
☐	Security — Need to protect the answer key.	← *security*
☒	Elasticity — There can be 20 to 200,000 students— the very definition of elasticity.	*maintainability*
☒	Responsiveness — We have to deliver the next question right away.	*observability*
☐	Availability — If the system isn't available, students can't take a test.	
☒	Data integrity — We absolutely cannot lose student answers.	
☐	Recoverability — We don't want the students to have to start the test over if the system crashes.	

Possible Candidate Architectural Characteristics

performance	data integrity	deployability
responsiveness	data consistency	testability
availability	adaptability	configurability
fault tolerance	extensibility	customizability
scalability	interoperability	recoverability
elasticity	concurrency	auditability

Exercise Solution

From page 411

Using the space below, draw your logical components and their interactions.

Logical Architecture Key

- Component
- Actor
- Data Entity
- Report
- • • • Async • • •→
- —— Sync ——→

These components are part of the test-taking functionality

Student

- interacts → **Student Sign-in**
- interacts → **Next Test Question**
- interacts → **Capture Answer**

This is async so the student doesn't have to wait.

Student Sign-in — reads ← **Student Information**

Next Test Question — reads ← **Test Questions**

Test Answer Key — reads → **Automatic Grading**

Test Schedule

Student Information

Test Questions

Test Answer Key

Automatic Grading — writes → **Student Answers**

- **Test Schedule** ← writes — **Test Scheduler**
- **Student Information** ← writes — **Student Maintenance**
- **Test Questions** ← writes — **Test Maintenance**

Student Answers — reads → **Test Reporting**

Test Scheduler

Student Maintenance

Test Maintenance

Test Reporting

- interacts → **Test Scheduler**
- interacts → **Student Maintenance**
- interacts → **Test Maintenance**

The proctor needs to know when the test is taking place.

interacts

Proctor (Teacher)

Test Administrator

This is the administrative functionality.

Test Reporting ← generates — Report

Head of Dataville Public Schools

Exercise Solution

From page 413

Outline the pros and cons of each architectural style to help you make a choice about which one might be most appropriate for Make the Grade.

Microservices Architecture Analysis

Pros

A microservices architecture provides good elasticity, scalability, and fault tolerance—things Make the Grade needs.

Partitioning data, so that each microservice owns its own data, provides a good level of fault tolerance and data access control.

Make the Grade has lots of separate, independent parts—test taking, grading, maintenance, and reporting—so it lends itself well to separately deployed, single-purpose services that don't require much interaction.

Cons

Microservices gets a low performance rating, but we could address this by using caching and minimizing communication between services.

The test administrator's functionalities write to a database that other services need to read (for test questions, student sign-on information, answer keys, and so on). This implies that we need to share data, something for which microservices is not well suited. However, this data is fairly static and can be shared through in-memory caching.

Event-Driven Architecture Analysis

Pros

Event-driven architecture (EDA) is highly responsive and provides the elasticity, scalability, and fault tolerance Make the Grade needs.

A student submitting an answer can be considered an event; the responses would be to deliver the next question and automatically grade the answer. However, this is a fairly isolated event—really the only one in the system.

Cons

The test administrator's functionalities (student and test maintenance and test scheduling and reporting) are not really suited for EDA.

There aren't many <u>events</u> in this system—mostly, requests are being made to the system. The only event we identified was a student submitting an answer, but that event only has one listener (the auto-grading functionality).

Remember, this isn't the only answer, just our choice based on our analysis.

List your winning choice here: Based on our analysis, we selected <u>microservices</u> for Make the Grade.

Exercise Solution

From page 415

Architectural Decision Record

Title: O11: Use of the microservices architectural style for the Make the Grade system

Status: Proposed

Context:
Make the Grade is a test-taking system that needs high levels of responsiveness, fault tolerance, elasticity, and data integrity. Because there are separate parts of the system (admin, reporting, grading, and test taking) that require different architectural characteristics, a distributed architecture is appropriate. The two choices are microservices and event-driven architecture.

Decision:
<u>We will use the microservices architectural style</u>.

Microservices provides the necessary fault tolerance, elasticity, and scalability.

Performance deficiencies and high responsiveness needs are addressed through minimal inter-service communication, caching to minimize data retrieval needs (student information, test questions, and test answer keys), and asynchronous communication for automatic grading and storing students' answers.

Data integrity (preventing data loss) is addressed by using persistent queues between the Capture Answer and Automatic Grading components, along with client acknowledgment mode in the Automatic Grading component, to make sure that each student answer stays on the queue until it is persistent in the Student Answer Database.

The test administration functionality will be a single microservice that combines the test scheduling, test maintenance, and student maintenance functionalities. Reporting will be a single microservice as well.

Consequences:
Technically partitioned teams will need to be reorganized into cross-functional teams and will work in parallel in order to finish the system in six months.

We will need to use in-memory caching to address the system's performance, elasticity, and data sharing needs.

We will need additional infrastructure to support microservices: specifically, a service orchestrator like Kubernetes and a more effective CI/CD deployment pipeline.

Exercise Solution

From page 417

Use this space and refer to the key on the page 416 to sketch your physical architecture for *Make the Grade*.

Microservices Architecture Diagram

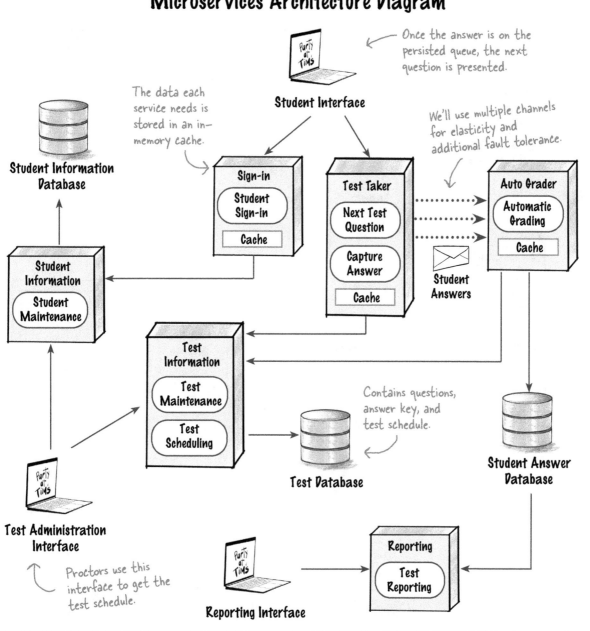

Once the answer is on the persisted queue, the next question is presented.

Student Interface

The data each service needs is stored in an in-memory cache.

Student Information Database

We'll use multiple channels for elasticity and additional fault tolerance.

Sign-in
- Student Sign-in
- Cache

Test Taker
- Next Test Question
- Capture Answer
- Cache

Auto Grader
- Automatic Grading
- Cache

Student Answers

Student Information
- Student Maintenance

Test Information
- Test Maintenance
- Test Scheduling

Contains questions, answer key, and test schedule.

Test Database

Student Answer Database

Test Administration Interface

Proctors use this interface to get the test schedule.

Reporting
- Test Reporting

Reporting Interface

Exercise Solution

From page 417

Use this space and refer to the key on page 416 to sketch your physical architecture for *Make the Grade*.

Event-Driven Architecture Diagram

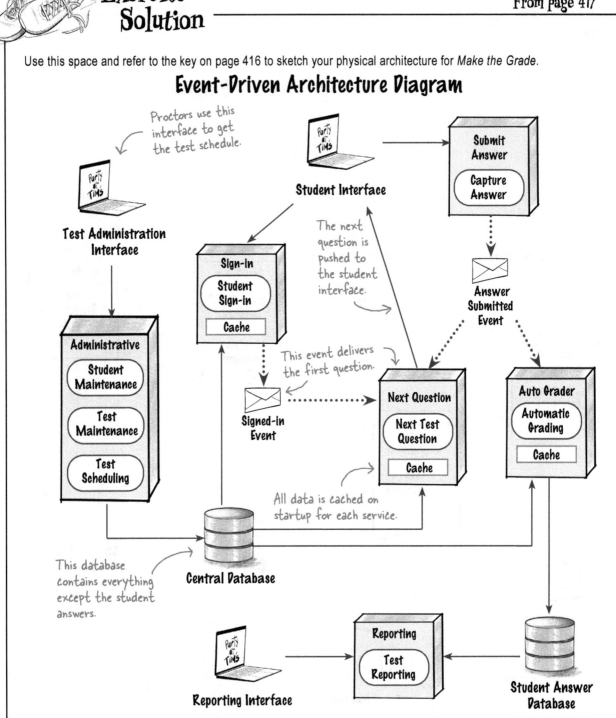

Proctors use this interface to get the test schedule.

Test Administration Interface

Student Interface

Submit Answer

Capture Answer

The next question is pushed to the student interface.

Sign-in

Student Sign-in

Cache

This event delivers the first question.

Answer Submitted Event

Administrative

Student Maintenance

Test Maintenance

Test Scheduling

Signed-in Event

Next Question

Next Test Question

Cache

Auto Grader

Automatic Grading

Cache

All data is cached on startup for each service.

This database contains everything except the student answers.

Central Database

Reporting

Test Reporting

Reporting Interface

Student Answer Database

The Top Six Topics We Didn't Cover

There's a lot more to be said about software architecture. We promise, you're done with this book. But reading this book is just the first step in your journey to thinking architecturally, and we couldn't in good conscience let you go without a little more preparation. So, we've gathered a few additional juicy bits into this appendix. Each of the topics that follow deserves as much attention as the other topics we've covered. However, our goal here is just to give you a high-level idea of what they're all about. And yes, this really *is* the end of the book. Except for the index, of course—it's a real page-turner!

#1 The coding architect

After reading this book, I'm interested in becoming a software architect—but I also really like writing source code. Can I still do that as an architect?

Yes! We firmly believe that software architects should still write source code. Not only does it help you maintain your technical skills, but it also shows you how your architectural decisions play out in real life.

However, it's not always easy to balance hands-on coding with software architecture. As you've seen, there's a lot to software architecture. It will take up most (if not all) of your time.

Don't worry though—we'll share some tips and techniques for writing software while being an effective software architect.

Don't become a bottleneck

Be careful not to take ownership of code that is on the product's critical path. Leave things like the underlying framework code and really complex or crucial parts of the system to your development team. That way, if you get pulled away by architecture-related stuff, you won't hold up your team.

Write proof-of-concept code

Having trouble making an architectural decision? How about writing some code to demonstrate each option? Writing proof-of-concept code is a great way to better understand the implications of your architectural decisions while maintaining your technical expertise. A word of advice, however—unless you know for *sure* you're going to throw it away, take the time to write the **best** *production-ready code* you can. It could very well end up in production.

Here are some more ways to make sure you don't become a bottleneck.

Pay back some technical debt

Almost every development team accumulates **technical debt** (needed changes that are deferred to a later time). Help your team out by addressing some of it. They'll appreciate it, and if you get called away, it won't hold them up.

Get involved during production outages

When an outage strikes, step in to assist, if you can. Help your development team identify the root cause and make the code changes needed to get the system back up and running. This also gives you an opportunity to see the detailed implementation of your architecture.

And here are some ways to stay continuously involved.

Do lots of code reviews

No one *likes* doing code reviews. But it's a good way to stay involved, and it helps you make sure the source code stays aligned with your architectural decisions.

#2 Expectations for architects

We've talked a lot in this book about architecture, but not so much about the **role** of a software architect. While the specifics will vary from company to company, here are some things any software architect will be expected to do, regardless of title.

Make architectural decisions

An architect is expected to define architectural decisions and design principles and use them to guide technology decisions within the team, the department, and/or across the enterprise.

Continually analyze the architecture

An architect is expected to always be analyzing the current architecture and technology environment and making recommendations for solutions and improvements. This continuous analysis is a way of checking for *architectural vitality*—that is, how viable the architecture still is, given constant changes in business and technology.

Keep current with the latest trends

To remain relevant (and retain a job!), developers must keep up to date on technical and industry trends. For architects, it's even *more* critical to keep current. Doing so helps you prepare for the future and make correct decisions.

Ensure compliance with the architecture

Architects should continually verify that the development teams are following the approved architectural decisions and design principles. This is called *architectural governance*. Regardless of how good the architecture is, the system won't work unless everyone adheres to your architectural decisions.

Cultivate diverse exposures and experiences

As an architect, it's important to know a little about a lot of things.

More about this in a few!

An architect is expected to be familiar with technologies, frameworks, platforms, and environments of all sorts. This doesn't mean you need to be an *expert* in all of them, but you should have some knowledge of what's out there.

Know the business domain

Effective software architects understand the business domain of a problem space. Without knowing what the business does and how, it's difficult to understand the problem, goals, and requirements well enough to design an effective architecture.

Possess exceptional interpersonal skills

Having exceptional leadership and interpersonal skills is important. Typically, technologists, developers, and architects prefer to solve technical problems, not *people* problems. But an architect is expected to provide technical guidance to the team *and* lead them through implementing the architecture. Leadership skills are *at least half* of what it takes to become an effective software architect, regardless of your role or title.

The American computer scientist Gerald Weinburg is famous for saying, "No matter how it looks at first, it's always a people problem" (https://oreil.ly/wyDB8).

Understand and navigate office politics

Many people will challenge your decisions. Product owners, project managers, and business stakeholders may see a solution as too costly or not fast enough to implement. Developers and other architects may challenge your approach if they feel theirs is better. You'll be expected to make a case for what you propose. You must navigate office politics and apply basic negotiation skills to get your decisions approved.

#3 The soft skills of architecture

Like we said on the last page, at *least* half of being a software architect is having great people skills. You'll need them to lead and guide your development team, gain the respect of your peers, and get everyone to agree to a common vision and direction.

We call these "soft" skills, but they are hard skills to acquire. Using them effectively requires years of practice and trial and error. Here are some soft skill techniques to help you become a more effective software architect.

Demonstrate, don't discuss

Rather than arguing a point with another architect or development team, *demonstrate* it. Every environment is different, which is why simply Googling never yields correct answers. When you compare the options in a production-like environment and show the results, there's little room for argument.

> Say it with us: "Demonstration defeats discussion."

Know when to fight and when to let go

Choosing your battles wisely is the mark of a great leader and makes you a reasonable person to work with. It gains you respect. Fight to the death for something that's crucial to making the architecture work, but let things go if they're not so important.

> Choosing your battles is good advice, even outside of software architecture. You're welcome.

Focus on business value

When talking with business stakeholders, describe your decision or solution in terms of its *business value*. Business stakeholders aren't interested in things like fault tolerance or testability—they care about things like time to market, regulatory compliance, and mergers and acquisitions. Translate your technical concerns into business ones and you'll be speaking their language.

$$$

This is the ADR
from Chapter 12.

Involve developers in your architectural decisions

We have learned two basic leadership rules over the years:

Rule Number 1: If developers don't know *why* you made a decision, they are less likely to agree with it.

Rule Number 2: If developers aren't *involved* in a decision, they are less likely to follow it.

Keep your developers involved. Collaborate by asking their opinions about a particular decision, involving them in a risk-storming exercise, or using the Request for Comment status in an ADR. Always justify your architectural decisions—and make sure everyone on the development team understands that justification.

Divide and conquer

In the book *The Art of War*, the ancient Chinese warrior Sun Tzu advises, "If your enemy's forces are united, separate them." You can use this tactic when faced with all-or-nothing situations. Do *all* parts of the system need 400 ms response times or 99.999% availability? Dividing the problem into parts can help you identify what's hard to achieve, which makes negotiation easier.

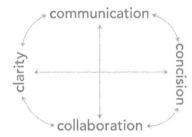

Keep things simple, clear, and concise

Nothing helps an architect gain respect and trust better than being able to explain things in clear, concise terms. It makes you more approachable. People will *want* to ask you things and get you involved. We call this the "four Cs" of architecture—be **C**lear, be **C**oncise, **C**ommunicate, and **C**ollaborate. You need all four to become an effective software architect.

Be available to your development team

Nothing is more frustrating for a developer or business stakeholder than having a critical question come up when you aren't around to answer it. Make sure not to spread yourself too thin—*be there for your team*.

Blocking out your calendar early in the morning or late in the afternoon is a great way to ensure you don't get cooped up in meetings all day. Use that time to collaborate with your development team and be available to answer their questions. They'll be grateful for it, and you will gain a lot of respect.

#4 Diagramming techniques

Back in Chapter 3, we discussed ADRs as the best way to document the analysis process that leads to a decision. Another common method architects use to document architecture is **diagrams**. Architecture diagrams illustrate many important details that team members benefit from visualizing, such as structure, topology, communication, dependencies, and integration points.

Communication Patterns by Jacqui Read is a great resource, if you'd like to learn more.

This topic can (and does) fill entire books. We're just here to provide some quick tips to make your diagrams better, regardless of how you create them.

Keep it simple

Don't try to create comprehensive architecture diagrams that include *every detail*. If you do, your diagrams will suffer from the "hairball effect"— becoming too complex and dense to understand.

> **Trading platform:**
> **Major information flows**

Use clear titles for your diagrams.

Always include a title

Most architecture diagrams represent a view or perspective, and your title should make yours explicit.

Use unidirectional arrows to represent communication

Double-headed arrows are ambiguous. Did the author intend to indicate two-way communications, or is just that the default arrow?

Using **unidirectional arrows** removes all ambiguity and makes documentation more explicit.

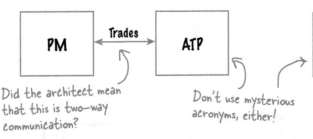

Did the architect mean that this is two-way communication?

Don't use mysterious acronyms, either!

Single-headed arrows remove ambiguity.

Use real labels, not acronyms

Only insiders understand acronyms. **Spell things out** whenever possible to avoid confusion and eliminate the need for extra documentation.

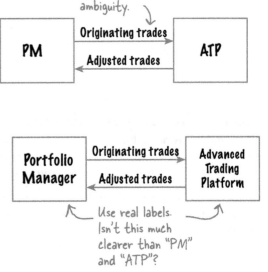

Use real labels. Isn't this much clearer than "PM" and "ATP"?

Use solid lines for sync and dotted for async communication

Architects need a way to specify whether communication is synchronous (blocking) or asynchronous (nonblocking). A solid line is common shorthand for synchronous communication, and a dotted one represents the asynchronous alternative.

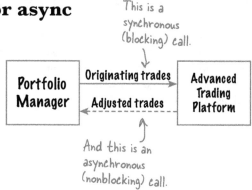

This is a synchronous (blocking) call.

And this is an asynchronous (nonblocking) call.

Use consistent shapes and colors

Don't use arbitrary shapes to try to save room; consistent shapes and colors cut down on the visual "noise" created by needless inconsistency.

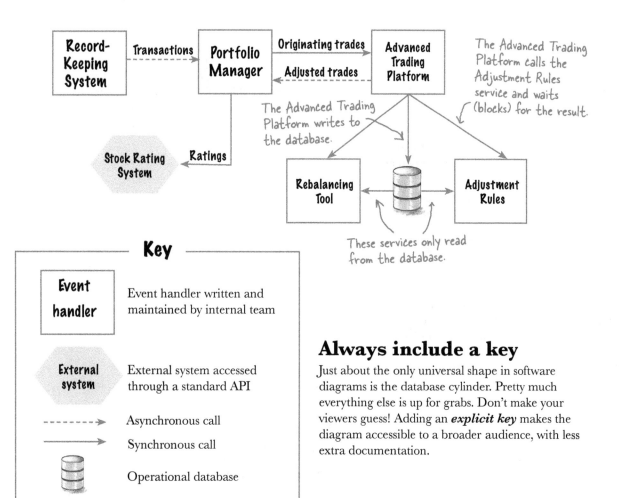

The Advanced Trading Platform calls the Adjustment Rules service and waits (blocks) for the result.

The Advanced Trading Platform writes to the database.

These services only read from the database.

Key

Event handler — Event handler written and maintained by internal team

External system — External system accessed through a standard API

- - - - -▶ Asynchronous call

——▶ Synchronous call

🛢 Operational database

Always include a key

Just about the only universal shape in software diagrams is the database cylinder. Pretty much everything else is up for grabs. Don't make your viewers guess! Adding an **_explicit key_** makes the diagram accessible to a broader audience, with less extra documentation.

#5 Knowledge depth versus breadth

An unexpected thing happens to your brain when you become a software architect—the new role *changes the kinds of things you seek out and learn.* Consider this structure, which categorizes all the information in the world, as far as you know at the beginning of your career.

The knowledge base of a super-excited junior developer—"I can't believe I get paid to do this!"

Early in your career, there's a lot you don't know that you'll need to know.

Junior developer knowledge pyramid

Paying attention to projects over time makes you proficient with more technical stuff.

As you move along in your career from a junior software developer to a tech lead, the "stuff you know" grows—things like programming languages, frameworks, tools, and platforms. You're also able to help and mentor other developers in this role.

Senior developer/tech lead

Over time, as you gather more expertise and become the go-to person, you start to grow the middle part of the pyramid—the "stuff you know you don't know." Because you're maintaining your hardcore technical skills as well (the "stuff you know"), it takes a lot of effort to get to this point. Congratulations!

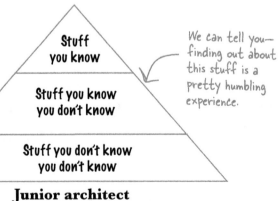

We can tell you—finding out about this stuff is a pretty humbling experience.

Junior architect

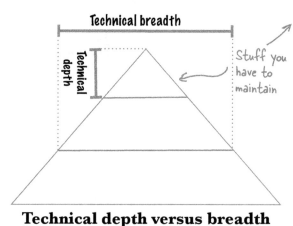

Technical depth versus breadth

Your *technical **depth*** consists of every topic on which you have expertise.

Remaining an expert in any technology requires investing time to keep up with constant change. Thus, maintaining technical depth takes time.

Your *technical **breadth*** includes the areas in which you have expertise, what you know about the existence of other solutions, and what you know about some of these solutions' trade-offs. As an architect, knowing that there are five different ways to solve a problem is better than deeply knowing *one* way to solve it.

New architects' knowledge pyramids start out looking like those of tech leads, but you should make an effort to broaden your experience base. If you have expertise in .NET, for example, see if you can do some work on a Java project, a user interface–heavy Javascript project, or a hard data architecture problem… you get the idea.

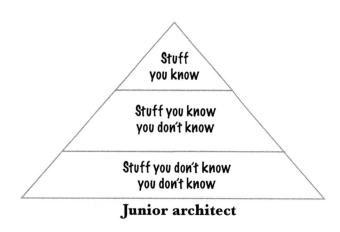

Junior architect

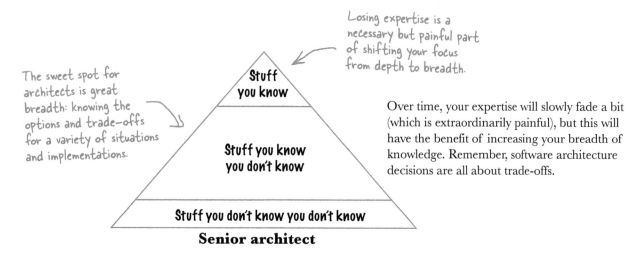

The sweet spot for architects is great breadth: knowing the options and trade-offs for a variety of situations and implementations.

Losing expertise is a necessary but painful part of shifting your focus from depth to breadth.

Over time, your expertise will slowly fade a bit (which is extraordinarily painful), but this will have the benefit of increasing your breadth of knowledge. Remember, software architecture decisions are all about trade-offs.

Senior architect

#6 Practicing architecture with katas

How do you get better at anything in life? Practice, practice, practice.

The legendary martial artist and actor Bruce Lee once said, "I fear not the man who has practiced 10,000 kicks once, but I fear the man who has practiced one kick 10,000 times." So how do you attain that kind of proficiency with software architecture? Glad you asked! We recommend *architectural katas*.

A *kata* is an individual form of exercise used in many martial arts to practice moves until they're perfected. In the same spirit, architectural katas simulate the process of designing a real architecture.

Architectural katas are intended for several small groups of three to five people. Each group becomes a project team and works on a different kata. (We sometimes get two teams to do each kata, just to see what differences arise.) A moderator keeps track of time and facilitates the exercise.

The moderator assigns each group a project needing development. The team meets for a while, asking questions of the "customer" (the moderator) for clarification. They discuss technology options that could work and sketch out a rough vision of their solution. Then they present their solution to the other project teams and answer challenges (hard but fair questions). Choosing an overall winner is optional.

The key to getting better at software architecture is to practice it—even in a simulated exercise.

Do we have your attention? Keep reading to find out more.

How to run katas

Katas are meant to be an adaptable exercise, so follow the rules below **when they make sense** for your organization, context, and needs. Any questions not covered by these rules are the domain of the moderator.

Preparation

Gather several teams of three to five people. (We prefer odd numbers, so disputes can be decided by a majority.) Generally, people who work together in the real world should not be on the same teams; this exercise stresses collaborating with other architects you don't already know.

Gather supplies like poster paper or whiteboards. The artifacts you produce may be very low-tech, depending on the time, complexity, and resources you commit.

Speaking of time, a kata exercise could take as little as 45 minutes or last as long as several weeks!

Your authors have done several katas for real companies that gave teams eight weeks to work out a solution.

Discussion

The teams get together and work through the exact process outlined in this book: analyzing architectural characteristics, determining logical components, choosing an architectural style, and documenting their decisions.

Any technology is fair game, although you should honor reasonable constraints (you won't have an unlimited budget or get to hire new developers). The focus is on architecture and trade-off analysis.

Presentation

Each team presents its solution and answers questions.

When you are listening to another project team presenting, your job is to ask questions. Try to keep them constructive. Don't focus on only the good parts of the solution or only the deficiencies. Strive for balanced feedback.

I feel like there's so much more to know. Are there are any other resources I can reach for?

You don't know about the website? It has updates, interesting links and posts, and much more!

Don't worry. This isn't goodbye.

Congratulations on reading all the way to the end and doing all the exercises! Job well done.

In case you haven't noticed, you've come a long way in this book—and your software architecture journey is just getting started. We'd like to suggest some next steps.

First, point your browser to *https://www.headfirstsoftwarearchitecture.com* to learn what's next! Then check out the books below.

What's next? So much more!

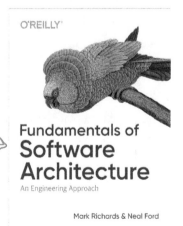

Start here. While some of the material may seem familiar, it's a worthy successor to this book.

O'REILLY
Fundamentals of Software Architecture
An Engineering Approach

Mark Richards & Neal Ford

O'REILLY
Software Architecture: The Hard Parts
Modern Trade-Off Analyses for Distributed Architectures

Neal Ford, Mark Richards, Pramod Sadalage & Zhamak Dehghani

This title is most apropos. Dive deep into the really hard parts of software architecture with this book.

Index

A

Accepted status (ADRs) 100

access control 313

accessibility 55, 56, 74

actor/action approach to logical architecture 135, 137

ADRs (architectural decision records) 97, 114, 292
  benefits of 112
  collaboration and 107
  Consequences section 107, 114, 120, 288
  Context section 104, 114
  context versus justification 106
  decision-capturing tools 111
  Decision section 105, 114, 119
  documentation and 414
  editing 102
  exercises 297–299
  file naming 111
  Governance section 109, 114
  immutability 102
  multiple projects 111
  Notes section 109, 114
  opinion and 105
  Status section 100–101
  storage 111
  Title section 99, 114
  visualization flowchart 103

afferent coupling (CA) 146, 154
  measuring 148–149

agility 52, 85

architects
  coding architects 428–429
  development team and 433
  soft skills 432

architectural characteristics 4, 6–7, 27
  abundance 48

accessibility 55, 56, 74
architectural style and 43
auditability 44
balancing 69
capabilities and 68
categories 48
composite 63
consistency 44
cross-cutting 55
data integrity 44
defining 45, 46
deployability 56, 74
domain requirements 60
domains 44
driving 292
explicit 50
from environmental awareness and 61
from holistic domain knowledge 61
from problem domain 60
implicit 50, 292, 408
limiting 48, 70
maintainability 56, 74
modularity 56, 74
modular monolithic architecture 235
numbers 69
operational 54
overengineering and 48
planning stages 281
priorities 64
privacy 55
process 52
reliability 44
robustness 56, 74
scalability 44, 56, 74
security 44
sources 59
structural 53
synergy 48–49

O'REILLY®

Learn from experts.
Become one yourself.

Books | Live online courses
Instant answers | Virtual events
Videos | Interactive learning

Get started at oreilly.com.

Printed in the USA
CPSIA information can be obtained
at www.ICGtesting.com
JSHW051912080324
58883JS00006B/7

9 781098 134358